John Alexander Henderson

History of the Parish of Banchory-Devenick

John Alexander Henderson

History of the Parish of Banchory-Devenick

ISBN/EAN: 9783337428648

Printed in Europe, USA, Canada, Australia, Japan

Cover: Foto ©ninafisch / pixelio.de

More available books at **www.hansebooks.com**

HISTORY
of the Parish of
BANCHORY-DEVENICK

BY
JOHN A. HENDERSON

WI
ILLUSTRATIONS BY WILLIAM TAYLOR

ABERDEEN: D. WYLLIE & SON
MDCCCXC

INTRODUCTION.

LIKE many works of a similar character, the following History of the Parish of Banchory-Devenick is more or less a compilation drawn from material published and unpublished. While of a fragmentary nature, and in many respects incomplete, the subject-matter has been carefully verified as far as possible, although, for the sake of brevity, cumbrous lists of authorities have not been stated.

The illustrations throughout the work have been introduced with a view of interesting the reader, and at the same time pictorially preserving several objects which are likely, in the course of time, to be lost sight of.

The Author tenders his most grateful thanks to the many kind friends who have aided him in the collection of matter. He acknowledges his special indebtedness to Mr. A. M. MUNRO, Town House, Aberdeen, and Mr. J. MALCOLM BULLOCH, M.A., Aberdeen (the latter is responsible for the chapter on the Bridge of Dee), both of whom have rendered signal service.

AVONDALE,
CULTS, *January*, 1890.

CONTENTS.

	Page
BOUNDARIES OF THE PARISH,	1

Boundaries, 1. Derivation of name, Banchory, 2.

BANCHORY LANDS, - - - - - - - -   3

Kirktown granted to the See of Old Machar—Banchory-Devenick granted to the Abbot and Convent of Arbroath; thereafter to Lord Alan Hostiarius, 3. History of Lord Alan—Succession of the Meldrum Family, 3, 4. History of the Meldrums, 5-8. Rental of Fishings, 8. Purchase by the Garden Family, and their History, 8-12. Forbes Family and their History, 12-14. Murder of Alexander Irvine of Kingcausie by William Forbes, 14-17. Purchase by Robert Cruickshank, Provost of Aberdeen, 17. James Gordon, 20. Purchase by the Thomson Family, and their History, 21-28. Stewart Family and their History, 28-31.

PARISH CHURCH AND HISTORY OF SAINT
DEVENICK, - - - - . - - -   32

Account of the Saint, with legends, 32-38. First Historical mention of the Church—Glebe in Old Aberdeen—Introduction of Episcopacy, 38, 39. Account of the old Parish Church, 39, 40. Account of the new Parish Church,—Notice respecting old Church Bell, 41.

MINISTERS OF THE PARISH, - - - - -   42

John Clatt, 42. Alexander Campbell—Alexander Cabell—Henry Forsyth—Patrick Dunbar—David Menzies, 43. Robert Merser—Robert Merser (son), 44. Andrew Melvin or Melvill—William Robertson, 45. David Lyell, 46. James Gordon, 46-51. John Maitland, 51, 52. John Lumsden, 52. James Nicolson, 53, 54. George Ogilvie, 54, 55. George Morison, D.D., 55-58. William Paul, D.D., 58-61. William Fyfe Lawrence, 61-62.

CONTENTS.

	Page
PARISH CHURCHYARD,	63

Early History, 63. Visit of Resurrectionists, 64-65. Ancient Funeral Customs, 66. Cases of Longevity, 66-67.

BANCHORY-DEVENICK FREE CHURCH, - - - 68

History of Erection, 68. Account of Ministers—David Findlay Arthur, 68-70. James Ironside Still, 70.

HILLDOWNTREE, - - - - - - - - 71

Origin of name, 71. Banchory Wedding, 71-73. Versified Narrative, 73-74.

PARISH SCHOOL, - - - - - - - - 75

Early History, 75. Ancient Scale of Fees, 76, 77. Teachers: William Mar — Robert Jamieson — David Martin—Charles Cay, 78. James Clark—James Hogg—George Skene Keith, 79. Robert Cormack, 81. Robert Adams—Patrick M'Gregor Grant, 82. John Webster, 83. William Skinner, 85. John Black, 86. Robert Ogilvie, 87. John Garden, 88. Robert Gray, 89. William Reid, 90.

ESTATE OF ARDOE, - - - - - - - - 91

Extent and Situation—Early History, 91. Mar Family—George Garden—Cheyne Family—Merser Family—Fraser Family—Mowat Family, 92. Menzies Family—Gordon Family, 93. Fordyce Family, 94, 95. Andrew Watson Fordyce—Alexander Ogston—Alexander Milne Ogston, 95. History of the Ogston Family, 96, 97.

BRIDGE OF DEE, - - - - - - - - 98

Account of erection 98-102. Handed over to the town, 102-105. History of its Chapel, 106-108. Erection of ports and guarding, 109-111. Catholic Rebellion quenched, 112. Siege by Montrose, 112-125. Two timber ports erected, 127. Captain Keith defeated, 128. History of upkeep and repairs, 128-130. Inscriptions, 131-134. Suicide of James Grant, 134.

DOWNIES, - - - - - - - - - 135

CONTENTS.

	Page
ESTATE OF FINDON, - - - - - - -	136

Early History, 136. Owned by the Crab Family, 136-137. Chalmers Family, 137, 138. Richard Vaus, 138. Menzies of Pitfodels—Murder of Alexander Menzies, 139. History of "the Finnan Haddie," 141-142. Landing of six Saint Andrews Students who had been driven out to sea, 143-145.

ESTATE AND VILLAGE OF PORTLETHEN - - 146

David Menzies Proprietor, 146. Sir Wm. Forbes of Monymusk and Banchory, 147. Robert Buchan Proprietor, 147. Sir Robert Patrie, 147, 148. Chalmers Family, 148, 149. Alexander Thomson, 149. Notices respecting Yeats' Family, the Family of Gammel, and the University of Aberdeen, 150. Erection of a Public Hall, 150, 151. Notices respecting the School and its Teachers, 151.

PORTLETHEN CHURCH, - - - - - - - 152

Early History, 152. Mr. Wilkins appointed minister, 153. Notices regarding Mr. Scorgie and Mr. Pirie, 155. William Law appointed minister, 155. William Bruce, 156. Alex. R. Grant, 156, 157.

AUCHORTHIES, - - - - - - - - 158

Early History, 158. Owned by the Irvines of Kingcausie, 158-160.

MANNOFIELD, - - - - - - - - 161

Population—Situation—Established Church, 161.

TWO MILE CROSS, - - - - - - - 162

Situation—Citizens of Aberdeen Encamping—Montrose Encamping, 162. Letter by Montrose to the Magistrates, 162, 163.

ESTATE OF PITFODELS, - - - - - - 164

Owned by the Family of Moray, 164. Family of Reid, 166-173. Family of Menzies and their History, 165-190.

	Page
ESTATE OF CULTS,	191

Owned by the Family of Thomson, 191. Family of Irvine, 191-192. Provost Alex. Livingston, 192, 193. George Chalmers—William Durward, 193. John Burnett—George Symmers—George Gibb Shirra Gibb, 194-195.

CULTS FREE CHURCH, - - - - - - - 196

Early History, 196. Notices respecting ministers—William Anderson, 197, 198. C. A. Salmond, 198, 199. Robert William Barbour, 199. Hugh Morrison, 200.

CULTS MISSION CHURCH, - - - - - - 201

History of erection, 201. Appointment of Charles S. Christie as minister, 203.

MURTLE, - - - - - - - - - - 204

Conveyed by Malcolm IV. to the Bishop of Aberdeen, 1163—History of the Chalmers Family, 204-206. Andrew Buk and Matilda Menzies, 206, 207. Strachan—Cheyne and Murray, 207. Dr. William Guild and Katherine Rolland, 207-209. Irvine Family, 209, 210. John Gordon, 211. John Thurburn, 211, 212. Thurburn Maclaine, 212.

CRIMINAL AND ECCLESIASTICAL TRIALS, - 213

Two cases of theft and one of debt, 213. Slander and assault, 214. Two of murder, 215, 216. Witchcraft, 216, 217. Ecclesiastical, 217.

ANTIQUITIES, - - - - - - - - 218

Druidical Stones at Portlethen, 218, 219. Stone Cairns near Cults House—Find near Findon—Stone Coffins at Clashfarquhar, 220. Stone Coffins found at Cults, Ardoe, and Banchory, 221. Finds at Clashfarquhar and Ardoe, 222, 224. Find of Axe Head at Lynwood, Deebank—and of Quern below West Cults, 224, 225.

EXTRACTS FROM THE SESSION RECORDS, - - 226

Parochial Board and Relief of the Poor, 226-231. Career of Lieutenant-Colonel Joyner, 230, 231. Disbursements, Bequests, &c., 232-239. Church Laws, 239-241. Ancient Form of Oath, 241. Offences against the Church, 242-252. Special Services and Intimations, 253-260. Church and Parish Property, 260-263.

	Page
APPENDIX,	265

Estate of Banchory—Notices respecting Lord Provost Stewart and Provost Robert Cruickshank, 265. Charter by Alexander II. to the Abbot and Convent of Arbroath—Charter to Lord Alan Hostiarius, 266. Charters to William of Melgdrum, 267-269. Description of lands in Mr. Thomson's Deed of Entail, 269, 270. Additional particulars concerning the Parish Church and its belongings, 270-273. Inscriptions on Tablets in Church, 274. Letter by James Calder, Merchant, Aberdeen, intimating Bequest of £500 to the Poor, 274-277. Disposition of Saint Devenick's Bridge in favour of the Kirk-Session, 277-279. Boundaries of Findon as settled in 1654, 280, 281. Versified Legend of the Baron of Petfoddils quha was Wirriet by his awin cat, 282-288. Contract between the Lord Forbes, Johne Leslie of Balquhane, and Thomas Menzes of Pittfoddelis, 288-291. Band of protectioune Huntlie to Pitfoddellis, 291. Charter of Murtle by Malcolm IV. in favour of the Bishop of Aberdeen, 292. Savings Banks, 292-294. Agriculture, 294-296. Population Statistics, 296. Inscriptions on Tombstones in the Parish Churchyard, 297-319.

LIST OF ILLUSTRATIONS.

PEN AND INK.

	TO FACE PAGE
MAP OF THE PARISH, - - - - - - - -	1
BANCHORY HOUSE, from the South-East, - - - -	26
PARISH CHURCH, from the South-East, - - - - -	41
REV. GEORGE MORISON, D.D., - - - - -	55
SAINT DEVENICK BRIDGE, with part of Cults, from the South-East, - - - - - - - - -	56
ARDOE HOUSE, from the West, - - - - - -	96
BRIDGE OF DEE, from the East, - - - - - -	98
JOHN MENZIES OF PITFODELS, the last of his race, - - -	188
VIEW IN THE POLICIES OF BANCHORY, - - - - -	265

MISCELLANEOUS.

	Page
BANCHORY DEVENICK FREE CHURCH, - - - - -	70
ARMS OF OGSTON OF THAT ILK, - - - - - -	97
SEAL OF WILLIAM DE CAMERA OF FINDON (Mar Charters, 1440),	145
FACSIMILE OF THE SIGNATURE OF PROVOST PATRIE OF PORTLETHEN, - - - - - - - -	148
FACSIMILE OF THE SIGNATURE OF PROVOST AULDJO OF PORTLETHEN, - - - - - - - - -	150
PORTLETHEN CHURCH, - - - - - - - -	157
ARMS OF PROVOST ALEXANDER REID OF PITFODELS, - -	168
ARMS OF THOMAS MENZIES AND MARION REID ON TOMBSTONE IN COLLISON'S AISLE, ABERDEEN, - - -	173
SEAL OF PROVOST THOMAS MENZIES (Pitfodels Charter, 1573),	175

LIST OF ILLUSTRATIONS.   xv

	Page
ARMS OF JOHN MENZIES OF PITFODELS, - - - -	189
ARMS OF PROVOST LIVINGSTON OF CULTS, - - - -	193
CULTS FREE CHURCH, - - - - - - - -	200
CULTS MISSION CHURCH, - - - - - - . -	203
DRUIDICAL STONES AT PORTLETHEN, - - - - -	218
URNS FOUND AT ARDOE, - - - - - - -	223
AXE HEAD FOUND AT LYNWOOD, - - - - - -	224
QUERN FOUND BELOW WEST CULTS, - - - - -	225
FACSIMILE OF THE SIGNATURE OF PROVOST CRUICKSHANK OF BANCHORY, - - - - - - - -	265
ARMS OF ALEXANDER THOMSON II. OF BANCHORY, - -	271
ARMS OF THE REVEREND GEORGE MORISON, D.D., - -	279
ARMS OF BISHOPS WILLIAM ELPHINSTONE AND GAVIN DUNBAR,	279

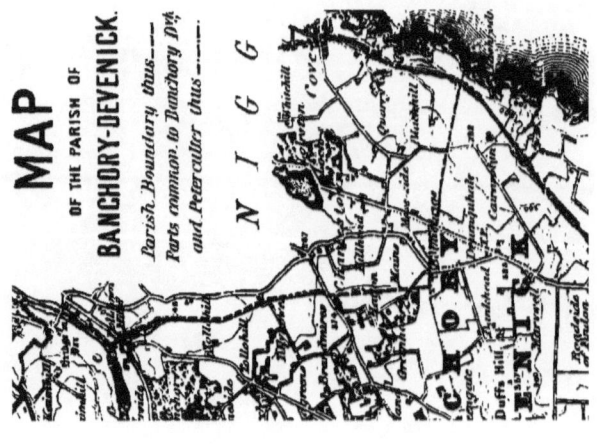

HISTORY OF BANCHORY-DEVENICK.

BOUNDARIES OF PARISH.

THE Parish of Banchory-Devenick is divided into two parts by the river Dee, one part lying in Aberdeenshire, and the other in Kincardineshire. The portion lying to the north of the river is the smaller, containing about 2374 acres. It is bounded on the north by the parish of Newhills, and partly by Old Machar; on the east by Old Machar and the Burgh of Aberdeen; on the south by the river Dee; and on the west by the parish of Peterculter. It forms a strip about one mile in breadth, and four in length, and stretches both farther east and farther west than the part of the parish upon the opposite, or Kincardineshire, side. This portion of the parish contains the properties of Pitfodels, Cults, part of Murtle, and part of Countesswells.

The south or Kincardineshire portion is almost three times the size of the other, containing nearly 7000 acres. It is bounded on the north and on the south-east by water,—on the north by the river Dee, and on the south-east by the German ocean, where it has a coast line of about three miles. On the north-east it is bounded by the parish of Nigg, on the south by Fetteresso parish, and on the west by Fetteresso and Maryculter. The estates of this part are Banchory, Ardoe, with Findon and Portlethen on the coast, and Auchorthies in the south-west corner.

The word Banchory, according to the *View of the Diocese of Aberdeen*, signifies the white choir, or beautiful church. Some believe it was derived from the Gaelic, and means the hollow between two hills. Devenick was the name of the tutelar saint of the parish, sent north by Columba to Christianise the country.

As the larger portion of the parish, the Kincardineshire part is historically of the most importance, and as the estate named after the parish, the lands of Banchory occupy the first place.

BANCHORY LANDS.

Banchory proper embraced two different properties—Banchory-Devenick, and the Kirktown of Banchory—each of which has a separate history up to 1618, when the proprietor of the former purchased the latter, and merged both lands into one. At first they were both church lands granted by different kings, but as the lands of Banchory-Devenick left the hands of the church earlier than the other, they have a more varied history.

Kirktown of Banchory was granted to the See of Old Machar in 1163, by Malcolm IV., and Banchory-Devenick, subject to a yearly annuity of one hundred shillings, together with certain forensical service, to the Abbot and Convent of Arbroath by Alexander II., in 1244. Twelve years later the Abbot parted with the property, disponing it to Lord Alan Hostiarius, justiciary of Scotland. The justiciary was a powerful noble. His real name was Lundie or Lundin, but his predecessors having been appointed door ward, or hostiarius, to the king, an appointment which became hereditary, they afterwards assumed the name of Durward. Lord Alan, who was the son of Thomas Durward, had married the natural daughter of Alexander II., by whom he was created Earl of Athole, and in 1242, made great justiciary of Scotland. His influence at court was of the most powerful character, but he fell into disgrace in 1251 through intriguing against the Crown. Being afterwards restored to favour, however, he became Regent of Scotland during part of the minority of Alexander III. In 1257 he renewed the claim, which had been made before 1228 by his father, to the Earldom of Mar, which even at that time was a matter of dispute. Though defeated in his claim to the title, he succeeded to the extensive domains in Mar, extending from Invercanny on the Dee to Alford on the Don, and from Banchory-Devenick and Skene on the east to Coull on the west, which had been acquired by his father under the compromise arrived at of the dispute in his case. As "the most accomplished knight, and the best military leader of his time," he got the lands of Banchory-Devenick in return for his homage and service, and paying three merks of silver, together with the annual annuity of 100 shillings, as stipulated for by the King in the original charter. Under the new titles, which converted the lands of Banchory into "a free barony," Lord Alan and his heirs were prohibited from alienating or feuing any portion of the ground to third parties, under penalty of forfeiture and escheat. This prohibition was shortly afterwards contravened, and the whole of the lands thereupon reverted to the Abbacy.

The next stage in the history of Banchory-Devenick is its passing into the hands of the Meldrum family. William of Melgdrum, who had got possession of a considerable portion from Lord Alan, ultimately succeeded in getting a charter of the lands in 1333 *(see Appendix)*. Prior to this, however, Robert the Bruce granted his annuity of £5, exigible annually from the lands, to Elizabeth Durward, one of the daughters of Lord Alan. In 1346, William Melgdrum got another charter of confirmation and infeftment *(see Appendix)* under which he and his heirs were prohibited from selling any of the land. The family of Melgdrum is of great antiquity. Philip de Fedarg, a distinguished gentleman in the reign of Alexander II., was ennobled, and subsequently held considerable sway in the north. He disputed boundaries with the Abbot of Arbroath, and their differences were finally adjusted in 1236—the Abbot afterwards granting him for his homage and service the territory of Auchineve. It is uncertain whether this Philip or his son relinquished the designation of Fedarg, and assumed that of Melgdrum; but this happened in the reign of Alexander III., about the year 1249.

Sir Philip de Melgdrum, son of Philip de Fedarg, who was the first Meldrum of Meldrum, married Agnes Cumyn, sister of Alexander, Earl of Buchan. He had powerful influence in State affairs, and in 1252 was one of the Justiciars of Scotland. The dispute with the Abbot of Arbroath appears to have been interminable, for Sir Philip and his Lady contested the right of presentation to the Church of Bethelny, the tithes of which had been given to the Abbey by William Cumyn, first Earl of Buchan, the brother or uncle of Philip's wife, and had been confirmed by Alexander II. in 1221-2. The Bishop of Aberdeen had to try the case, and he held a court at Inverurie, on 21st January, 1262, to which all interested were summoned. Judgment was pronounced in the following month, and the decreet was witnessed by Richard, the vicar, by William Lamberton, rector of Turriff, Roger Stainforth, vicar of Banchory-Terny, Thomas de Bennin, rector of the schools of Aberdeen, and Roger Scharcheburg, official. Sir Philip died in the reign of Alexander III., and was succeeded by his eldest son, Sir William de Meldrum, who espoused the cause of Baliol in his competition with Bruce for the Crown of Scotland. Sir William was succeeded by his eldest son, John, of whose history little is preserved. He left two sons, of whom the eldest, Sir Philip, became his heir. His second son, William, who acquired the lands of Banchory, as before mentioned, and was ancestor of the Meldrums of Fyvie, acted as one of the ambassadors nominated to negotiate the liberty of David II., who had been taken prisoner by the English at the battle of Neville's Cross in 1346. In October, 1353, the King confirmed to him, and to his heirs, the lands and barony of Meldrum.

Nine years later the King, who frequently visited Aberdeen, granted a charter, in January, 1362, in favour of the Dominican or Black Friars, whose church was situated in the vicinity of the East Church, of an annual annuity of 100 shillings from the Barony of Banchory-Devenick, for the endowment of a chaplain to serve in their Church at the altar of the Blessed Virgin, or of Saint Michael; and the donation bears to be made for the welfare of the soul of the King, of his beloved Margaret de Logy, and the souls of his ancestors and successors. James III., by charter dated 30th September, 1477, confirmed this annuity.

The Meldrums of Fyvie continued as proprietors of Banchory down till almost the close of the sixteenth century. In 1544 the proprietor was Sir George Meldrum, whom Bishop Lesley calls "ane valyeant and wyse gentleman." In that year he was sent on an embassy to Henry VIII., who was then besieging Boulogne, in France.* His instructions were "to commoune upon certane abstuonce, to the effect that Commissioners should meit, quhilk was aggreit qntill his returning in Ingland in the moneth of August thairafter." In 1554 he secured a tack of the fishings, described in the deed as "foure cobillis," upon the water of Dee, "payand thairfoir yeirlie fiveteen barrellis salmond gude and sufficient." In these times the fishings had been very productive, for, according to the *Scots Magazine*, 900 salmon were caught in one day in April, 1749, at the Raick fishings alone; whilst the other fishings on the Dee and Don had even greater catches in proportion. Difficulty of transit, however, kept down the price, and what would now secure a yearly

---

* Bishop Lesley's *History of Scotland*, p. 187.

rental of £60 or £80 could have then been had for as many shillings. So accustomed were the lower orders of Aberdeen and district to salmon dinners, that it was no unusual circumstance for farm servants, on being engaged for the half-year, to stipulate that they would not get salmon beyond three times a week. The present rents of the parish salmon fishings are:—Sea: Clashfarquhar, £50; Portlethen, £180; Findon, £270; Cairnrobin, £90. River: Murtle, £19; Ardoe, £70; Inchgarth, £40; Banchory, £38; Kaimhill, £115.

The estate then passed into the hands of the Garden family, during whose proprietorship the two portions of Banchory merged into one. Under charter, dated in 1555, granted by Sir George Meldrum of Fyvie, with consent of William Meldrum of Hatton, his son, George Garden, then designed as proprietor of Dorlaithers, acquired the estate. At the same time, Garden obtained a charter of the lands of Hatton and Auchterless in warrandice of the lands of Banchory. The Gardens were a very ancient and highly respected family, and this George, who was frequently called of that Ilk,* married Isobell Keyth, daughter to the laird of Troup, "wha wes lawfull sone to the Erll Mershall."† He was a burgess of Aberdeen, but on 18th September, 1562, he, along with twelve others, "tint the freedom" through remaining "not

---

* The Arms of Garden of that Ilk were *argent two chevrons ingrailed gules.*—Nisbet's *Heraldry.*
† Birth Brieves, Miscellany, *Spalding Club*, Vol. v., p. 326.

actually within the Burgh." In 1589 he was one of the gentlemen sent by James I. to Denmark in connection with the marriage treaty of the Princess Anne. He left a son and a daughter.

Arthur, the son, succeeded his father in 1590, in which year a Patrick Bissett, " his Maiesties rebell," took shelter in Banchory House, which was surrounded by a mob from Aberdeen, who claimed him as their prisoner. Considerable mischief had evidently been done, for the Town Council afterwards ordered fifty merks to be paid out of the town's funds as compensation. Beatrix, the daughter, had an eventful history. She was one of Queen Mary's maids of honour, and was celebrated for her beauty and her skill as a harpist. Miss Strickland relates a well-known story of her. Once, when the Queen "proclaimed a music meeting, offering her own favourite harp as a prize to the best performer, the fair Beatrice Gardyne of Banchory was adjudged by her majesty to have surpassed all the courtly competitors, and even her own musicians, in skill and taste, as well as in the sweetness of her voice. Neither Michelet, Mary's newly imported French musician, nor even her old established favourite, David Rizzio, was excepted. The Poet-Queen acknowledged the superiority of the native melodies of Scotland to the most elaborate harmonies which foreign science could produce; and when she felt the soul-thrilling power of a Scottish ballad from the lips of a sweet-voiced Scottish lassie, the generous Sovereign hailed her young subject as the 'Queen of Song,' and accorded the harp to her with this compliment, 'You alone are worthy to possess the instrument you touch so well!'" Queen Mary's harp is now deposited in the museum, in Edinburgh, of the Society of Antiquaries of Scotland. It was originally graced with a portrait of the royal donor, and the arms of Scotland in solid gold, enriched with several gems—two of which were considered of great value—but these were stolen during the Civil Wars. By her marriage Beatrix again figures prominently. She became the second wife of the redoubtable Findla Mhor, and thus ancestor of the Farquharsons of Invercauld and Finzean, and they had issue five sons and five daughters. Of the sons, Donald, the eldest, got Castleton of Braemar; Robert, the second, Invercauld; Lachlan, the third, through marriage with Grizel Campbell, the lands of Broughdearg; George, the fourth, through marriage, the lands of Deskry and Glenconry; and Finlay, the youngest, Achreachan, in Glenlivat. In 1547, Findla was royal standard-bearer at Pinkie. "Surrounded by the men of Strathdee," says an interesting writer, "he cleared the way with his huge claymore, before which man and horse went down. The English cavalry, under Lord Gray, were in a moment overthrown, and the General himself wounded. But then the main body of the invaders advanced, pouring in volleys of musketry, and Findla Mhor fell on the field, shrouded in the royal banner he had borne with such honour. He lies interred at Musselburgh—Burke says at Invercauld—happy no doubt in that he did not live to see the triumph of England." It is not clear when Arthur Garden died. He had married Elizabeth, or Elspet Gordon, daughter of the laird of Gight, and left a son, Alexander. It was with this laird that the lands of Banchory-Devenick and Kirktown of Banchory merged into one.

Kept in the hands of the church for four centuries, Kirktown of Banchory at last, in 1571, reached a distinctive point in its history. In that year the Bishop of Aberdeen, with consent of the Dean and Chapter, granted a feu charter of the lands, which was confirmed by the King, in favour of William Blinshell, one of a family that had taken a leading part in the history of Aberdeen for two centuries. As they had long been under one proprietorship, they now, for the next few years, rapidly changed hands. Blinshell, in the same month that he got his feu charter of them, granted a charter of alienation in favour of Robert Menzies, elder, burgess of Aberdeen. He was succeeded in 1586 by his son, David, who married Marjory Gray, by whom he had an only danghter, Marjory. She became the wife of the Rev. Andrew Milne, minister of Maryculter, and inherited her father's property. The Milnes, however, parted with it in 1618, when they sold it to Alexander Garden for 3000 merks, but subject to a wadsett of 2000 merks upon the Mains of Banchory, held by Gilbert Club, burgess of Aberdeen.

Henceforward the history of the two properties becomes

one. Garden was married to Janet Straquhan, by whom he had two sons, both of whom went abroad. One of these, Alexander, who had entered the army, in which he held the rank of Major, proceeded with the troops sent by Charles I. to assist Gustavus Adolphus, and was present at the battle of Lutzen, in 1632, when the gallant king lost his life. Major Garden remained many years at the Swedish Court, where he attained to great distinction. On the abdication, however, of Queen Christina, in 1654, he returned to Scotland, and purchased the estate of Troup, from Troup of that Ilk. He married Betty, daughter of Alexander Strachan, of Glenkindy, and had issue—Alexander Garden, of Troup, who married Bathia, daughter of Sir Alexander Forbes, of Craigievar, and whose grandson, Peter Garden of Delgaty, heir to his brother Francis, Lord Gardenstone of the Court of Session, married the heiress of Campbell of Glenlyon, and thereafter assumed the additional name and arms of that family.

It is strange that the laird who united the two parts of Banchory into one should have also had to let both go out of his family. His financial affairs became embarrassed, and five years after his purchase of Kirktown of Banchory, the property passed into the Forbes Family, who held it for the next half century.

It was in 1623 that Garden "disponed to William Forbes of Monymusk, and Elizabeth Wishart of Pitarrow, his spouse, the haill lands of Banchory with the pertinents." Forbes was created a knight baronet, of Scotland and Nova Scotia, by Charles I., in 1626, and in 1629 he was formally infefted in the lands of Banchory, and also part of Torry. He had issue, three sons and three daughters. The eldest son, William, succeeded; the second son, Robert, became proprietor of Barns; and the third, Alexander, was subsequently designed of Aberswithark. The eldest daughter, Jean, married Alexander Lunan, minister of Monymusk, and afterwards of Kintore. Isobell married John Forbes of Asloun; and the third, Anna, died young.

In 1630 Sir William granted a deed of wadsett over Banchory for 13,840 merks, paid to him by his brother, John Forbes of Leslie, and William and Alexander, his sons. The deed contained a special clause, which provided that in the event of the latter family paying the further sum of 6000 merks within seven years from the date thereof, they should get infeftment of Banchory, the same as if they had purchased it outright. Litigation subsequently followed as to the legal rights of parties, but, ultimately, John Forbes of Leslie secured the proprietorship of Banchory, and had his title ratified by Parliament. He was the second son of William Forbes of Monymusk, and Lady Margaret Douglas, daughter of Sir William Douglas of Kemnay, who in 1588 became ninth Earl of Angus. He obtained the lands of Leslie about 1620, from George, the last Leslie of that Ilk, through paying the debts lying upon them. He married

Jean Leslie, sister of Patrick, second Lord Lindores, from whom it is believed he got for a trifling amount a large portion of the estates of that lordship. He bought Edingarroch and Licklyhead from Patrick Leith in 1625. Along with John Leslie, younger of Pitcaple, he made a representation to the Covenanting Lords against the blockade of the Harbour of Aberdeen, 31st May, 1639. In 1645 he was engaged in the burning of Pitcaple Castle, where Jaffray and Cant were prisoners. Spalding, who calls him "ane gryte covenanter," records that in April of the previous year his "girnillis in Banchorie wes plunderit" for the upkeep of the Marquis of Huntly's army, quartered in Aberdeen.

He was succeeded in his large estates by his son, William. This laird had, in 1644, rendered himself notorious through murdering his neighbour, Alexander Irvine, of Kingcausie. Spalding relates the story with his usual minuteness :—" Vpone Setterday, 17 August, 1644, about 11 houris at evin, Alexander Irving, of Kincousie, cuming quyetlie to Abirdein (becaus he durst not ryd vpone day licht for being at the rode of Montroiss). Williame Forbes, sone naturall to Johne Forbes of Leslie, hapnit to be cuming out of Abirdene going to Banchorie, quhair his father wes duelling, and met with him about the Crabstane, who wold haue takin him and had him perforss to Abirdene, luiking to get for him 5000 merkis conforme to ane ordinans of the Estaitis, that who suld tak him and bring him in sould get the same soume.

Kincovsie being ane fyne gentilman stormit to be tane with the lyk of him, and wnder speiking this Williame Forbes schootis the gentilman with ane pistoll deid, and thairwith cruellie strikis him two straikis in the heid. Thus is this brave gentilman mischantlie mvrdreist, wnder scilens of nicht, (never wining to his armes to defend him self), for greid of this gane set out be the Estaitis, without ground of godliness. Many wes sorrowfull at his death, being mervalouslie weill belovit both in brughe and land. He left behind him his dolorous wyf and fyve fatherles children. Vpone the morne he is takin up and bureit within the Laird Drumis Iyll in Sanct Nicholas' kirk of New Abirdene with gryt mvrning and lamentatioun. This innocent blood is noways pvnishit according to the law of God and man, bot is esteimit and publictlie approvin as good and loyall seruice, in manifest contempt of oure dreidfull God and the kingis lawis. For vpone the 21st of the said moneth of August, four dayis immediatlie efter this bloodie mvrther, the said Williame Forbes is avowitlie brocht in befoir the committe of Abirdein, and found to be ane volunteir in Schir Williame Forbes of Craigiewaris company of trovperis, and declairit him to haue done good seruice to the publict for mvrthering of this gentilman, for no vther ressone bot becauss he wes at Montrose with his young cheif the Laird Drum, drawin thair also aganist his will, as sum said ; for this fault the taking of his lyf is approvin good seruice, and absoluit thairfra. Likeas the said committe sent ane trumpettour to the cross of Abirdene, and be oppin proclamatioun absoluit him fra this mvrther frielie, and ordanit 5000 merkis to be liftit af of his estait, being about 12 chalderis victuall, quhairof 2000 merkis sould be givin to the malefactour, and 3000 merkis to Craigiwar, ritmaister, conforme to ane ordinans set out be the generall committe of Estaitis. Likeas thairefter he wes of new agane declairit to haue done good seruice, and to get his rewaird, strictlie charging and commanding that no maner of man sould speik or say aganis the samen bot lavdablie. Bot the Lord luikit to their presumptuous sinis and bloodsched, for in August, 1645, the said Williame Forbes, being keiping his fatheris hous of Likliheid, schuiting ane mvscat, schot his richt hand fra him self; a token that the Lord thocht not this innocent blood good seruice. And that same hand who schot this gentilman wes schot fra him be him self; but it wes his left hand quhilk fyrit, and wes cuttit at the elbo." Gordon, in his history of the family of Gordon, says that after the Restoration the eldest son of the murdered laird of Kingcausie, "having obtained an order from the Council to apprehend Forbes, went to Caithness, where the assassin then lurked (as he thought in safety), took him prisoner, and carried him to Edinburgh, where by the Council he was remitted to a Justiciary Court to be holden at Aberdeen for that effect, and was by that Court condemned to be hanged at the Crabstane, a place as near as could be guessed to that where the murder was committed; and which sentence was accordingly executed."

This, however, was not the case. The loss of his hand had evidently satisfied his enemy for the loss of his head, for he succeeded his father, and married Janet, sister of Lord Duffus, and by her had several children, among whom were John, his successor, and Jean, who became Lady Hatton Meldrum. According to his tombstone in the churchyard of Leslie, he " lyved fifty-fyve yeirs, and depairted this lyfe, November 12, 1670 yeirs." He is believed to have been the continuator of Matthew Lumsden's *Genealogy of the family of Forbes*, from Lumsden's death in 1580, to 1665. Leslie Castle, now a picturesque ruin, which might have been preserved at little cost in a habitable condition, was rebuilt by him, as appears by an inscription on the wall, dated 17th June, 1661.

John Forbes, his son and successor, married in 1662 Helen Scot, daughter of the laird of Ardross, in Fife, by whom he had several daughters. One of these, Christian, was married, first, to John Skene of Dyce, and, secondly, in 1734, to John Paton of Grandholm.

With this laird the estate of Banchory left the Forbes family. In 1682 he disposed of the whole estate to Robert Cruickshank, merchant in Aberdeen, and Sarah Leslie, his spouse. Cruickshank was the son of John Cruickshank, burgess of Aberdeen, and he was elected Provost for four successive years, beginning in 1693, besides being Member of Parliament for the city from 1694 to 1702. In 1694 he returned the following information for the poll taken in that year:—" Hath one wyfe, and five children in familie, two servant lasses and one man servant." Of the family, three sons appear in the burgess register of Aberdeen as having been made Guild Brethren, viz.: George, Robert, and James. The first named passed as an advocate in Aberdeen, and married Elizabeth Geddie. The second became a merchant in London. The third qualified as a doctor, and was afterwards designed as "Chirurgeon in Kent, County in Maryland." One of the daughters, Helen, married the Reverend John Whyte, minister of Coylton, in Ayrshire; the other, Elspet, became the wife of John Johnston, merchant in, and one of the baillies of, Aberdeen. At Michaelmas, 1697, Johnston had exception taken to his election as provost by several members of the Council. These dissentients raised an action of reduction before the Lords of the Privy Council, and, among other grave charges, declared that Johnston, and his father-in-law, "disregardful of the laws of God and the sett of the Burgh, have arranged for the future to get themselves alternately returned as Provost. The laird of Banchory has already had himself re-elected four several running years." The objections were sustained, and, accordingly, in December following, "the haill Council" elected as provost, Alexander Walker, who was the grandfather of Principal Campbell.

This dispute led to a very curious episode in connection with the Bridge of Ruthrieston. The council register of date, 23rd Feby., 1698, contains the following entry which shows that the spirit of Town Councils has been pretty much the same for a considerable length of time. "The Councill, finding that, when the Bridge of Ruthreston was perfyted, Robert Cruickshank, of Banchorie, being then [1693-4] provost, he did clandistinly cause put up his armes on the sd. bridge without any act of councill, albeit he contrabute nothing for building thereof, and yet the same was begune and near ended in provost Cochran's time, And was builded on the money of the Bridge of Dee, Doe therefore appoint the sd. Robert Cruickshank's armes to be taken down, and to be given to him, he paying the pryce thereof, And appoints the Mr. of Kirk Work to cause put up in the place where the sd. arms, stood ane handsome cut stone with the following inscription thereon, viz. :—" Senatus-Abredonensis hunc pontem, impensis ex Ære ad pontem Dee spectante extruendum Curavit, 1693." Notwithstanding this order, Cruickshank's arms are still to be seen on the bridge. The reason is this—the grandiloquent inscription of the Council is on the reverse of the stone on which Cruickshank's arms are cut. Under date, 13th Sept., 1705, the Council " appointed the Mr. of Kirk work to cause turn the stone whereon the Inscription is that Robert Cruickshank, of Banchorie, his Arms qch are on the back thereof may be seen, and to add Provost of Abd. to his designation when this Bridge was built, and to put on vpon another stone of the sd.

Bridge the former latin inscription, that the sd. wes built at the expense of the Bridge of Dee."

Johnston, his son-in-law, died within the next year or two, being survived by his wife who had no issue, and Cruickshank died about 1st May, 1717, and was buried in Saint Nicholas Churchyard, Aberdeen. Two years previously he bequeathed 1000 merks to form a fund for "relieving decayed Burgesses, their wives and children." His grandson, Robert Cruickshank, son of the before designed George Cruickshank, succeeded, and with him the estate again changed hands.

In 1724, Cruickshank, who was then resident with his widowed mother in Saint Andrews, sold the estate to James Gordon, merchant in Aberdeen, who was then proprietor of Ardmellie, in the parish of Marnoch, Banffshire. Gordon was a keen Episcopalian, and took an active interest in the raising of funds for the erection of a "meeting house in Aberdeen, for that body." In 1736 he secured an obligation from the Governors of Robert Gordon's Hospital, Aberdeen, agreeing to grant 30 "spidarrock" of peats—a spidarrock being what would be dug in one day by a spade—to be cast annually out of the moss of Findon and Cookston by the tenants of Banchory, for sale in Aberdeen for the space of 29 years after Candlemas 1737, each "spidarrock" to pay 48 shillings Scots yearly. He married Mary Buchan, and his eldest daughter, Anne, married in 1757 John Gordon of Craig, by whom she had three sons—John, who died in infancy; James, the successor; and Francis. Another daughter, Mary, married in 1768 Sir Alexander Bannerman of Elsick.

The next change of proprietor brought the estate into the hands of the Thomsons, with whose name it is best known. Gordon sold the property, in 1743, to Alexander Thomson, advocate in Aberdeen, who also acquired, in 1765, part of the fourth lot of the lands of Portlethen, called Balquharn. He married Katherine Skene, daughter of George Skene of Rubislaw, who survived him, and died 4th March, 1776, aged 73. One stirring incident in his life was undoubtedly due to his connection with the Skene family. He lived in the fine old mansion in the Guestrow, now known as the Victoria Lodging House. It had belonged to his wife's family, and he had either bought or leased it. At all events, when the Duke of Cumberland came to Aberdeen in February, 1746, in pursuit of the Jacobite rebels, he pronounced Marischal College, which had been prepared for him, as too small, and took up his abode in Thomson's mansion, which was roomy enough for him. For six weeks he occupied his unwilling host's house, and during that time "made use of every kind of provisions found in the house, coals, candles, ales, or other liquors in the cellars, and the milk of his [host's] cow : bed and table linen, which were very much spoiled and abused; he broke up a press in which Mrs. Thomson had lodged a considerable quantity of sugar, and whereof he took every grain weight. When about to march from Aberdeen, he left six guineas to the three servants of the house, but did not make the least compliment or requital to Mr. Thomson for the so long and free use of his house, furniture, and provisions, nor so much as call for his landlord or landlady to reward them thanks."

In 1768 Thomson mortified to the minister and Kirk-session of Banchory-Devenick, for behoof of the poor of the parish, the sum of £5, payable yearly after his demise, from the lands of Kirktown of Banchory. The Session's right to the annuity was constituted "by gift and delivery to their Treasurer of earth and stone of the ground of the foresaid lands of Kirktown of Banchory, an hand full of corn, stubble, straw, and grass, together with a penny and other symbols used in the like cases." The deed of mortification, which was registered in the Baillie Court books of Aberdeen, declares " that the foresaid annuity shall never be redeemed upon any consideration, but shall remain as a perpetual burden in all time coming on the said lands of Banchory." He also mortified £20 to be paid annually out of the lands of Balquharn to the master of mortification of Aberdeen, for payment of annuities to certain relatives, at whose decease the fund was directed to be applied in all time coming "towards the support and maintenance of old infirm Burgesses of Guild of Aberdeen ; and their wives ; or to their widows; or to their sons or grandsons; daughters or grand-daughters of Burgesses of Guild—

the persons receiving the benefit being old, infirm, and not able to gain a livelihood, and being of pious disposition."

At the same date he executed a deed of entail *(see Appendix)* of the whole of his extensive estates. He left a most curious array of reasons for doing so, for the special guidance of his trustees and factor. " It may be proper to let my friends know some of my reasons for executing the Deed of Entail of my lands of Banchory, Rainieshill, &c. I many times considered the circumstances of my ancient friends and relations now dead, that those who made any figure in the world, and acquired a competency of means, their eldest sons and successors squandered away their Estates, and spent the same in a foolish profuse idle way. *First*—To give some instances, A—— died, leaving his estate to his eldest son, B ——, who sold it. He lived and died in great want, being a sluggard. *Second*—C——, who was an eminent lawyer, died leaving a plentiful estate to his only son, D——, who became an Edinburgh lawyer. He afterwards squandered away his substance, neglected his business, though he was one of the best writers of his time, and at last died in low circumstances, and his sons after him turned debauchees. *Third*—E——, who was a man of great knowledge and activity, acquired a considerable estate in money, which he divided amongst his five sons, who went abroad, made no figure, but spent their patrimonies without doing any good. *Fourth*—F——, acquired the estate of. . . . with several feus, houses, and fishings. He left all his children competently provided for. His eldest son, G——, succeeded to all his means and estate, with the burden of his mother's liferent and the younger children's provision. He would have had a very good reversion if he had managed well and applied to business. Other instances could be given, but I shall not mention them on account of their surviving friends. *Fifth*—None of these friends executed any Deed of Entail of their estates. When I considered how those before me were represented, I thought a Deed of Entail might be tried to see if that would preserve my small estate from being squandered away . . . " Mr. Thomson died in 1773, at the advanced age of 81 years.

He was succeeded, under the deed of entail, by his nephew, Andrew, the eldest son of his brother, Andrew, an advocate in Aberdeen, and proprietor of Cammachmore, in the Mearns. Andrew Thomson, senior, who died in 1766, was married to Margaret Muir, by whom he had issue, Andrew, James, Margaret, Anne, and Helen. Andrew, the eldest son, who was born on 28th October, 1747, married in 1769 Mary Skene, daughter of Dr. Andrew Skene, a lineal descendant of the great Scottish reformer, John Knox. "Knox left three daughters, one of whom was married to a Mr. Baillie of Jerviswood, and by him had a daughter, who was married to a Mr. Kirkton, of Edinburgh." By this marriage there was a daughter,

Margaret, who married Dr. Andrew Skene, of Aberdeen, the grandfather of Thomson's wife. He had issue, Margaret, Andrew, and Alexander. During his proprietorship the third lot of the lands and Barony of Portlethen, called Glashfarquhar, was acquired from James Thomson of Portlethen, and "added, annexed, and conjoined to the tailzied lands and estate of Banchory, Rainieshill, &c., from which it was never to be disjoined." Thomson died in 1781, at the age of 34.

Andrew Thomson, his eldest son, succeeded. He was born on 27th December, 1774, and educated at the University of Aberdeen, at which he studied medicine. He married Helen Hamilton, second daughter of Dr. Robert Hamilton, professor of natural philosophy in Marischal College, Aberdeen. He died on 13th April, 1806, in the 32nd year of his age. Smeaton says, " He is remembered as a man devoted to literary and scientific pursuits, with a considerable genius for music, and an enthusiastic love of chemistry. He erected a building out of doors where he could carry on his chemical experiments."

He was succeeded by the last and most venerable of the Thomsons, his son, Alexander, who became laird at the age of eight. His early training devolved entirely upon his mother, who was known as a very superior and most pious woman. He studied at the Grammar School, and thereafter at Marischal College, where he graduated in 1816. Proceeding to Edinburgh, he studied for the bar, and passed as an advocate in 1820. He never practised—preferring the life of a country gentleman to the worry and bustle of a lawyer. On 14th February, 1825, he married Jessy, daughter of Alexander Fraser, ex-Lord Provost of Aberdeen, who survived him.

Securing disentail and devoting great attention to the improvement of his estates, as also to county business, Mr. Thomson speedily became one of the most popular proprietors in the north. The old house of Banchory, which was erected in middle of the seventeenth century, having become ruinous, he had a massive new mansion erected on same site. The foundation-stone was laid with much ceremony on 21st January, 1840. He was ordained an elder of the Parish Church at Banchory; but subsequently becoming more of the evangelical turn of mind, he resigned office. In the Disruption controversy, he took a very prominent part, sparing neither time nor money in advancing the cause of the Free Church. On 1st June, 1843, he laid the foundation-stone of a Free Church at New Machar, on his estate of Rainieshill, and he was the means of forming a congregation and procuring a minister for the Free Church of Banchory-Devenick, which was built almost entirely at his own expense. In September Dr. Chalmers paid a week's visit to Mr. Thomson at Banchory House, and, on the 10th of that month, preached on the lawn to an immense congregation, drawn from many miles around, including Aberdeen. At the Free Church

General Assembly of 1844 Mr. Thomson suggested a scheme for providing manses for the clergy, and the establishment of the Theological Hall at the Free Church College, Aberdeen, was mainly due to his exertions.

Between the years 1847 and 1857 Mr. Thomson's time was greatly taken up by antiquarian and geological studies; as also with enquiries into the social condition of the people. In 1859, when the Prince Consort visited Aberdeen to take part in the business of the British Association, of which he was president, Mr. Thomson had the honour of entertaining him at Banchory House.* About this time symptoms of failing health began to manifest themselves, and he was thereafter compelled to forego several of the investigations in which he had hitherto taken such an active interest. With diminished strength, however, he pursued his studies, issuing many pamphlets on scientific and antiquarian subjects. He died on 20th May, 1868, aged 70. Under his trust disposition and settlement he bequeathed to the Free Church College in Aberdeen about £16,000 in cash, and the valuable library and interesting museum he had collected at Banchory House. The collection included

* In commemoration of the Prince Consort's visit Mr. Thomson caused a granite monument to be erected at Tollo Hill on the estate, which is thus inscribed:—
"IN REMEMBRANCE OF THE VISIT OF
H. R. H. ALBERT PRINCE CONSORT,
TO THIS SPOT.
XV. SEPTEMBER, MDCCCLIX."

a watch said to have been given by Queen Mary to John Knox at the time when she was anxious to conciliate him. The watch came into the Thomson family through Mr. Thomson's grandmother.

The *arms* of the Thomsons are—Argent, a stag's head, cabossed, gules; attired or; on a chief wavy of the second, a lozenge between two spur-rowels of the field. *Crest*—A crane holding a palm-branch in the beak, all ppr. *Mottoes*—Over the crest—*Curæ cedit fatum* Under the Arms—*Secum cuique.**

In 1872 the estate was sold by Mr. Thomson's Trustees to Mr. John Stewart, comb manufacturer, Aberdeen, for £76,000. The career of the late Mr. Stewart was a remarkable one, and might be cited among the many examples of what a determined, persevering, and sound-headed Scotchman can accomplish. Born in Perth in 1810, he started the business of combmaking in Edinburgh about 1828, in partnership with a friend of the name of Whitehead. The venture did not succeed; but, nothing daunted, Stewart removed to Aberdeen, where he started a similar business in Mealmarket Lane, this time in partnership with his brother-in-law, Mr. Joseph Rowell. Combs were then made by hand, but gradually, as the concern increased, it became imperative to introduce machinery. In 1835 the manufactory was removed to larger premises in

---

* Burke's *Landed Gentry*, p. 1200.

Hutcheon Street, where the business grew and flourished till it became the largest combmaking centre in the world. Such handsome annual profits were realized that in 1848 Mr. Rowell retired with an ample fortune. Mr. Stewart, on the other hand, embarked the larger share of his savings in the Great North of Scotland Railway Company. This interest induced him to become also a shareholder and director of the Aberdeen and London Steam Navigation Company, with the avowed object of making Aberdeen the great competitive point for the traffic of the north-east of Scotland, and compelling the southern railways to compete with the Steam Company for such traffic, and thus to modify their rates. To do this effectually he laid down the policy that the fine old paddle passenger boats should be ultimately superseded by screw steamers capable of working at a saving of coal, that the sailings should be bi-weekly instead of weekly, and that the tariff rates and fares should be substantially reduced. The older directors and shareholders, however, dreaded the effect of such drastic changes, and, a bitter opposition springing up against him, Mr. Stewart started three rival screw steamers—the *Stanley*, *Kangaroo*, and *Gambia*—under the title of "The Northern Steam Company." After a tough contest an amalgamation of both companies took place, under which Mr. Stewart became chairman, and his policy may be fairly called the foundation of the present active and prosperous state of the concern. The fight had, however, cost him upwards of £46,000, and as the Highland Railway from Perth to Inverness, which was opened shortly afterwards, got a contract for the carrying of the greater portion of the mails to the north, which had previously been carried by the Great North Railway, a panic set in amongst the shareholders of the latter, and its stock was depreciated to such an extent that Mr. Stewart was obliged to relinquish everything, including his estate of Craigiebuckler. His firm of S. R. Stewart & Co., however, weathered this crisis, and after a few years of successful trading, he was enabled in 1872 to purchase the estate of Banchory, as before mentioned. He died on 25th January, 1887, and was interred in the Free Church burying-ground, Banchory-Devenick. His wife, Mary Irvine, died at Craigiebuckler 24 years previously.

He was succeeded by his eldest son, David, who was educated at the University of Aberdeen, of which he is a graduate. He has for several years been at the head of the combworks in Aberdeen. He is a very active business man, and has filled many public offices. After acting as president of the Aberdeen Chamber of Commerce, he was elected Dean of Guild. A few years ago he was appointed Judge at the Horners' Exhibition held at the Mansion House, London, and at the same time he was elected a Liveryman of the City of London. He married Margaret Dyce, eldest daughter of Principal Brown, and has issue four sons—David Brown Douglas, William Dyce, George Irvine, and Charles—and five daughters—

Mary, Alexandra Catherine Dyce, Julia Charlotte, Jessie, and Margaret Isabel. Mary is married to Mr. Charles Niven, professor of natural philosophy in the University of Aberdeen, who was senior wrangler of his year, and has since been elected a Fellow of Trinity College, Cambridge.

THE PARISH CHURCH AND HISTORY OF SAINT DEVENICK.

The patron Saint of Banchory-Devenick was one Devenicus, a disciple of St. Columba. Like most of the good men of Iona his history is obscure. Trained in the rigorous school over which the great Saint presided, he was sent forth, like the other disciples, from the little island to the rough mainland with its rougher people, to endeavour to convert them from Paganism. After wandering on his mission through various districts of Scotland, he founded a church at Methlick, in which parish, on the second Tuesday of November, till within recent years, a fair or market, called St. Devenick's Fair, was regularly held. His chief connection, however, lay with the parish of Banchory-Devenick, which took its name from him.

The following legends, in prose and verse, are translations from latin biographies of the Saint :—" While the most blessed Fathers, Columba and Mauricius, were preaching the faith of Christ in Scotland, St. Devenicus, the celebrated Confessor of Christ, famous for his life and sanctity, flourished; a man, indeed, given up in an unusual degree to holy and religious works, after the manner of the age : who, burning with divine love, being inspired by the Holy Spirit, said to St. Mauricius, 'You see, O

Master, what a great number of people there is in this province given up to the worship of idols, and how few works of the ministry of God : therefore I ask that if it please you we separate in the work of ministry through the breadth of the kingdom. You, indeed, tell the Word of God to the nation of Picts. I will depart to the province of the Cathini, and proceed to announce the doctrine of Christ to them.' St. Mauricius said, 'Now, Brother, we will again be joined,' and he said, 'We will also be joined forever in the heavenly life, and there be glad and rejoice with Christ. Only, this more do I ask of you in the name of our Master, that since near death enshrouds me, when I am dead you will cause my body to be carried to this place and buried here.' St. Mauricius also assenting, St. Devenicus departed to the Cathini, boldly preaching the Word of God there, and converting many persons to the faith of Christ. Mauricius, the blessed man, wandering through the whole kingdom of the Picts, by praying and exhorting them, and by doing many wonderful things, and making many signs, brought an infinite multitude of them under the faith. He even caused the chiefs and leaders and also the nobles of the land to believe on Christ; and, having there destroyed the temples of the idols, and having overthrown their altars, he ordered houses of meeting to be built. In these days it happened that the most holy old man, Devenicus, of whom we have made mention, having advanced to a long old age, spent his life in this manner. When he came to the end of his life, having called some of his servants to him, said, ' When I am dead, take up my body, and carry it to one of the meetings of St. Mauricius, and say to him that I remember his promise which I got from him when I was going away.' Having said these things he gave up the ghost, and his men, carrying out his orders, carried him to a certain hall which was in a neighbouring monastery. And on the following night, whilst the blessed Mauricius was keeping watch at his orisons, he saw angels descending on the house in which the body of St. Devenick was. The holy man said to his brothers, ' The most holy man came to us a guest, come let us visit him and perform the duty of humanity which we owe to him.' But when they came to the house they did not find the body, for they passed the porters and ascended into the mountain, there desiring to rest for a short time. The Saint with his men, following on their track, found them in a place which is called Crosta. There, therefore, the devoted man stayed beside the remains of the holy old man, keeping watch with psalms, prayers and preachings, and unwearied with assiduous watching. These finished, they carried the body to a place of which the name is Banchory-Devenick, and there gave it up to be honourably buried. They built a hall which is called, even to this day, after the name of that old man, Banchory-Devenick, where the merits of that Saint intervening, many benefits are conferred on the erring by the assistance of our Lord Jesus Christ, to whom be the honour, forever, Amen !"

So much for the prose story. The versified one is hardly less interesting :—

>Nocht lang eftire apone a day
>(To) sanct Machor a mane cane say:
>That sanct Dewynnik In-to Catnes
>Thru gret eilde falyeit and ded was ;
>And quhene he one his dedstra lay,
>To thaime that nest war he cane say:
>Sene that ye se ded sall me tak,
>I coniure you for godis sak
>That yhe for na trawall be Irke
>To bere my body to sume kirk,
>Quharfor sanct Machor has keping,
>And pray hyme for the hewynnis king
>That he meyne one and thochtfull be
>Of his hicht that ye mad to me
>Of his gud will at our partyng.
>With this of spek he mad ending
>And yaulde the gast but mare abad.
>And thai that this commawndment had,
>To tak his body war nocht Irk
>And one a bere brocht till a kirk
>That was bot litill fra that place
>That befor to thaime lentyne was.
>And quhene that sanct Machor this tale
>Has herd as I haf tald yu hale,
>He mad regrat and had disese.
>But, for he durst nocht god disples,
>That nycht but slepe all haile he lay
>In his prayere, till it wes day:

And in that kirk with fleschely eyne
Full feile brycht angelis he has sene
Fle upe and doune, makand thaire play.
Quhar at the cors of Dewynnik lay.
Thane was sanct Machor blyth and glad
For this fare sicht that he sene had.
And one the morne quhene it was day,
Till his discipulis this cane say:
Lowe we all god, my brothir dere,
That has ws send a gud gestenere!
Tharfor mak we ws redy tyt
Hyme, as a spe afferis, to visidte
And yeld till hyme forout delay
That office that we acht to say
For worthi mene, quhene thai ded are!
With that thai passit furthmare
To the kirk quhar at sanct Machor
The angelis play had sene befor.
Bot thai that the cors brocht thiddire,
With It had gane thar way to-giddir
Ner-by of Creskane to the hill,
And thare abad, to reste in will.
Bot sanct Machor forontyne firste.
Folouit and fand thaime thaire tak reste.
And he and his thar with thame abad
Till thai the seruice all had mad
That to sic deide mene suld parteyne
Ar ony wink come in thar eyne.
And syne bare the cors deuotely
Till a place callit Banchory.

And thare solempni with honoure
Thai grathit for it a sepulture,
And one hyme thare thai mad a kirk.
Quhar god yeit cesis nocht to wirk
Thru his prayere ferleis full fele,
To sek and sar folk gyfand heile.
Mene callis that place quar he lay
Banchory Dewynnik till this day.

These legends represent St. Devenick as an old man at the time St. Machar was preaching in the northeast of Scotland; and then, as dividing the work between himself and St. Machar, he going to Cathini while St. Machar remained at Aberdeen. In consequence of a prior compact entered into between the two Saints, the body of St. Devenick was brought back to Aberdeen, and buried at Banchory-Devenick. He had a dedication at Creich, in Sutherland, where he was known as "St. Teavnich." Boece calls him, 'Archdeacon,' but King, Keith, and others style him 'Bishop.' Though the first legend represents him as a contemporary of St. Columba, the Scottish Annalists record his death as occurring, A.D., 887, in the reign of Soluathius. But the Scotch Kings, named Selvach, Latinised, Soluathius, were both in the sixth century, and thus the time of the Saint is left in doubt, though the balance of authority leans to the sixth century.* His feast day, 13th November, was long religiously held by the inhabitants

* Dr. Gammack, on *St. Devenick.*

of the parish, and a special altar was afterwards raised to his memory in the Cathedral of Aberdeen.

The kirk of Banchory-Devenick, however, does not appear prominently in history till the year 1163, when Malcolm IV. granted a charter (its authenticity is doubted) in favour of the Bishop of Aberdeen, confirming and conveying large tracts of land throughout the country, for the benefit of the See which his namesake, Malcolm II., is said to have founded at Mortlach in 1010. It had been removed to Old Aberdeen in 1137, and among the lands mentioned in the charter of Malcolm IV., is "the kirk of Banchory-Devenick, with the land and pertinents."

Nearly a hundred years later, 1256, the parson of Banchory-Devenick was eleventh prebend of the chapter. Each prebend had a manse and glebe, in Old Aberdeen. "His manse, yard and gleib," says Orem, describing the prebend's property, "lie on the west side of the Chanry; having on the north the Parson of Oyne's manse, and on the south the Parson of Ellon's; which manse was a great lodging, with a large yard, and a gleib of arable land, consisting of a rigg at the end of said yard, lying towards the Kettle Hills." This manse continued to be occupied by the minister of Banchory-Devenick, for some considerable time after the Reformation.

Banchory-Devenick is interesting as being one of the last parishes in Scotland into which Episcopacy was attempted to be introduced. In the Spring of 1712, upwards of two hundred copies of the English prayer book were sent down from London, for gratis distribution among the parishoners. On 19th October, following, the assistant minister, Robert Jamieson, intimated from the pulpit, that "the excellent liturgy of the church of England was to be used in the public worship of God in this congregation, and accordingly the people were seriously exhorted to perform this method of worship with a true spirit of devotion, and with that becoming gravity and decencie that was expected from those who had been so exemplary heretofore in the public worship of God." On the following Sunday, therefore, "the liturgy was first used," and two months thereafter, "all the dasks in the church were made fitt for kneeling in the time of prayers, by fixing kneeling boards in every dask." This mode of worship appears to have been followed for only a very brief period, probably not beyond December, 1714, when the Rev. James Gordon the minister, who was a staunch Episcopalian, died. It is a singular circumstance that, seventy years after, not a single copy of the two hundred books remained in the parish, and that a tempting offer by Dr. Morison, to the booksellers in Aberdeen, failed to secure one.

It is impossible to state at what date the church previous to the present one was erected, but on the back of an old pewter plate belonging to the church is a rude tracing of what is believed to represent it. It had been a small low roofed building with two windows on the south side, and a sort of belfry with entrance door at one end.

The date given is 1642. In the beginning of last century the fabric had fallen into a somewhat unsatisfactory state. "Divots" or "sods" were frequently required to fill up gaps in the walls; and although no great attention was paid to comfort, the parishioners had evidently had a desire to improve the appearance of the structural arrangements. On 23rd November, 1712, "the minister and elders, taking to their serious consideration that whereas the pulpit in the church was very mean and insufficient, it was judged proper for the greater decencie and ornament of the church that there should be a new pulpit, and reading dask made of firr wood, and handsome and good work, and the management and ordering thereof was committed to the assistant." After the wear and tear of another century, however, the whole building became decayed; and in 1821 the state of the church was such that it became imperative on the heritors either to substantially renew the old structure or provide a new church in its stead. A strong movement was made by certain parishioners resident on the coast side of the parish to have the church removed from the old site to the top of the hill of Banchory, but the minister and several of the heritors were opposed to it. Ultimately estimates were taken for the renewing and enlarging of the old building, and also for erecting a new church from the foundation. It was then found that the one would cost about as much as the other, and, as the leading heritors were in favour of the latter scheme, it was unanimously agreed that the old building

Kirk of Banchory Devenick

should be pulled down, and a substantial one, capable of accommodating nine hundred sitters, erected in its place. The kirk-session records show that the new church was opened for divine service on 29th September, 1822, and that on the previous twenty-five Sundays the congregation had met for worship in the churchyard, where the pulpit and seats had been temporarily set up. It is worthy of note, that on none of these twenty-five Sundays had a single drop of rain fallen during the services, whilst on the day the church was opened rain fell heavily. It was not till the year 1865 that the area of the church was floored with wood and a system of heating introduced. Prior to this, rough blocks of stone served as a floor, and the idea of heating would have been considered grossly extravagant.

The old church bell, believed to have been cast in the year 1597, having become useless, was sold in 1868. It bore the following inscription, which is old German :— H B. Alleine . Got . In . Der . Hoge . Sei . Ere . 1597. The translation is. *Alone to God in Heaven be Praise.* A new bell was provided and hung, but it possesses nothing like the rich and mellow tone of the old one.

MINISTERS OF BANCHORY-DEVENICK.

. . . .

1425. John Clatt, vicar.* The probabilities are that this is the same John Clatt referred to by Kennedy as being the original founder of Saint Thomas' Hospital, which stood near Saint Nicholas Church, Aberdeen. "By the charter of foundation, dated May 28, 1459, Clatt granted all his lands and tenements in the Netherkirkgate for erecting the hospital in honour of God, the blessed Virgin Mary, and all Saints, and particularly for the honour of Saint Thomas, the martyr; and appointed Mr. John Chawmers to be master and rector. After his and the founder's death, the patronage of the institution was to devolve upon the provost and community for ever. The founder also endowed it with annuities in perpetuity, amounting to £1 4s. 8d., arising from certain tenements in the town; and also with an annuity of 6 merks, to be levied from the lands of Mondynes, in the county of Kincardine, for celebrating, in the hospital, masses for the salvation of his own soul, and for the souls of James II., and of Alexander Stuart, Earl of Mar, of his own father and mother, and of all the faithful departed, according to the custom of the age."†

* *Antiquities of Aberdeen and Banff*, Vol. iii., p. 517.
† Kennedy's *Annals of Aberdeen*, Vol, ii., pp. 78, 79.

. . . .

1497. Alexander Campbell, prebendary.

1508. Alexander Cabell, successor. He mortified £10 of yearly rent to be paid from the land of Muriecroft, with its pertinents, to pray at the altar of St. Devenick. Adam Hepburn of Craggis "oblist hym and his airs to Alexander Cabell, persown of Banchory Dewynyk that forsamekle as the said Alexander had resignit the haf land of Murcroft, the foresaid Adam or his airis shuld deliver ane mortification of ten punds of annual rent to ane chaplainry fundit at Sanct Dewynik altar situat in the cathedrale kirk of Aberdeen and shuld present nain thereto bot quhom that pleiss the said Mr. Alexander."* It was expressly stipulated that after mass the tomb of the founder should be sprinkled with consecrated water, and the psalm, *De Profundis*, repeated. Cabell was one of the umpires chosen, in 1508, to define the marches between the lands of Ardefrie and those of Ardendracht and Ashallo.

1526. Henry Forsyth, successor.†

1541. Patrick Dunbar, successor.

1567. David Menzies, minister of Nigg and Banchory-Devenick, with Robert Merser, person, exhorter and administrator of the sacraments at a stipend of £34 13s. 4d. Scots. Nothing is now known of the

* *Registrum Aberdonensis*, p. 352.
† *Fasti Aberdonenses.*

history of Menzies, but it is evident that he had not held the appointment for any lengthened period.

1571. Robert Merser. In this year, Merser, who had acted as assistant under Menzies, succeeded to the full charge. He was of the family of Innerpeffry, in Strathearn, senior cadets of the Mersers of Meiklour. He had possibly secured the appointment through the influence of Erskine of Dun, superintendent of Angus and the Mearns, to whom the Mersers were related by marriage. In the assembly of 1575 a complaint was lodged against Erskine for admitting him to the office, on the ground "that he was unable to discharge his cure;" but, as it was stated that he had been duly put upon trial by his brethren of Aberdeen, nothing came of it. He died before 25th February, 1578-9, leaving three sons—Malcolm, rector of Crieff; Robert who succeeded to the benefice of Banchory-Devenick; and Thomas.*

1578. Robert Merser, son of the foregoing, succeeded. For some time previously he had acted as a regent in King's College, and as such was the teacher of John Johnston, the eminent Latin poet and scholar, who by his last will and testament bequeathed to Merser, his "auld kynd maister," his "white cap with the silver fit in taikin of thankful dewtie." The Presbytery in 1602 "fund Mr. Merser negligent in teaching and exercising of discipline," yet there was "a rare

---

* Jervise's *Epitaphs and Inscriptions*, and Scott's *Fasti*.

commendation of the people, and quhen they are assemblit litill reverence or attendance geiven to the word teached, and therefore he was scharplie admonishit." In the following year it was reported that "he teaches better and oftner now sen he has his residence in Aberdeen, than he did quhen he was resident with them, notwithstanding he was ordained to reside." The Presbytery in 1610 "fund him sumquhat cauld in his doctrine and delyuerie thairof, and that he has delapidat his benefice, and therefore the auld processe to be reuiset." The stipend in 1606 was given up at 200 merks.* Merser was one of the assenting parties to the Disposition, granted in 1613 to the "minister of sanct Nicolas of 200 lb. yeerlie out of the salmound fischerys teyndis vpon Done Water,"

1627. Andrew Melvin or Melvill, M.A., successor, was admitted about 1627, and subscribed the Covenant in 1638. Spalding says he was recognized as a shrewd business man, and adds, that when he, along with two other ministers, was chosen to represent the Presbytery at the Assembly of 1641 "Mr. Androw is vrgit to dimit, whiche ignorantlie contrair his credit, he did."†

1651. William Robertson, who had been educated at King's College, Aberdeen, succeeded. He married in 1630 Isobel Gordon, who, with three sons and three daughters, survived him. He died 16th June, 1656, aged about 46 years.

*Scott's *Fasti*; *Presb. Reg.'s*; *Book of the Kirk*; Gordon's *Aberdeen* &c.
† Scott's *Fasti*; Spalding's *Trubles*, &c.

1657. David Lyell, eldest son of Walter Lyell, town clerk of Montrose, and licensed as a preacher of the gospel by the Presbytery of Brechin in 1656, was presented to the charge of Banchory-Devenick in the following year, and ordained there by the Presbytery of Aberdeen. The famous Andrew Cant, who then held a city charge, was present at the ordination, and when Lyell, three years later, pronounced the sentence of deposition upon him, the latter, who was in church at the time, stood up and in a sorrowful voice exclaimed, " Davie, Davie, I kent aye ye wad do this sin the day I laid my hands on your heid." Cant, by the way, once "teichit at Banchorie-Devnik, to whome flokkit sindrie puritanes out of Abirdein to heir him—a gryte covenanter—veray bussie in thir alterationis and mortall enemy touardis the bischoppis." Lyell was translated to the the third charge of Aberdeen in 1666, and thence to the first charge in Montrose in 1673. He was elected minister of Edinburgh (Trinity College Church) 18th December, 1678, but he did not accept it, and died in March 1696, in the 62nd year of his age. He had a "thundering way of preaching," was very popular with his parishoners, and mortified a considerable sum for behoof of the poor of Montrose.*

1667. James Gordon, M.A., was the son of Dr William Gordon, physician, and professor of medicine in

---

* Scott's *Fasti*, and *Memorials of Angus and Mearns*.

King' College, Aberdeen. Spalding describes him as "ane of the foundit memberis of the colledge of Old Abirdein, and common procuratour thairof, a godlie, grave, lerned man, and singular in commoun warkis about the colledge, and putting wp on the stepill thairof most glorious, as you sie, ane staitlie crowne throwne doun be the wynd abefoir." He had no sooner secured the pastorate of Banchory-Devenick, at Martinmas 1667, than he threw himself with the utmost zeal into the fierce contest then raging throughout the country, whether the Presbyterian or Episcopalian form of church government should obtain the supremacy. Dr. Grub, in his *Ecclesiastical History of Scotland*, says that "from conviction and hereditary feeling, strongly attached to the hierarchy, the parson of Banchory submitted with reluctance to those defects which the prudence or timidity of the Bishops did not attempt to remedy. Having considerable family influence, he was probably looked up to as a leader by the younger clergy, who composed the discontented party. The records of the diocese show that he was of a hasty temper; and, according to the statements of his opponents, his zeal was sharpened by disappointed ambition." He was present at the meeting of the Bishop's Court on 23rd May, 1676, when the "masters of aither of the colledges," were "appoynted to think upon the most feasable way for restraining the students from Inglish speaking within the Colledge gates, from swearing and obscene talking."* In 1679 he published a book entitled *The Reformed Bishop, or XIX. Articles*, tendered by a well-wisher of the present government of the Church of Scotland (as it is settled by law) in order to the further establishment thereof. The work, which was remarkable for its erudition and argumentative tenor, denounced in the most scathing terms the so-called corruptions prevailing throughout the Church. No names of individuals were mentioned, but the references were of such a pointed character that it was impossible to mistake for whom they were intended. The author concluded by urging the establishment of such a moderate Episcopacy as Charles I. was ready to grant—a system he stated, which, in that king's own words, "would at once satisfy all just desires and interests of good bishops, humble presbyters, and sober people; so as church affairs should be managed neither with tyranny, parity, nor popularity, neither bishops ejected, nor presbyters despised, nor people oppressed."†

The publication of the work caused the utmost anger and bitterness, not only in Aberdeen, but throughout the whole country. A pasquil of the period, epigrammatically told the parson, who became nicknamed the "Reformed Bishop,"

> "If your book had never been seen,
> You had been Bishop of Aberdeen,
> If you had been Bishop of Aberdeen,
> Your book had never been seen."

* *Fasti Aberdonenses*, p. 342.
† *The Reformed Bishop.*

He was summoned for trial in January, 1680, before an Episcopal Synod at which Archbishop Burnet presided. The Synod, while acknowledging the error of the parson, took a charitable view of the case. "For all which malicious, slanderous and impious defamations," runs the closing passage of the sentence, "notwithstanding that the said Mr. James Gordon hath rendered himself justly obnoxious to the highest and heaviest censure of the Church, as having incurred the curse of wicked Cham in the most eminent degree, yet we have, in order to the vindication of the honour of the Church and its governors, and for the reclaiming, if possible, of the said Mr. James out of the snare of the Devil, into which, through his malice and ambition, he hath wilfully thrown himself, thought fit at this time to proceed only to the sentence of deposition." In an Act of the Privy Council in November, 1680, the book was classed among seditious and forbidden works, such as Buchanan's *De Jure Regni*, Calderwood's *History*, and *Naphtali*. This sentence was considered by many as more severe than the offence warranted; but Mr. Gordon having expressed his sorrow, and craved pardon of all whom he had offended by publishing the work, the Bishops recalled their former sentence, and, on 14th March following, he had the satisfaction of being re-instated to his office and benefice at Banchory-Devenick. In 1689 he and the minister of Cruden were appointed by the Synod of Aberdeen to draw up an address relative to the proposed abolition of Prelacy, &c. ; and, five years later, he appeared before a Commission, and lodged a formal protest against the authority exercised by the late Assembly. Besides publishing *The Reformed Bishop*, he was the author of many other works—*Request to Roman Catholics*, 1687; *Some Observations on the Fables of Æsop*, 1700; *Reflections on L'Estrange's Translation of Æsop's Fables*, 1700; *The Character of a Generous Prince*, 1703; *Some Charitable Observations on Forbes' Treatise of Church Lands and Tithes*, 1706; *Some Just Reflections on a Pasquil against the Parson of Banchory*, 1706—(the two latter were answered by Mr. William Forbes, afterwards professor of law in the University of Glasgow); *Queries about Popery*. He was married to Elizabeth Forbes, by whom he had issue. His eldest son, James, who married Catherine Collison, was for sometime a rector in Yorkshire, and afterwards episcopal clergyman of Montrose. Like his father he also fell into the bad graces of his brethren, for "intruding upon the paroche of Foveran"— an offence for which he was summoned before "a considerable number of the clergy of the country," at the instance of the laird of Udny. "It would fill a volume to give an account of this affair," wrote Wodrow's correspondent, Langlands, " but, in short, after a prepared speech, larded with Latine phrases, had by Mr. James Gordon of Banchrie, they gave in some queries to which they got an answer, then gave in an appeal with these queries in its bosome." The appeal was withdrawn from, however, and the matter thereupon dropped. Gordon's other son was George, who graduated M.D. at King's College in 1696. Notwithstanding the strong episcopalian tendencies which all along pervaded the parson of Banchory-Devenick, he took a keen interest in the temporal, as well as the spiritual welfare of his parishioners. It was no doubt through his personal influence over his hearers that he got them to submit to the introduction of Episcopacy. As proprietor of the lands of Ardoe, and a connection of the powerful family of Seaton, he was possessed of a considerable annual income. In 1710 he mortified 40 pounds Scots, to be paid annually in all time coming from the lands of Ardoe, for the benefit of the poor of the parish. The deed of mortification is of the most exacting and unalterable character, winding up by insisting that the minister and members of session, as patrons, "shall duly maintain and administrate the same in all time coming, and adhere thereto in the terms expressed without any change or alteration whatsomever, as they will answer to God; and as they would wish to be saved at the great day of judgment." He died 24th December, 1714, aged 74.

1716. John Maitland, son of an advocate in Aberdeen, was licensed by the Presbytery of Aberdeen in May, 1700; ordained minister of Skene in September following; was called by the Presbytery to Banchory-Devenick, *jure devoluto*, 17th August, 1715; and inducted there on 1st March following. He married Agnes, daughter of Mr. Thomson, advocate in Aberdeen, and she survived him. He died in March, 1727, in the 27th year of his ministry. As a clergyman he was beloved and respected by his parishioners, who deeply regretted his premature demise. His son, James, became minister of the parish of Sorbie on the south-east corner of Wigtonshire.

1728. John Lumsden, son of Alexander Lumsden of Auchenlett, schoolmaster of Chapel of Garioch, ordained minister of Keith-hall and Kinkell in 1721, and presented to the charge of Banchory-Devenick in 1728. He married a sister of the last laird of the Leslie family, who was proprietor of Pitcaple. This laird, who was an officer in the army, died in 1757, when the property fell to Mrs. Lumsden. Her two daughters subsequently sold Pitcaple to Henry Lumsden, grandfather of the present proprietor, Mr. Henry Lumsden.* Lumsden, who was an excellent preacher and a shrewd business man, was about 1734 honoured with the appointment as one of the Deans of the Chapel Royal. Two years later he was appointed professor of divinity in King's College, Aberdeen, when he demitted his pastorate of Banchory-Devenick, and preached his farewell sermon there on 7th November, 1736. He was moderator of the General Assembly of 1746, and died in 1771.

* *Inverurie and Earldom of Garioch ; Castles of Aberdeenshire,* &c.

1737. James Nicolson, who had been licensed by the Presbytery of Haddington in 1734, was presented to the charge of Banchory-Devenick by George II., in January, 1737, and ordained there on 13th September of that year. The way in which the presentation fell to him was remarkable. More than a century before, Thomas Garden, a younger son of one of the lairds of Banchory, and a prominent member of the incorporated trades of Aberdeen, leased from Mr. Menzies of Pitfodels the lands of Gilcomston, at the annual rental of £27 15s. 6d. He acquired a competency, and left to his eldest daughter 27,000 merks Scots—a very considerable sum in those days. To the regret of her relatives she married a Lieutenant Cadogan, at that time a subaltern officer in Oliver Cromwell's army. But the marriage, though at first disappointing, proved in the end to be both advantageous and honourable. Her husband rose to be a colonel, a general, and latterly was created a peer. From him were descended the Lords and Earls Cadogan, the Dukes of Richmond and Leinster, Earl Verney, Lord Holland, the Right Hon. Charles James Fox, and other persons of the highest rank in England, through intermarriage with the Cadogan family. What is still more to their honour, they did not neglect their Scotch relatives, who at first thought themselves affronted by Miss Garden's marriage. On the vacancy occurring at Banchory-Devenick through the resignation of Mr. Lumsden, Lord Cadogan used his influence at Court, with the result that the King gave the living to Mr. Nicolson, who was a son of the second daughter of Mr. Thomas Garden, and thus nephew of the first Lord Cadogan. In 1760 Mr. Nicolson instituted a process against the heritors which depended for six years, when he got decree establishing his former stipend out of the parsonage teinds, and throwing the vicarage on the heritors at 400 merks per annum. He was twice married: first, to Janet, daughter of George Haliburton, Lord Provost of Edinburgh, and by her he had issue one daughter and two sons. Out of respect to Lord Cadogan, he named the daughter Cadogan, and one of the sons Charles, the other being named George Haliburton. Charles was for sometime minister of Amsterdam, and afterwards chaplain to the British Embassy at Constantinople. Mr. Nicolson's second wife was Helen Thom, to whom he was married in May 1772. According to the quaint entry in the session book on 4th June following, "at 7 o'clock in the morning," he "paid the debt of nature, aged 65 years." Mr. Nicolson was deeply regretted by his parishioners with whom he was an especial favourite, for he was eminently a man of peace, who found his chief delight in the faithful and conscientious discharge of his parochial duties.*

1773. George Ogilvie, schoolmaster of Auchterhouse, licensed by the Presbytery of Dundee in 1747, was presented to the charge of Cortachy by its patron, John, Earl

* Scott's *Fasti*, Skene Keith's *Agricultural Survey*, and *Session Records*.

of Airlie, in 1748, and received a presentation to Banchory-Devenick from George III., in 1772, being inducted on 8th July of the following year. He died, 17th April, 1785, in the 65th year of his age and 37th of his ministry, survived by his wife, Katherine Anderson, who died, 28th March, 1800, aged 81, and two sons. One of these, Skene Ogilvie, was laureated at the University and King's College, Aberdeen, in 1773; was licensed in 1776; ordained minister of Skene 1777; translated to Old Machar in 1784, and died 12th December, 1831.*

1785. George Morison, M.A., fifth son of James Morison of Elsick (who was Lord Provost of Aberdeen at the time of the Rebellion of 1745-46), was educated at the University and King's College, Aberdeen, where he graduated in 1776. Passing through the Divinity course with distinction, he was licensed by the Presbytery of Aberdeen in 1782, received a presentation to the parish of Oyne in the Presbytery of Garioch in the same year, and in 1785 he was presented by George III. to the parish of Banchory-Devenick, being inducted 10th November of same year. From the outset he took the liveliest possible interest in his parishioners to whom he became greatly attached. In the discharge of the various parochial duties of the parish he was ably assisted by his wife, Margaret Jaffray (they were married 26th June, 1786), who was a descendant of the Jaffrays of Kingswells,

---

* Scott's *Fasti, Session Records of Skene*, &c.

Aberdeen, so well known from their connection with the Society of Friends. Mr. Morison's brother, Thomas, who was at one time a physician in London, and subsequently proprietor of the estates of Elsick and Disblair, aided in the introduction of the benefits of vaccination into the parish. On the decease of this brother, the Rev. Mr. Morison succeeded to the estates mentioned, and the large annual income he subsequently derived enabled him to do many acts of benevolence. In the year 1800, when there was all but a famine in the district, he bought meal at exorbitant prices, stored it in a granary, and by his own hand doled it out from time to time to such as were in want. By these means he kept many from actual starvation. He had the degree of D. D. conferred upon him by the University and King's College, Aberdeen, in 1824. He contributed handsomely to the fund for endowment of Portlethen Church *(quoad sacra);* erected a school and schoolhouse at Portlethen, and bequeathed large legacies for the support of the teacher, as also for a female school teacher at Banchory-Devenick. Perhaps his greatest act of liberality, however, was the erection in 1837 of the suspension bridge across the Dee at Cults. Previous to this a parish boat was the only method by which communication could be maintained between the north and south side of the parish. Owing, however, to frequent floods of the river and floes of ice in the winter season, this mode of transportation could not always be depended on. The construction of the bridge cost

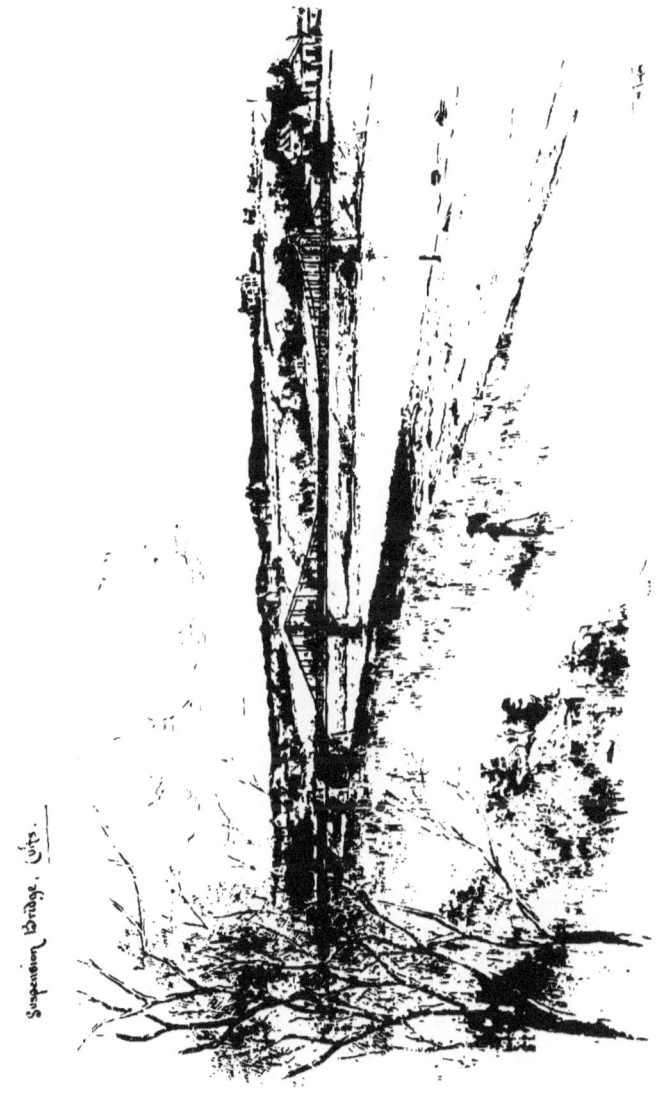

Suspension Bridge, Cliften.

about £1400, which was borne entirely by Dr. Morison, who also left a large sum to the minister and kirk-session of the parish as trustees "to maintain and uphold it in time coming." The bridge, which is popularly known as the chain or shaking bridge, bears the following inscription on a cast-iron plate which is built into the south-east parapet :—

MDCCCXXXVII.

SAINT DEVENICK BRIDGE,

ERECTED BY GEORGE MORISON, D.D. OF ELSICK, FOR THE ACCOMMODATION OF THIS PARISH, OF WHICH HE HAS NOW BEEN LII. YEARS PASTOR. JOHN SMITH, ARCHITECT ; J. DUFFUS & CO., G. DONALDSON AND G. BARCLAY, CONTRACTORS.

In recognition of his munificence and liberality the parishioners presented him with a handsome testimonial on the occasion of his jubilee. He was the author of several publications—*two single Sermons 1831-32*; *A Brief Outline of the External Framework and Internal Constitution of the Appointments of the Church of Scotland, as by Law established, 1840*; *State of the Church of Scotland in 1830 and 1840 Contrasted, 1840*; *Accounts of the Parish* (Sinclairs IV. and *New Stat. Acc.* XI. XXI). He died on 13th July, 1845, father of the Church of Scotland, in the 88th year of his age, and 63rd of his ministry. The tribute paid in the minutes of the kirk-session on his death represents the feeling of the whole district. "To enumerate instances of his private benevolence would be endless, as in this way he was continually doing good. As moderator of this court the session bear testimony to his excellent judgment and enlightened views in the management of the whole business, to his great anxiety to economize the poor's funds, and to supply the poor at the same time with the necessaries of life, to his mixture of impartiality and tenderness in the exercise of church discipline, and to his conciliatory, kind and friendly demeanour towards the other members of the session. In fine, the session feel with deep regret that, in the death of Dr. Morison, the parish has sustained a great public loss, the extent of which is perhaps not yet fully felt, and which, in many respects they fear it is not probable will in their day ever be repaired." At his death his nephews, Captain Robert Farquhar of the Madras Infantry, succeeded to Elsick, and Professor Mearns of King's College, Aberdeen, to Disblair, respectively. Elsick was subsequently sold to the deceased Sir Alexander Bannerman, Bart. of Crimonmogate, whose ancestors had previously owned it; and Disblair now belongs to Professor Mearns' son, the Rev. Dr. Mearns, minister of Kinneff. The Rev. D. G. Mearns, the only son of Dr. Mearns, is the present minister of Oyne, to which Dr. Morison was first called.

1826. William Paul, M.A., eldest son of the Rev. William Paul, minister of Maryculter, afterwards professor of natural philosophy in King's College, Aberdeen, was born at the manse of Maryculter on 27th September, 1804. His mother was daughter of the Rev. John Hutcheon,

minister of Fetteresso. He attended the Grammar
School, Old Aberdeen, and subsequently King's College,
at which he graduated in arts in 1822. In that year
he went to England, where he taught for sometime
very successfully, in a private academy in Colchester.
Even whilst attending his divinity course in Aberdeen, he
contrived between the sessions to visit England, and find
work there as a tutor. In the spring of 1826, when
little more than 21 years of age, he was licensed by the
Presbytery of Aberdeen, and thereupon became assistant
to his grand-uncle, Dr. Morison, at Banchory-Devenick.
In the autumn of the same year he was ordained as a
minister, but it was not till eight years later that he
received the formal appointment as assistant and success-
or, in the charge of Banchory parish. By this time Dr.
Morison, the senior minister, was getting old and infirm,
and the burden of the ministerial work now devolved
almost entirely upon his ordained assistant. In July,
1845, on the decease of Dr. Morison, he succeeded to
the full charge. He discharged his duty well and faith-
fully. "As a preacher," in the words of a newspaper
obituary notice, "he was earnest, simple, and persuasive,
adapting his language to the understanding of the
humblest of his flock; but by his elegance of style and
lucidity of arrangement, attracting and instructing the
most cultured. But in his parochial, as distinguished
from his ministerial work, he took special delight. To
visit the fatherless and widows in their affliction, to

attend the sick beds of his people, and to minister advice, encouragement and consolation, he accounted the highest privilege and the most sacred duty of a Christian minister." As a linguist and educationist, he had few, if any, equals in the ministry, and as such he attained much distinction. In 1857 he published, *Analysis and Critical Examination of the Hebrew Text of the Book of Genesis, preceded by a Hebrew Grammar and Dissertation on the Genuineness of the Pentateuch, and on the Structure of the Hebrew Language.* In recognition of the excellence of this publication his *Alma Mater* conferred on him the degree of D.D. Continuing his biblical studies with earnestness and assiduity, he produced in 1870 another work, entitled *The Scriptural Account of the Creation Vindicated by the Teaching of Science, or a New Method for Reconciling the Mosaic and Geological Records of Creation.* Again in 1878 he published a third book, entitled *The Authorship and Date of the Books of Moses*, which was followed two years later by *The Past and Present of Aberdeenshire.* Through having for many years acted as presbytery-clerk he acquired an excellent knowledge of church law, and his opinions were recognized alike in the General Assembly as in the inferior Church Courts. During the trying time of the Disruption, when some fifteen of the churches within the bounds of the Aberdeen Presbytery were without ministers, the work of finding substitutes lay entirely on his shoulders, but so completely did he combat the difficulty that not one was even temporarily closed. For this signal service the members of the Presbytery subsequently presented him with a magnificent salver and handsome tea service, both of silver. Again on the occasion of his jubilee in 1876 he was presented by the congregation and friends with an illuminated address and valuable purse of sovereigns. He was twice married—first to a daughter of the late Baillie Stewart of Aberdeen, and secondly to Miss Margaret Smith, daughter of the minister of the parish of Bower in Caithness. The latter survived him, and is now resident in Edinburgh. By his first wife he had a large family, of whom five daughters and four sons are still alive. Of the latter, William is an advocate in Aberdeen; George is partner of the well-known legal firm of Dundas & Wilson, W.S., Edinburgh; David is minister of the parish of Roxburgh; and the fourth, Edward, is principal of a college in America. From 1881 Dr. Paul's health gradually declined, and, though carefully nursed, he passed quietly away on Sunday, 27th April, 1884, in the 80th year of his age, and 58th of his ministry.

1881. William Fyfe Lawrence, M.A., only son of Mr. William Lawrence, farmer, Kirkbuddo, near Forfar, and nephew of the Rev. John Fyfe, M.A., professor of moral philosophy in the University of Aberdeen, was born in the parish of Carmyllie. He received his early education at the parish school, thereafter at the Grammar School, Old Aberdeen, and entered King's College as a bursar, graduating in 1878. Choosing the ministry as a profession, he was licensed by the Presbytery of Aberdeen in 1881. In the summer of that year he acted for three months as assistant to Dr. Paul, who, a month or two later, owing to his failing health, applied to the Presbytery for an assistant and successor. Mr. Lawrence became a candidate for the vacancy, and, in December following, when the election took place, obtained a majority of votes, and was thereupon elected. His ordination took place in the church on 26th January, 1882, when the deceased Rev. William Oliver of Greyfriars, Aberdeen, presided. On the decease of Dr. Paul in April 1884, Mr. Lawrence succeeded to the full charge. In 1888 instrumental music was introduced into the services, and the congregation willingly raised the necessary amount to liquidate the cost of the instrument. An additional £50 was at the same time collected as an augmentation to the minister's income, which had been materially reduced owing to the fall in the fiars' prices, by which four-fifths of the stipend of Banchory-Devenick is regulated. Mr. Lawrence who is possessed of excellent mental abilities, is a powerful preacher, and takes an active interest in the affairs of the Parochial Board. In January, 1885, he married Miss Lizzie Milne, daughter of Mr. William Duncan, who is a large quarry owner near Arbroath.

PARISH CHURCHYARD.

The probabilities are that simultaneous with the erection of the first church, the ground immediately adjoining had been set apart as a place of sepulture. Undoubted evidence could be furnished that for long it formed the only public place of interment in the parish, and so largely had its capacity been taxed, that in 1783 it was found to be "in such a crowded state as to cause serious danger to the church walls." Prior to this any parishioner was entitled to secure burial space within the church, on payment of a small fee, but an Act of Session was then passed that "in future none excepting an heritor or his family, and the minister of the parish shall be buried within the church." Since then three separate extensions of the burial-ground have taken place, the last one being of such a substantial character, that there is now ample space available for the requirements of the parish for many years to come. Up to the present time it may safely be computed that upwards of 15,000 persons have found their last resting place in this hallowed spot.

In the beginning of the present century, owing to each student of medicine being required before qualifying as a doctor to furnish a body for dissecting purposes, various expedients were fallen upon to meet the demand. The usual one followed, however, was that of exhuming and stealing newly interred bodies out of the country churchyards. The persons engaged in the nefarious trade went by the name of "Resurrectionists," and such a feeling of terror and alarm did they instil in the minds of the common orders throughout the country, that in the end it became imperative, not only for the Legislature to pass strong measures of repression, but for each parish, independently, to take steps for guarding the graves of their newly buried dead. So expeditiously, and at the sametime so secretly were the thefts committed, however, that in spite of all the vigilance of watchers, bodies were repeatedly lifted and carried off. On a dark and wintry night in the year 1813, three medical students from Aberdeen visited the churchyard of Banchory-Devenick for the fixed purpose of removing a body,* which

---

* The old churchyard of Nigg, from its proximity to Aberdeen, and secluded situation near the bay of Nigg, was frequently visited by bodysnatchers. On 22nd December, 1808, the remains of Mrs. Spark, an aged woman who had died in Aberdeen, were ferried across the Dee, and decently interred in the churchyard. Next morning it was discovered that during the night the body had been taken up, and carried off. The grave was left in a most gruesome fashion—broken pieces of the lid of the coffin, tatters of grave linen, and marks of blood, being left scattered about the grave. It was afterwards discovered that the perpetrators of the outrage were medical students belonging to Aberdeen. They had evidently been disturbed in their transporting of the body, and, to avoid detection, had hid it in the sand on the north side of the bay of Nigg. A storm subsequently arose and washed it out to the bay, where it was discovered and again interred. The ringleader in the escapade, who was described as "a forward, impudent, not well behaved

had that day been interred. The relations of the deceased, however, were on the outlook, and secured the three, after a stiff tussle. They were carried to Stonehaven, and committed to prison on the double charge of attempting to steal a dead body, and for an assault upon the watchers. At the trial, which afterwards took place before the sheriff, their guilt was clearly established, and they were ordered to pay a fine of £20. This amount having been recovered, the procurator-fiscal handed over a considerable proportion of the fine for behoof of the poor of the parish.

For the comfort and protection of watchers a small building was erected on the south side of the churchyard, where it still stands, being now used as a tool-house by the sexton. As many poor people could not afford to pay the expense of "watching," the late Mr. George Barclay, builder, Cults, designed, and got cast two massive iron chests or safes—coffin-shaped—each weighing about nineteen hundredweight, for placing around the coffin when lowered into the grave. The iron safe was lowered by block-and-tackle, and being correctly set, the grave was filled up. Six weeks later, when it was considered that decomposition had made such progress as to preclude the chance of a visit from the "body-snatchers," the grave was again opened and the safe removed. These safes of Mr. Barclay's were likewise used in many of the neighbouring churchyards, but by the passing of the Act of

young man," was obliged to leave the country for a time to escape the wrath of the people.—*Session Records of Nigg.*

Parliament, ordering all unclaimed bodies to be delivered up for purposes of dissection, their further use was happily unnecessary. One still lies in the churchyard and forms a source of considerable attraction to visitors. Till within comparatively recent years it was usual, on the morning of an interment, for a lighted candle to be placed near the dead body, and left to burn itself out. Another custom was to stop all clocks in the house at the moment a death occurred, and not to set them in motion again till the corpse had been removed from the house. In some instances there was placed on the breast of the deceased person a platter containing a small quantity of salt and earth, unmixed, the earth as emblematical of the corruptible body, and the salt as symbolical of the immortal spirit. These customs, however, together with the treating of the funeral party to refreshments, are now rarely observed, and the funeral rites usually followed are of the simplest possible character,

Of instances of longevity which have occurred in the district, the following are perhaps the most remarkable :—

1759. 27th March. Died, William Cushnie, from an attack of the measles, aged about 100 years.

1761. Feb. Died, George Forbes, a farmer in the adjoining parish of Maryculter, aged 106 years.

1764. 30th April. Died last week at Wardhead of Countesswells, in the 98th year of his age, Robert Williamson, who was married 74 years previously, to Isobel Wagrel, who is now left a widow in the 100th year of her age, and in so good a state of health that she has for these last two weeks attended the weekly market in Aberdeen, selling her butter, poultry, and eggs.

1771. 1st April. Died, George Keith, who resided on the south side of the parish, in the 100th year of his age. He followed his ordinary business till within twenty days of his death, and continued sensible to the last. Thirty-eight of his children and grand-children, and fifteen of his great-grand-children, followed his remains to the grave.

1823. In this year there died at Greenhead, in the neighbouring parish, the widow of a farmer, aged 102. She is interred in the churchyard of Maryculter.

Some of the inscriptions on the present tombstones are given in the Appendix.

BANCHORY-DEVENICK FREE CHURCH.

This church was erected in 1844 on a site surrounded by trees, about a mile to the south of the parish church. The ground, along with a sufficient space for a graveyard, was given off, gratuitously, from the estate of Banchory, by the proprietor, Mr. Alexander Thomson, who also contributed handsomely to the funds of the church.

The first minister was David Findlay Arthur, who is a native of the parish of New Cumnock in Ayrshire, where his forefathers had been farmers for many generations, and had taken an active part in the struggles of the Covenanters. He was educated at Glasgow University, in which he was for some time class assistant to Dr. Buchanan, subsequently acting as tutor in the family of Captain McLeod, who, with his wife, family, and shepherds formed at the time the sole inhabitants of the island of Rum. Duly licensed by the Church of Scotland, Mr. Arthur acted for some time as assistant to Dr. Main of Kilmarnock, after which he removed to Manchester, to take charge of the Church of Scotland mission station there. At this time the Disruption controversy was agitating the country, and, as a crisis in church matters was imminent, Mr. Arthur refused the presentation to his native parish, which had been offered to him by its patron and proprietor, the Marquis of Bute. When the actual separation came he was still at Manchester, but at once resigned and threw in his lot with the dissenting body. Being ordained at Banchory-Devenick in 1844, he found hard and very trying work before him in his new charge. Dr. Morison and his assistant, Dr. Paul, were both popular in the parish, and as they remained in the Establishment, there were not over fifteen available worshippers from whom to make up a congregation. By faithful attention and kindly acts, however, Mr. Arthur soon succeeded in gathering around him an active and earnest congregation, which he had the pleasure to see yearly increasing. The labour and responsibility devolving upon him at Banchory were great ; for, not only had he to discharge the whole ministerial duties of his own congregation, but he had also to attend to the duties of moderator of the session at Cults and Bourtriebush, till regularly ordained ministers were appointed there. He married Miss Brown, daughter of Mr. Brown of Cardens Haugh, by whom he had four sons and one daughter. In 1883, owing to failing health, he was reluctantly obliged to apply to the Presbytery of the bounds for an assistant and successor. The request was at once complied with, the members of the Presbytery embracing the opportunity for expressing the high respect and esteem in which they held their venerable brother. His congregation and private friends, anxious to show their favour in a more tangible form, presented him with an illuminated address and purse of sovereigns. He retired to Cults

House, where he lives with two of his sons, who are physicians, enjoying a deservedly large practice there.

James Ironside Still, who had been educated at the University of Aberdeen, and afterwards at the Free Church College there, succeeded as assistant and successor. He is an active and energetic clergyman, and a member of the School Board of the parish. He had the manse repaired, and the church repainted at an expense of some £500, which he succeeded in raising by means of two bazaars held in the grounds of Banchory House in 1887-88. . The congregation now numbers upwards of two hundred and thirty communicants, and is steadily increasing.

HILLDOWNTREE.

The few houses bearing this title stand a few hundred yards west of the Bridge of Dee. Tradition gives us to understand that the name was assumed "from a huge tree, which long ago had been floated down from the hills and landed here, where it took root and grew to an enormous size. It was blown down by the storm of 3rd October, 1860, but its root is still visible."* At one time public executions are believed to have taken place here, and for many centuries there was an hostelry at which travellers could regale themselves when they were on the road. In the beginning of the present century, the lessee of the inn was a man named Kirton, who was a sort of character in his way, and the hero of the following curious episode—

James Selbie, a blacksmith in Aberdeen, had long courted Betty Tamson, the only daughter of a worthy neighbouring couple. Unfortunately his advances were not looked upon with favour by the parents of Betty, who expected a better match for their daughter. Jamie, however, having received the full consent of his sweetheart, had the necessary proclamations made, with a view to the celebration of the happy event. At this juncture, Betty's parents peremptorily refused to allow the marriage to

* Jervise's *Epitaphs*, Vol. ii., p. 284.

proceed, and, acting on their resolution, "put her under lock and key in a back closet." Jamie, smarting under the indignity, communicated his case to a few of the weavers at the Rigg and Windmillbrae factory, and, after being duly fortified, a large relief party sallied down to the residence of Betty, to rescue her from such parental tyranny. With the assistance of a ladder the window was reached, and the fair enchantress was tenderly and lovingly lifted out, and laid in the arms of her faithful Jamie. Acting under the advice of friends the party at once set off by way of Hardgate for Banchory-Devenick, assured that Dr. Morison would tie the knot on production of the necessary papers. Off they went, a motley crew of weavers in their working garb, and others of a nondescript order, bent on a bit of fun. Refreshments were obtained at Watson's in the Hardgate, after which they pushed on to Kirton's celebrated house. Here a fresh fortification of courage was obtained, and a section of the more respectable members of the *cortege* accompanied the pair to the Doctor's. He refused, however, to have anything to do with them; so, considerably crestfallen, they returned to Kirton's. That worthy, however, was equal to the occasion, for over a "tappit hen" he told them that, by the law of Scotland, the due acknowledgment before witnesses of their taking one another for husband and wife was quite sufficient. The form was gone through—as was also a considerable amount of Kirton's best—and they returned to town—"a' fu' an' a' happy." A meeting with the parents took place, and, after considerable ado, they agreed to be pleased if the pair would get Mr. Gellatly in the Shiprow to marry them like decent folk, which he did, and so ended "the Banchory weddin'." The wedding has been commemorated in a ballad by George Smith.*

An excellent idea of the city and its suburbs is obtained in walking between Murcar and Hilldowntree, which doubtless gave rise to the composition of the following doggerel lines, which appeared in the *Aberdeen Almanac* for 1722:—

"'Twixt *Murcur* and the *Hilldown Tree*
These following things a man may see:
Two Noble Rivers there doth run,
Adorn'd with Splendid Briggs of Stone;
One of one Arch without compare,
The other of Seven, and very Fair,
And yearly throughout every Arch
Cathedral Fish in Legions march
Long time these have the Fronteers been
Of the Antient towns of ABERDEEN
For if these Briggs were quite away
They would be a *Peninsula ;*
Bounded on East with *Neptune's* Fleet,
With Braid-hill, Block-house, Canno-Sweet
With famous Town of antient *Fittie*
Where dwelleth Women wise and wittie

* Walker's *Bards of Bon-Accord*, page 406-407.

On West with a large fertile Field
Which Parsneps, Turneps, Carrets yeeld
With finest Cabbage, Sybows, Leeks,
(Which women sell who wear the Breeks)
Potato's, Beans, & *caetera*,
Abound in this *Peninsula*,
Wake, Wind and Water Mills these Towns
Do separate from Rustick Clowns:
In midst of these there may be seen
The beauteous Towns of ABERDEEN
Whose UNIVERSITIES discover
Their learning all the World over,
Their Musick, stately Buildings, Bells,
Their spacious Streets and Suggared Wells
Which any may observe who will,
'Twixt *Tillidron* and *Ferrihill:*
Inverurie Battle and *Harlaw*,
Did their Ancestors Valour shaw,
All which demonstrate in a Word,
The comeliness of BON-ACCORD."

PARISH SCHOOL.

The date when a school was first opened at Banchory-Devenick for the education of the young must be mere matter of conjecture; but the old parish records show that in the year 1711 the building used for that purpose, and believed to be on same site as the present school, was in a very dilapidated condition. The following suggestive entry occurs of date 1st July, 1711, " The said day it being represented to the Session that whereas in moist and foggy weather the roof of the schoolhouse pours down so many soot drops that scarcely it is habitable : to remove this inconveniencie the Session did unanimously ordain that the said school house should be lafted with dails upon the publick charges." On 24th June, 1714, "the sum of 10 lib. was paid for casting 900 divots, and 13 lib. scots for meal and meat to the man who laid on the divots on the roof." In 1732 the school had fallen into such a ruinous state that the erection of a new building was contracted for at a cost of £36 13s. scots.

The kirk-session, having had the strongest voice in the appointment of schoolmaster, invariably gave with it the session clerkship and sometimes the precentorship. The emoluments of the appointments are thus recorded in 1707. " There is due from the possession of every pleugh in the Parish twenty shillings scots, which in all amounts to above fourty eight payed at Candlemass. There is payable out of the Kirk Box for officiating as Session-Clerk twenty punds scots, and four punds four shillings scots for writing all testimonials gratis. Every husbandman pays for clerking his childs Baptisme ten pence and every subtennant payes halfe a merke, and for clerking of every marriage ten pence. Every Scholar learning to read and write payes to the Schoolmaster a merk (1s. 1⅓d.) quarterly and every Latin Scholar twenty pence quarterly." In addition, it had been customary for the session to allow the schoolmaster £1 Scots "for the casting and winning peats for the children's use who are at School in the winter time." Later on "a crown" was repeatedly granted "to the Clerk for a hat as usuall." It does not appear that the income of the schoolmaster had been in any way improved till the passing of an Act of Parliament in 1803 "for the bettering of Parochial Schoolmasters." Under this Act the minister and heritors of the parish met at the schoolhouse on 10th September of that year, when the following resolutions were passed:—" That the Schoolmaster's salary for the first period fixed by the Act shall be three hundred and fifty merks Scotch, to be proportioned amongst the several Heritors agreeably to the said Act. Also that a garden, containing a quarter of a Scotch acre, shall be set aside and enclosed from the adjoining field belonging to Mr. Thomson of Banchory. The meeting was unanimously of opinion that the school fees, which had not been raised for at least half a century, should be augmented in the following proportions, all payable on entering to the School, and to commence on the expiry of the present vacations, vizt: For a quarter of a year at reading English, *One Shilling and Sixpence*. For Reading and Writing, *Two Shillings and Sixpence*. For Arithmetic, *Three Shillings*, and for Latin, *Five Shillings*." This scale of fees was repeatedly amended in subsequent years, with a view to still "further encouarge the Teacher in the discharge of his duties."

As early as 1738 the catechising system began, "intimation being given from the pulpit that a Committee of Presbytery would visit the school, when all concerned were warned to attend." These visitations were continued annually down to a comparatively recent date. In October, 1799, in consequence of the distracted state of the country, all schoolmasters were ordered by the sheriffs of counties to take a formal oath of allegiance to his Majesty, George III. In 1807 the number of scholars in attendance was thirty. Of these, sixteen studied English only, twelve writing, twelve arithmetic, and two book-keeping. The gross income of the teacher, including emoluments of session-clerkship, &c., amounted to £44 6s. 10$\frac{8}{12}$d.*

The parish has been unusually fortunate for the last two centuries in the selection of teachers. For this too much credit cannot be assigned to the parish ministers,

---

* *Table No. IV. Agricultural Survey.*

especially to Dr. Morison and his scholarly successor, Dr. Paul, whose respective efforts and influence secured the appointment of the best possible men. Indeed, it is questionable if any rural parish in the north, with a like limited population, could produce a list of such distinguished teachers.

TEACHERS.

. . . .

1569. William Mar held the offices of schoolmaster, reader, and session-clerk. As " reidar" he had a salary of " xx lib" per annum.

. . . .

1693. Robert Jamieson was elected to the same offices, and in 1703 "he being before in holy orders commenced Preacher and Assistant to the Minister of Banchory Mr. James Gordon." Having, however, secured a charge of his own at Inverness, he removed there in the summer of 1714.

1714. David Martin officiated for a year or two as schoolmaster under Mr. Jamieson, at whose removal he was appointed to the three offices.

1716. Charles Cay succeeded him, but he does not seem to have held the appointments beyond about twelve months. He appears to have likewise acted as precentor and session-clerk, and to have taken a great interest in the ministerial affairs of the parish. Having secured another appointment he left at Whitsunday, 1717.

1717. James Clark, who had been temporarily officiating as precentor, was formally elected to the vacancy in 1717. He left the district in the summer of 1726.

1726. James Hogg, who had previously been schoolmaster at Drumoak, succeeded Clark in 1726. He held the post for forty-five years, when he retired through old age. According to the minute of session, " he had filled the office with great abilities, diligence and success." He had a son, George, who was a very successful merchant in Aberdeen, and who latterly became proprietor of the estate of Shannaburn. Like his father, the son took the greatest possible interest in Banchory-Devenick, building a female school entirely at his own expense, and endowing it with a legacy of £100. This endowment was supplemented by Dr. Morison, who added another £100 to the fund. This female school, which stood about three hundred yards south of the parish school, is now closed, the pupils having been transferred to the parish school; but the annual interest on the fund is regularly paid by the kirk-session, who are the trustees, to the School Board, thus enabling the latter body to reduce the school rate exigible from the ratepayers. George Hogg died in 1826, in the 78th year of his age.

1771. George Skene Keith, the industrious reviewer of Aberdeenshire agriculture, "who produced the best attestations of his conduct from the Minister and Session of Peterculter, whence he came," was appointed both schoolmaster and session-clerk in February, 1771. He was the lineal descendant of Alexander Keith, third son of the second Earl Marischal, and had been laureated at King's College the previous year. Whilst discharging the functions of teacher at Banchory-Devenick, he contrived to attend the divinity course at Aberdeen, securing license from the Presbytery there in 1774. Two years later he received a presentation to the charge of Keithhall and Kinkell from the commissioners of George, Earl Marischal; but his lordship having the following day given a presentation to the same charge to Thomas Tait, one of the ministers of Old Machar, a serious question arose as to which should be preferred. The Court of Session, and the House of Lords, both decided in favour of Keith, who was accordingly ordained on 14th May, 1778. In 1822 he received a presentation to the parish of Tulliallan in Perthshire, and, accepting it, his younger son, John, who was a graduate of Aberdeen University, and licensed as a preacher of the gospel, succeeded him as minister of Keith-hall. The elder son was Dr. Keith of St. Cyrus, author of the well-known book on prophecy. A son of the latter is the celebrated surgeon and ovariotomist, Dr. Keith, who recently removed from Edinburgh to London, and who claims to be the oldest surviving representative of the Earls Marischal in the male line. Skene Keith, who had received the degree of D.D. from his *Alma Mater*, died at Tulliallan House on 7th March, 1823, in the 71st year of his age, and his remains were interred in the churchyard of Keith-hall, where a handsome monument, bearing the following inscription, was afterwards erected to his memory :—

"Near this wall are interred the mortal remains of The Rev. Dr. George Skene Keith, Minister of the Parish of Keith-hall for forty-four years, and of Tulliallan, in Perthshire, for eight months. Born at Auquhorsk on the 6th November, 1752, he died at Tulliallan House on the 7th March, 1823. Distinguished and beloved as the clergyman of a parish, and remarkable in a wider sphere for his learning and science, of great mental and bodily activity, he preserved in age the same vivacity and cheerfulness, the same love of knowledge, warmth of feeling, and untiring Christian benevolence which characterised his youth and manhood. Some gentlemen of this county who had intended to present him with a memorial of their high respect for his character, but were prevented by his death, have erected this monument to his memory."

He will be remembered best by his book on the *Agriculture of Aberdeenshire*, published in 1811. It is a wonderful collection of facts on a subject which was then in its infancy, and is thoroughly indispensable to a historian of Scotch agriculture. His other works are *Tracts on Weights, Measures, and Coins; The Excellence of the British Constitution*, and *A Short Sketch of the Life of Principal Campbell*.

1778. Robert Cormack was appointed successor in July, 1778, but only on the condition that "he should grant his obligation not to commence as a Student of Divinity, and likewise that he should find one sufficiently qualified to precent in the Church and teach Church Music." He was a painstaking and highly successful teacher, and was much esteemed in the parish. He continued to hold the double office down to the date of his death, which occurred on 13th January, 1813.

1813. Robert Adams, designed as "Student in Philosophy in King's College, Aberdeen, and having ample certificates of his literature and abilities to fill the office," was appointed successor in the following March. This being the first appointment under the Act of Parliament of 1803, it devolved upon the Presbytery, after Mr. Adams had been formally appointed by the heritors, "to make trial of his proficiency in Latin, English, Arithmetic, and Writing, and if found qualified to teach these branches of education, that they furnish him with an Extract from their Minutes in due form, so that his right to the endowments of his Office may be completed." He was a most careful teacher and excellent session-clerk—the minutes and accounts in his handwriting giving evidence of his ability as a caligraphist. He qualified for the Dick Bequest; and his literary attainments generally were of a high order. In January, 1836, he contracted a malignant fever and died after four days' illness. Under his deed of settlement he bequeathed a sum of money for behoof of the poor of the parish.

1836. Patrick McGregor Grant, M.A., "Preacher of the Gospel," was appointed successor on 10th March, 1836. He was an active and energetic teacher and won himself many friends. Amongst these was John Irvine Boswell of Kingcausie and Balmuto, who, as patron of the living of Auchterderran, in Fifeshire, presented it to him on a vacancy occurring in 1844. Grant was accordingly ordained and inducted there in the autumn of the same year. He took an active interest in the spiritual welfare of Lochgelly, a mining village three miles distant from the manse, and for many years he preached there twice every Sunday, until his exertions, backed by the assistance of outside friends, got the Chapel of Ease erected into a *Quoad Sacra* parish with a duly ordained minister. He never married, but lived a quiet retiring life on his stipend, which amounted to the handsome sum of £463 per annum. Unfortunately, about ten years ago, symptoms of mental derangement began to manifest themselves, and he became quite incapacitated from discharging his duty. A curator was thereupon appointed for him, and he was removed to a private lunatic asylum in Edinburgh, where he died on 28th March, 1889.'

1844. John Webster, M.A., who was educated in the parish school of Forglen and studied afterwards at the University of Aberdeen, where he also passed the divinity course, subsequently receiving license from the Presbytery of Aberdeen as "a preacher of the Gospel," was appointed successor to Grant on 24th October, 1844. Entering upon his duties at Banchory immediately thereafter, he speedily gave proof of his literary proficiency and rare power of imparting knowledge to others. His ability in these respects led the University of Aberdeen, in 1850, to appoint him Murray lecturer, and in that capacity, and whilst still teacher at Banchory-Devenick, he delivered the lectures at King's College during the sessions 1850-51, and 1851-52. In the autumn of 1852 he was presented to the charge of the parish of Strichen, and five years later he was translated to Anstruther Easter, in Fifeshire. In 1864 he removed to the parish of Cameron, near St. Andrews. At the end of 1876 the congregation of St. John's, Edinburgh, recognizing his power as a preacher and organizer of church-work, which eminently qualified him for a city charge, made the most strenuous efforts to get him to remove thither. With considerable reluctance he severed his connection with Cameron, and was inducted to St. John's on 23rd December, 1876. For the next seven years he discharged the multifarious duties of his office with indefatigable energy and assiduity, which resulted in a very large increase of the congregation. In the spring of 1884 a call from Cramond, one of the most beautiful parishes in the outskirts of Edinburgh, gave him an opportunity of again removing to the country, and, accepting it, he was inducted there on 11th March, 1884. Next year his *Alma Mater* conferred on him the degree of D.D.; and in May, 1888, when the convenership of the Education Committee of the Church of Scotland became vacant, he was selected as being an experienced educationist and a shrewd business man.

1852. William Skinner, M.A., who was born in the parish of Clatt in 1830, received his early education at the parish school there. Afterwards removing to Aberdeen he attended the new town Grammar School, where he studied under the celebrated Dr. Melvin. In the bursary competition of King's College he took fifth place, and in the University classes carried off the first prize in moral philosophy. After graduating in 1849 he took to teaching. He first acted as assistant substitute to the Rev. Gordon Raeburn of Keig, then an old man, who had been for many years unfit for duty. From Keig he was appointed schoolmaster of Banchory-Devenick in 1852. While teaching there he attended the divinity classes in Aberdeen, and was licensed to preach by the Presbytery of Aberdeen in 1854. Of his work at Banchory-Devenick Dr. Paul wrote: "He (Mr. Skinner) was selected by me from about twenty candidates, as being the best qualified, as regards his literary and scientific attainments, and his aptitude for communicating knowledge. I can certify with great confidence that his scholarship is of a high order, and extremely accurate, and that I have never seen a better teacher, or one who more thoroughly understands the business of instruction." After teaching at Banchory-Devenick for about three years he was, in 1855, appointed assistant to Dr. Paterson, minister of the second charge at Montrose, In 1857 he was appointed to the West Church, Dalry, and, in the following year, he accepted a presentation to the parish of Coull. Ten years later he removed to the parish of Tarland where he still ministers to an attached congregation.

1855. John Black, M.A., was born in the parish of Glenrinnes in 1834. After studying for a time at the parish school there, he went to the school at Keith. When only about thirteen he entered a law office in Keith as a clerk, but did not take to the drudgery of the desk; and, after some preliminary training, took the third bursary at Aberdeen University. He subsequently became one of the most brilliant students, not only taking either the first or second place in all his classes, but carrying off the Simpson mathematical prize of £60. His abilities and distinction as a student secured for him a large amount of private teaching in Aberdeen, and, immediately on his graduating M.A., Dr. Paul selected him as schoolmaster of Banchory-Devenick, where he entered upon his duties in the autumn of 1855. In addition to gaining the Milne Bequest he competed for the Dick Bequest, making the best appearance of any candidate up to that time. As a recognition of the scholarship displayed he received the highest possible grant and a premium of £30. Whilst still acting as teacher at Banchory-Devenick, he received an appointment as one of Her Majesty's inspectors of schools, an office in which he was at first associated with Dr. Woodford of Edinburgh; but, after a time, he came to Aberdeen as inspector for the counties of Aberdeen, Kincardine, and Forfar. In 1868, on death of Dr. Maclure, he was appointed professor of humanity in the

University of Aberdeen, and afterwards had the degree of LL.D. conferred upon him. No gentleman in the north commanded greater esteem and respect than did the portly and dignified professor of humanity. He died suddenly on 17th November, 1881. He was married to a daughter of the Rev. Mr. Strahan, some time headmaster of Gordon's College, and she, along with two sons and four daughters, survived him.

1858. Robert Ogilvie, M.A., was the youngest of the seven sons of Mr. W. Ogilvie, a highly respected farmer in Rothiemay. He was born there towards the close of 1834, and received the rudiments of his education at a small side school. He attended the Rothiemay parish school for about a year, and was afterwards for a short time under the tuition of an elder brother. With a view to prosecuting his studies still further, he removed to Aberdeen in 1852, and after attending the Grammar School there for about three months, entered the University of Marischal College where he gained a bursary. His career thereafter was of the most brilliant character, for in almost every class he carried off the first prize, and finally won the Gray mathematical bursary of £60 and the silver medal. He studied at the Divinity Hall for some time, and, on the removal of Mr. Black from Banchory in the spring of 1858, was unanimously appointed his successor in the offices of schoolmaster and session-clerk. He continued to discharge his duties as such until the autumn of 1860, when he was appointed to succeed his eldest brother as rector of Milne's Institution, Fochabers. Eight years later he was appointed H.M. inspector of schools in succession to Mr. Black. It is a singular coincidence that in this appointment he should have followed a second time in the footsteps of Black, whose work in Aberdeen as inspector of schools he now took up. A year later he was transferred to the Stirling district, and in 1882 promoted to the senior inspectorship in succession to Mr. Hall, when he returned to Aberdeen. In 1888 he was appointed successor to Dr. Kerr as senior inspector for the West of Scotland, with his head-quarters in Glasgow. In recognition of his scholarly accomplishments and distinguished career the Universities of Aberdeen and St. Andrews simultaneously conferred on him the degree of LL.D. One of his brothers is principal of Gordon's College, and another is rector of the Church of Scotland Training College, both in Aberdeen.

1860. John Garden, M.A., who was born in the parish of Rathven on 15th August, 1835, received his early education at the parish school there. Thereafter he for a short time attended the parish school of Keith, then under charge of the famous Mr. Smith. Removing to Aberdeen he attended the bursary competition and carried off the second prize. His college career there was of a bright character. In each of the Greek, Latin, and moral philosophy classes he took a high place, finally graduating M.A. in 1857. From the University he went to Wakefield, Yorkshire, where he taught for a short time under Dr. Bewglass. Thereafter he held an appointment in Daniel Stewart's Hospital, Edinburgh, from which he went to Arbroath as rector of the Academy there. In October, 1860, on the vacancy occurring at Banchory-Devenick, he was, out of many excellent candidates, unanimously elected. His duties as teacher were of an onerous nature ; but he continued not only to discharge them to the entire satisfaction of the parish, but also to win for himself fresh laurels by passing the Dick Bequest examination and obtaining a premium of twelve guineas. In 1863, on the rectorship of the Elgin Academy becoming vacant, he was induced to accept the appointment ; but, not finding the duties of that office altogether congenial, he secured the mastership of Rothes parish, where he has continued ever since, and is still active in the discharge of his duties.

1863. Robert Gray, M.A., who was educated at the Gymnasium, Old Aberdeen, and at Marischal College, Aberdeen, where he graduated in 1853, was appointed successor on the last day of 1863. For the previous eight years he had taught Mr. Thomson's private school adjoining Banchory-Devenick Free Church, but on his receiving the new appointment this school was closed. He continued to discharge the duties of teacher till the summer of 1887, when failing health compelled him, very reluctantly, to seek retirement. The Education Act of 1872 being then in operation, the School Board of the parish, under its powers, voted him a handsome retiring annual allowance, while, at the same time, many of his old pupils and friends presented him, through Mr. Ogston of Ardoe, chairman of the Board, with an illuminated address and a purse of sovereigns. He has for many years acted as registrar of the parish, and is a respected office-bearer in the Banchory-Devenick Free Church.

1887. William Reid, M.A., son of a wood merchant and fishcurer, was born at Portgordon on 10th December, 1861. He received his early education at Burghead and Sandhaven public schools. Subsequently he attended the Grammar School, Old Aberdeen, and King's College where he graduated in 1884. Choosing the profession of a teacher, he for some time held appointments in King Street School and Gordon's College; but in January, 1885, on a vacancy occurring in Glentanar public school, was unanimously elected as schoolmaster. In 1887, on the retirement of Mr. Gray, he was appointed successor, and entered on his duties at Banchory-Devenick after the autumn holidays. He is a most diligent and painstaking teacher, and keeps all departments of the work in a thorough state of efficiency. His success in the latter respect is remarkable, every scholar in attendance (about 140) having passed the last Government inspection.

ESTATE OF ARDOE.

This estate, which extends to about one thousand acres, forms the north western boundary and corner of the Kincardineshire portion of the parish. Its early proprietary history is intermingled with that of the Banchory lands, gifted in 1244 by Alexander II. to the abbot and convent of Aberbrothock, as for many years it was owned by the proprietors of Banchory. The earliest owners of whom record exists appear to be the Meldrums of Fyvie, who, as superiors, kept up their connection with the estate for a long period. William Meldrum of Fyvie granted precept of the lands of Ardoe to his son, George, in 1502; and in 1509 David Murray was served heir to his father, Andrew Murray, in the lands of "Ardoche and fishings, one net of the Fords on Dee, and an annual rent of fourty-four shillings scots from the lands of Cortycrome, in the Barony of Slains," acknowledging that the lord of Fyvie was superior of the holding so far as it affected Ardoe.

On 2nd May, 1511, William Murray was served heir to David, his father, in the same lands, fishings, and feu-duty; and the jury at the same time adjudged a reasonable terce from them to Agnes Strathachin, the widow of David Murray.*

* *Antiquities of Aberdeen and Banff*, Vol. iii., p. 256.

In 1582 David Mar, one of the baillies of Aberdeen, and several times its representative in Parliament, obtained a charter of confirmation of these lands from George Meldrum of Fyvie, to himself and his son, Thomas Mar, but they do not appear to have taken sasine till 1586, and that only for the purpose of enabling them to sell the lands. On the 18th May of the same year, Meldrum issued another charter of confirmation, in his capacity of superior or over lord, in favour of George Garden of Banchory. Two years later Garden granted a charter of the "Sunny half of Ardoe" in favour of Patrick Cheyne, burgess of Aberdeen, and proprietor of Danestown. The latter was married to Katherine Fraser, and their son, Thomas Cheyne, afterwards succeeded to the estate.[*]

In the same year, viz., 1588, Thomas Merser in Old Aberdeen, and Barbara Blinshell, his spouse, secured a charter of the "Shady half" of Ardoe, which was confirmed under the Great Seal of James VI. of date 24th March, 1598. George Merser, their son, who married Elizabeth or Eliza Garden, subsequently succeeded.

Shortly thereafter, John Fraser of Ferryhill, fourth son of Thomas Fraser of Durris, designed in his deed of infeftment as "of Tilbunes," and Ann Lorimer, his spouse, acquired both the sunny and shady halves, but in 1619 sold them to James Mowat, advocate in Aberdeen.

[*] *Title Deeds of Estate.*

In 1631 the famous Dr. William Guild purchased from the Mowats, who were possessed of extensive house property in Aberdeen, the ancient convent of the Trinity Friars, and gifted it to the trades as an hospital for the reception of decayed workmen. King William the Lion, tradition asserts, was the founder of the convent, and it is believed that it was occasionally the place of his Majesty's residence. The purchase price on this occasion was 40 shillings of annual feu-duty, and 40 pennies scots yearly during the lifetime of Thomas, one of James Mowat's sons. The latter must have died shortly afterwards, as his son James had a Birth-brieve granted him in 1641, in which he is described as " son to the late James Mowat of Ardoe." His remains were interred in Saint Nicholas Churchyard, Aberdeen, where a monument was erected to his memory. The following abridged translation is taken from it :—

"Whatever was of James Mowat of Airdo, a man singular both in private and publick lies here; if you enquire what it is look up to Heaven."*

In 1639 Sir Gilbert Menzies of Pitfodels acquired the whole lands, but in 1670 his son, William, sold them to James Gordon, designed as "Rector of Banchory-Devenick," and Elizabeth Forbes, his spouse. Gordon died in December, 1714; and his great grandson, "John Gordon, son of Dr. William Gordon, physician in

* *Theater of Mortality*, p. 92.

Montrose, son of James Gordon, episcopal minister at Montrose, eldest son of James Gordon, rector at Banchory-Devenick, as heir to the said James Gordon, his great-grandfather, in the lands of Ardoe," by disposition dated 10th November, 1747, sold the lands to John Fordyce, merchant in Huntly, for £21,400 scots.

Fordyce had previously acted as a gunner's mate on Commodore Anson's ship "Centurion," in its voyage round the world. Having survived repeated attacks of scurvy, which carried off nearly three-fourths of the ship's crew,* he returned to Britain on the 15th June, 1744, and, according to the late Dr. Paul, travelled from London to Aberdeen on horseback with all his prize money in specie in his saddle bag.† He married a daughter of Irvine of Cults, a niece of John Douglas of Tilwhilly and Inchmarlo, and died 4th June, 1794.‡ During his residence on the estate he did much to ameliorate the condition of his tenantry and their holdings, and the poor of the parish were also benefited through his liberality. He was succeeded by his only daughter, Agness, who never married, but lived a quiet retired life, making herself, however, like her father, popular with the tenants through her kindly interest in them. She died 20th November, 1834, in the 76th year of her age, and was buried in the parish church of Banchory-Devenick. By her last will and testament

* Anson's *Voyage.*
†*Past and Present of Aberdeenshire*, p. 115.
‡ Dingwall Fordyce's *Family of Dingwall Fordyce.*

she bequeathed £100 for behoof of the poor of the parish. Andrew Watson, advocate in Aberdeen, son of the Reverend Andrew Watson, minister of the parish of Tarland and Migvie from 1799 to 1845, was left the estate by Miss Fordyce, for whom he had, for a short time before her death, acted as law agent. He assumed the name of Fordyce, but did not live long to enjoy the handsome bequest, for he died on 4th April, 1837, in the 26th year of his age.

In 1839 his representatives sold the estate to Mr. Alexander Ogston, soap manufacturer, Aberdeen. In 1853 Mr. Ogston sold the "Shady half of Ardoe," now known by the name of Cotbank, to the Reverend James Gillan, D.D., minister of the parish of Alford. The latter never resided on the lands, but simply acquired them as an investment. Mr. Ogston, on 18th December, 1834, married Elliot Lawrance, daughter of Mr. James Lawrance, manufacturer, Aberdeen, by whom he had issue two sons, Alexander Milne, and James, and four daughters, Elliot, Helen, Sarah, and Amelia. He died on 11th December, 1869, survived by his wife, who died 1st August, 1886. Their remains are interred in the churchyard of Banchory-Devenick.

Mr. Alexander Milne Ogston purchased the estate from the trustees of his father in 1870, and three years later acquired the lands of Cotbank from the Reverend James Gillan, minister of Alford, whose father had bought them twenty years previously. On 16th April, 1872,

Mr. Ogston married Katherine Ann Mitchell Rennie, daughter of Mr. Charles Moray Hill Rennie, Aberdeen, by whom he has issue three sons, Alexander Gordon, Charles, and James Norman, and two daughters, Katherine Emily, and Elliot Mabel. In 1877-78 he erected a large and massive mansion house in the Scottish baronial style of architecture. The house is decorated and furnished throughout in an elaborate style, and in these respects has few equals in the North. Mr. Ogston some time ago claimed to be the lineal descendant of the Ogstons of that Ilk,* and, having satisfied the Lyon-King on the point, had his claim sustained. He is therefore entitled to bear the primitive arms of

* Ogston was the name of a parish in Morayshire which, along with Kinnedar, went, shortly after the Restoration, to form the present parish of Drainie. The Ogston family formerly owned extensive lands in the north. "In 1473 (26th October) Alexander Ogstoun of that ilk, had a licence under the privy seal of James III. to sell his lands of Ogstoun in the Lordship of Moray; reserving the orchard and chief chymmis thereof: and he accordingly, with consent of John Ogstoun his son and apparent heir, sold the lands of Ogstoun to James of Innes of that ilk, and Margaret of Culan, his spouse, under reversion and with regress on payment of 300 merks on the high altar of the Parish Kirk of Elgin, after 40 days warning at the chymmis of Innes—20 December 1473. James Innes and his wife had seisin of Ogstoun, which was never redeemed, and either by them, or in the next generation, the Plewlands were added to it. Out of these lands and others, bought about 1630-40, from the Inneses of Drainie; and Ettles, &c., from Innes of Pethnak, Sir Robert Gordon, Tutor of Sutherland, formed his estate of Gordonstown."—*Familie of Innes*, p. 80, 81. *Gazeteer of Scotland, &c.*

that ancient family, which are :—*Argent, three mascles sable, on a chief of the second two lions passant of the first, armed and langued gules.*—Patent. In 1880 Mr. Ogston purchased the estate of Heathcot, which lies contiguous to Ardoe, although in the adjoining parish of Maryculter. He takes a lively interest in county matters, having for many years occupied the position of chairman of the Lower Deeside District Road Trustees, and of the School Board of the parish. He is on the board of several of the leading public companies in Aberdeen, where he is otherwise largely engaged in business. By reclaiming waste land, forming plantations, and erecting commodious and substantial farm steadings, he has done much to beautify the appearance of his estate. Nor, with all these improvements, have the tenantry been forgotten, for he has ever shown himself ready to encourage and deal liberally with the diligent and industrious.

Arms of Ogston of that Ilk.

THE BRIDGE OF DEE.

"A bridge doth reach along the river Dee,
Wherein seven double stately Arches be :
Who built this sumptuous-work if ye would know,
The myter which is carv'd thereon doth show."
—ARTHUR JOHNSTON.

The bridge of Dee is one of the most interesting relics of antiquity in the north-east of Scotland. The interest centres, not only in the mere structure, but in its associations with the history of the town of Aberdeen, and more than once with great national events.

As early as 1384 there would seem to have been a bridge across the Dee—perhaps on the same site as the present one—with a paved road leading southwards across the mounth.* It had doubtless been of slim construction, for, in 1459, Master John of Levingston, vicar of Inuerugy, was appointed, by the alderman and common council of the burgh of Aberdeen, to be the master of work of a proposed bridge across the Dee. It would appear, however, that this design was abandoned, probably as too great an undertaking for the slender revenues of the town.†

To the forethought and liberality of Bishop Elphinstone the present bridge owed its origin. It was one of the last efforts of the church to exercise that function with which

---

* *Registrum Episcopatus Aberdonensis*, Vol. ii., pp. 286, 287.
† *Antiquities of Aberdeen and Banff*, Vol. ii., p. 398.

Bridge of Dee.

it was so closely identified in the Eternal City, the function that gave a title which its highest prelate bears to this day. It is strange—if we are to believe the statement of one writer*—that the only bridge that has been built by the clergy in this country since the Reformation, is the one erected by Dr. Morison across the Dee at Cults, in the same parish. The bridge was one of Elphinstone's greatest schemes—the keystone virtually of his many magnificent services to the country. In 1500 he set about the erection of the College which the famous popish bull had authorised, and in the same year it is believed he began building the bridge of Dee. The early history of the latter structure is not very clear, for, as an ecclesiastical enterprise, the records of it have not been kept. That the bishop died, however, before it was finished is certain. The enormous labour entailed in carrying out two such schemes as building King's College and the bridge of Dee, in the early years of the sixteenth century, can scarcely at this date be realized; but we cannot wonder that the latter work was not completed in 1514. The bishop's successor, Alexander Gordon, did not take up the work. Bishop Gordon occupied the See for the short period of three years, and in 1518 he was succeeded by Bishop Gavin Dunbar, a man after Elphinstone's own heart. It seems a doubtful point whether Dunbar finished the structure begun by Elphinstone, or made a

* James Bruce on *Eminent Men of Aberdeen*, p. 39.

new one altogether. A document, corroborating the latter view, was recently found in "a rare old folio" in the library of the Archiepiscopal Seminary at Mechlin.* The writer, Alexander Kennedy, is said to have been an Aberdonian living in Brussels, who had joined the Order of St. Francis. The translation of the document is as follows :—

"The testimony of Brother Alexander Kennedy, the Scot, monk of the order of S. Francis. I, the undersigned, bear witness and take my oath that I heard from my ancestors the following facts :—That the statue of the Blessed Mary the Virgin, called Of Good Success, and placed in the monastery of the Augustine Fathers at Brussels, gave audible indications to the Most Reverend Father Gavin Dunbar, Catholic Bishop of Aberdeen, whilst he was praying concerning the spot where he should lay the foundations of the bridge over the rapid river Dee, and pointed out to him on both sides the points between which he afterwards built the magnificent bridge of seven arches that to this day is to be seen. —Given at Brussels, 19th May, 1636, in the Monastery of S. Augustine, by the hand of Brother Alexander Kennedy, unworthy Minorite of the Regular Observance."

The evidence of this document certainly deprives Elphinstone of the honour of a share in raising the existing structure; but it is at best a legend founded on an

* *Aberdeen Journal,* August 18, 1887.

equally fanciful miracle. When we recall that Dempster and Bishop Leslie, writing at a much earlier date, set the *pons lapideus magnificentissimus* on *ten* arches, the story of the "unworthy Minorite" will not carry much weight.

A side glimpse is given of how the bridge was actually built from an entry in the Council Register in 1531, when the Town Council ordained that the master of work "suld gar amend the frame of the brig, and gif hir in keping to sum traist hand." A peculiar use was to be made of it, namely, to "lat hir and the prouestis greit Reile to fraucht to the losing and laidnyng of schippis, and to the hame bringing of elding, and the profitte to be equalie deuidit betiux thame, hir part cummand to the tovnis vtilitie." The town, it may be observed in passing, made excellent "vtilitie" of the bridge work, using the cooms for the arches of the Blockhouse at Footdee, in 1532, and nine years later the "lym, stanis, tymmer, and jrn, takin away fra the brig Wark," were used "to byg ane bryg of tre our the pot burne"—that is the Ruthrieston bridge. Dunbar carried out the idea of the early connection of the church with bridge building by appointing Alexander Galloway, parson of Kinkell, the architect. The master mason was Thomas French, who also built Dunbar's Aisle in St. Machar Cathedral. Little is known of the progress of the work, but it had evidently been at least once delayed by a spate in 1522, which brought down the "sentrice of the brig," sweeping them away, "broking, spylt, to the see haid, in gret skayth and damag to the noble wark." The "skayth" was estimated at "ane hundreth pundis and mair."

At last, in 1527, the bridge was finished. The bishop builder immediately offered it to the town, together with the lands of Ardlair in the parish of Kennethmont, which the bishops of Aberdeen had got before 1199 from David, Earl of Huntingdon and the Garioch, to uphold it. The most unaccountable wariness was exhibited by the Town Council in accepting the handsome gift. The first time it is mentioned in the town's records is 1st April, 1527. "The haill tovne, all in ane voce, thankit gretly thar lord and bischop of Aberden for the gret plesour and proffeit done to thame in the biging of the brig of Dee," but even on this occasion Elder John Anderson "saed he wad nocht mell with sik materis." It was, however, agreed to "give a finell ansuir to the said lord." "This is the ansuer of the tovnn of Abirden gevin to my lord of Abirdene anent the brig of Dee. (My lord, we your seruandis, prouest, bailzeis, consull, comunite, of Abirdene, hes ressauit your l[ordschipis] guid mynd exponit to vs be your commissar, Maister Alexander Hay, persoun of Turref tuching of your l[ordschipis] brig of Dee, fundit, biget, and endit one your grit, hie and exorbitand expensis, for the perpetuall commond weill of the cuntra and of ws; of the quhilkis guid deid and mynd God eternall revard yow, for we ma nocht; and quhar your lordschip desiris ws and our successouris to be bundin to the ouphaldin of the said brig, it beand completit one your expensis, in the maist souer wise cane be devisit be wismen and men of craft in all thingis necessaris; and at your lordschip will infeft ws and our successouris in your landis of Ardlar to be haldin of yow and your successouris in few, we ar hartlie contentit of the same, makand ws souer thairof be the pape, the prince your chartour, and all wther handis necessar, for we desyir na inconuenient, bot to be maid souer; quhilk ve vnderstand is your l[ordschipis] guid mynd. Nochtwithstanding, gif your l[ordschip] may eislie infeft ws in ony if your landis liand mair evnse to ws, or interchange the saidis landis with wtheris haiffand landis liand mair ewnse to ws, lik as Rudrestoun or ony vther sik lik, it var profetable for the canseruacioun of your said l[ordschipis] vark, and plesand, and ewnse; quhilk we refer haill to your l[ordschipis] plesour, besaikand you to labour the same gif ye ma guidlie. And atour, we consideraned the mony guid turnis done be your l[ordschip] within your diocy to your cathedral and vther places, and wnderstanden at your l[ordschip] hes na kyrk within your diocy appropriat to your mitar except our mother kyrk, we vald exort your l[ordschip] to help to sum notable turne to be done thairto; to the quhilk we sall put our handis in the largeist form be the sycht of your l[ordschip], that sum remembrance ma remain thairin of yow, lik as is of money of your reuerend predecessouris, Bischop Thomas Spens, and Bischop Wm. Elphinstoun. In this cause and all wtheris referrand ws to your l[ordschipis] plesour, to the quhilkis we are gritlie indettit, as knowis the gret God eternall, quhome mot conserue your l[ordschip] in sawill and body at your noble desyir. Your l[ordschipis] seruandis, Prouest, bailzeis, consail, and comunite of your burght of Abirdene."

As a specimen of Aberdonian caution this document ought to be preserved and become classic. The way in which the council looked the gift horse in the mouth, gently hinting that his lordship might "eislie infeft ws in ony of your landis liand mair ewnse to ws, or interchange the saidis landis with wtheris haiffand landis liand mair ewnse to ws, lik as Rudrestoun," is characteristic; and although no heed was paid to the council's hints on this occasion, yet nearly a century later—1610—they were given effect to, through the sale of Ardlair and the purchase of the lands of Caprastoune—the old name for Hilton, Woodside—" to the uphauld and manteining of the brig of Dee, in place and sted of the lands of Ardlair." Continuing the narrative of the original transfer, on June 3rd, 1527, twelve gentlemen objected to the making of the bond of indenting with the bishop to uphold the bridge, and the affair was not settled for two years, when, "efter diuerse and sundry consultatiounis at this time maid, and at diuerse wthyr tymes afor, it was fundin and concludit be the haill communite that the said bond vas ressonable." So it was agreed that "thair suld be ane kyst, denit in the souerest sort, quhilk sald haue four lokis, and four keyis," in which the funds for the support of the bridge were to be kept. Of the keys the "provest sall haue ane in keiping, and the merchandis ane wther, the maisteris of the kyrk wark the thrid, and the deikynnis of craftis the ferd." The council then swore " in jugment the grit bodelie ayth, the crucifixt being tuiching be thame and ilk ane of thame that thai suld neuer intromit with the money" for any other purpose, "and every future council was ordained to "sweir inlikvise the grit ayth." The bridge was formally handed over to the town in 1529 by its architect, the parson of Kinkell, and Robert Elphinstone, the parson of Kincardine, in "name and behalf of ane reverend father in God, Gauane bischop of Dunbar," and the council accepted it " without ony langer delay."

The city has always been proud of the Bridge of Dee, and a whole series of eulogistic couplets might be adduced to show this. The document just referred to waxes eloquent over the "nobill and substantius brig." "The greatest and brawest bridge now to be seen in Scotland," quoth Parson Gordon, but perhaps the most enthusiastic panegyric is by Boece, "that excessively Scotch Herodotus" as Masson cleverly dubs him. His life of Elphinstone leads him of course to speak of this part of the bishop's work, and it has been versified thus by Alexander Garden :—

>"And yet a work als great
>And necessar much more,
>Unto his oune, his countrie's good,
>And both their great gloir,

Annon their-after he
   Resolved and first intends,
That everie age and ey that vieus
   Admires and yet commends.
This was the bridge of Dea
   Which every man may mark,
Ane needful, most expensive, great,
   A good and gallant wark ;
Knit close with quadrat stones,
   Free all, incised and shorne ;
Of these the pend with arches sevine,
   Supported is and borne.
Sharpe poynted butresses ·
   Be both that breaks and byds
The power of winter speats
   And strenth of summer tyds
Above it's beawtified
   With posts and prickets four ;
And all alongst rayled is
   And battailed to look our.
A great and goodlie work
   Which how long t' stands and stayes
It aye shall mater ministratt
   Unto the author's praise."

Near the north end of the bridge stood a chapel which was dedicated to the Virgin Mary. The earliest mention of it is in 1530, when Sir William Ray is described as "vmquhyle chaplane to our lady chappell," but it had probably been built at the same time as the bridge itself. The habit of building chapels at bridges in those times was not uncommon, and in this case it had probably been set down for the benefit of passing strangers coming to the town, and townsmen speeding south. In that year, however, Sir William Ray gave to the council "ane challis of siluer, ane ymage of siluer of our lady, baicht our guilt; thre naipkingis, ane broodin, and tua quhyt, "ane altare towell, togidder with the key of the offerand stok, to be kepit to the vtilite and proffite of the said chappell." This image which the chaplain presented is now in a church at Brussels. An extraordinary story of how the statue found its way to the Continent is told by Father Blakhal in his tedious and misnamed *Breiffe Narration of the Services done to Three Noble Ladyes*— "I did ther, as I have oft tyms dun in the faire of St. Germains, behold many fyne things, and wish myself able to buy them, but, for want of moneys, leave them to others for I was very scant. I had non but what I gotte for saying the first messe, every morning, at Notre Dame, de bonne successe, a chapelle of great devotion, so called from a statu of our Ladye, which was brought from Aberdein, in the North of Scotland, to Ostend, by a merchant of Ostend, to whom it was given in Aberdein. And that same day that the shippe in which it was did arrive at Ostend, the Infanta did winne a battaile against the Hollanders, the people thinking that our Ladye, for the civil reception of her statu, did obteane that victorye to the princesse, who did send for the statu to be brought to Bruselle, when the princesse, with a solemn procession, did receave it at the porte of the tounc, and placed it in this chappel, wher it is much honored, and the chapelle dedicated to Our Ladye of bonne successe, which befor was pouer and desolat, now is riche and wel frequented. The common beleiff of the vulgar people ther is, that this statu was thrown in the sea at Aberdein, and carried upon the waves of the sea miraculously to Ostend. So easie a thing it is for fables to find good harbour, where verities would be beaten out with cudgelles." This is the statue referred to by Kennedy in his story of how Dunbar came to fix the site for his bridge. There has been a great deal of discussion over it, which has been revived within recent years. About twenty years ago, Father John Sutherland made strong but unsuccessful efforts to get it back to Aberdeen.

The chapel was protected by a bulwark, which was an eyesore to the laird of Abergeldy, who ordered the town to "mak ane esy gait and passage betuix the brig of Dee and chapell of the samyn, quhair throw thai may eselye, without impediment wyrk and laubour thair watteris." The council did not evidently see eye to eye with the laird, although he protested "aluayis quhat damnage or skaith thai sustenit thairthrow suld com on the toune and nocht" on him, and so he hewed down the obnoxious bulwark. He was immediately demanded to build it again, and "to keipe stane stabill," and, as if to punish him the more, "this to be extendit in the largest forme."

The bridge was of much greater importance in the

past than it is now. It was the only accessible land entrance from the south, and thus, if guarded, nearly all strangers from the south could be kept from entering the town. Two powerful factors compelled the town to keep watch and ward over the bridge—pestilence and war. This seems very primitive, viewed from the modern standpoint, but then the structure was of paramount importance ranking with the ports of the city, if not taking a higher position. The dreaded plague called in the guardianship of the bridge for the first time in 1529. It was then ordered that two persons should "pas dailie to the brig of De, and ramane thair continualie fray vj houris in the morning quhill vj houris at euin, during all the tym it hapnis this contagius plaige and pestilance to ring, for keiping of this guid tovne fra the samyn, and to lat nane our the said brig without testimoniall quhat place thai came fra." The duty of watching went by turns among the citizens. The next step was to get a port erected, and, in 1545, the dreaded approach of an enemy made the council ordain that "thair be ane port maid incontinent with all diligence on the south end of the brig of Dee with tymmer, to be fast lokit in the nycht, and weill keipit one day licht." Every neighbour of the town "and honest men" had to give twelve pence thereto, and "sobir folkis viijd.," or "sax d." at the least. While the port was being made, "tua trew honest fellowis" had Horatius-like to keep the bridge. A few months later the presence of the plague again demanded a watch, so that "na suspect personis of the contagius pest haue enteres thairat." Those antiquated sanitary precautions gradually became stricter. The punishment for a drowsy bridge watchman in 1566 was to pay forty shillings, and failing that "to haue his lug nailed to the trone and to be put in the branks." The severity of the order, however, reached its climax in the disastrous period of 1584-85 when Scotland was devastated by the plague. Seeing that it was "ringand in dyuerss partis, townis, and places of the south contrie," the council ordained "ane port of tree to be biggit and sett upoun the Brig of Dee; that thair be ane wache there of twa honest burgess men or craftismen, thât nane be sufferit to haue entrie thairat, without ane sufficient attentik testimoniall; and that na testimoniall be ressauit nor admittit, giffen at ony suspect place." A much more rigid restriction was enforced in the following year when the council, driven to desperation, ordered gibbets to be erected at the cross, the harbour, and the Bridge of Dee, "that in caice onye infeckit persoun aryue or repair be sie or land to this burght or fredome thairof, or in caice ony induellar of this burght ressaue, hous, or harbrie, or giff meat or drink to the infekit persoun or personis, the man to be hangit, and the woman to be drownit."

These ports were all more or less of a temporary character, being erected every now and again when the council became panic-struck at the threatening of a plague, or other invader. The erection of one of those ports was one of the good deeds for which, in 1597, William Dwn, the dean of guild, received some £47 odds. This dean has immortalized himself in local annals for "hes extraordinarlie takin panis in the birning of the gryt numer of wiches brint this year," 1597, and the hanging of four pirates. In the following year the first really substantial erection was made in the shape of an arched port on the south end "with a chamber above the arch for a watch tower." This, probably, was the tower constantly occupied for two years, 1604-6, by watchers. When all the other ports in the town had had their watch restrictions removed, the Bridge of Dee port was still occupied. We find mention in the town's accounts on one occasion, 1648, of "twa gryt lockis to the brig of Die, and for stokis to thame and for shots and yron work." There were evidently seats erected, for a mason is paid for "seating the same and for caring out a tril to be a baer." This arched gateway, which seems to have latterly been built of stone, was, in 1679, ornamented with Elphinstone's and the town's arms.

The building of ports leads to the occasion when they were really most in requisition—the time of war. In this connection the Bridge of Dee has figured very prominently in the city's history.

The first event of historical importance occurred in 1589, when the great Catholic noblemen of the north—Huntly, Errol, and Crawford—raised the standard of rebellion against the king, whose Protestant attitude struck terror to their hearts. James, advised of " sum interprises appeirandlie moved aganis the treu religion," hastily collected about 1000 men, and marched to oppose his noble subjects ; who, with 3000 followers, were then quartered in Perth. Both parties moved northwards, but at the Bridge of Dee, 20th April, according to Calderwood, "feare seazed upon the most part of Huntlie's faction, when they heard the king was in person in the feilds." So the Catholic rebellion was for the time quenched, although it was not the last time that its leaders were heard of. Indeed, the " Brig of Dee affair," as it was long called, was Huntly's first entry into a public life, which lasted for nearly half-a-century.

The part of history, however, in which the Bridge of Dee will always figure most conspicuously, was in the great Covenanting struggle. Built by the church, it is a noteworthy fact that in two religious struggles the bridge should have occupied a prominent place.

The part played by Montrose in the early struggle in the North is well known. Within three months, in 1639, he mulcted Aberdeen in 110,000 merks of penalty, and in May left the city for the purpose of punishing the Royalists elsewhere, carrying off Lord Huntly as a prisoner. A month later Huntly's son, Lord Aboyne, a spirited boy of nineteen, was on his way north, and on June 6th he landed with two armed vessels, and a Newcastle collier, and a few gentlemen and field pieces. His subsequent movements are familiar. On June 14th he marched against Montrose at Stonehaven, was beaten at Megray Hill, his men scattering like sheep before Montrose's guns. "Musket's mother," as the great guns were called, were too powerful for them, and even Spalding tremblingly writes of the artillery as "veray feirfull." The young general retreated to Aberdeen with his two colonels, Gun and Johnston, while his men fled helter-skelter. On Sunday the 16th he sent out a picket of seven men under Johnston; and these, meeting seven of Montrose's men some six miles from the city, soon knew that the energetic Covenanter was on the track. On the following day Aboyne issued orders to his men to re-muster, but they were not all forthcoming, One detachment, numbering 4000, never got further than Leggatsden, where they lay to see their comrades beaten. Before sunrise on the 18th, Johnston was sent to barricade the south port of the bridge, by casting up a "thik faill" rampart behind it. The river being swollen, and unfordable to the enemy, these preparations were deemed the most judicious for the safety of the town. Aboyne followed with 100 musketeers and a large number of cavalry, only to catch a glimpse of Montrose's army encamped in the Tollo hill above Banchory House. Here, in March, Montrose and the Covenanters had "stentit thair pavilionis" before marching upon the city. Montrose's force was estimated at 2000 foot and 300 horse. The arrival of Aboyne was greeted with a small volley, which, however, fell short of the defending cavalry. Then followed that quarter cannon, "haueing hir bullet of 20 pund wecht," which Spalding thought so "veray feirfull." But the defenders, under the courageous Johnston, stood firm. So bravely did they defend their position, that they won the admiration of the opposing musketeers. Their intrepidity inspired their servants and followers, who, in spite of the cannon and musket shot, went and came to the bridge with provisions and necessaries for the defenders.

"In the afternoon," says Gordon in his *Scots Affairs*, "the companies of Dundee, emulous of the Aberdeen citizens, desired to be letten storm the bridge, which Montrose readily yielded to. Two companies fell on, under the command of one Captain Bonar, but they found so hot a welcome from the Aberdeens-men that they made a quick retreat, which was seconded with whooping and hollowing of such as were looking on, who mocked their poor bravado." The battering rams which were brought into requisition against the barriers were of no avail. "Thus, this haill day, thay on the ane syde persewing the brig with cannon and mvscat, and on the vther syde thay ar defending with muscat and thair four brassin peices (whiche did littill service), yit," recounts Spalding, "no skaith on our syde except ane townes man callit John Forbes wes pitifullie slayne, and William Gordoun of Gordouns Mills rakleslie schot in the foot, both ante covenantaris." The gathering darkness of night put an end to the fight, for, says Gordon curiously, "there is no sky-set then in the north of Scotland," Watches were set, and the two forces went to sleep, only however, to renew hostilities as vigorously as ever on the morrow.

The obstinacy of the defenders irritated the dashing Montrose, whose whole military tactics were of an energetic character. He "thought such a delay little better than to be beaten," writes Gordon, and in the darkness of the night, he had drawn up his two half cannon nearer the bridge. The citizens were less active. In the early morning fifty of them foolishly left their post, leaving the other fifty to guard the bridge, and went to the town to bury Forbes, "quhilk wes veray vnwyslie done and to the tynsall of the brig." Montrose saw his advantage and was quick to embrace it. He levelled his guns against the barricade, " both to break the gates of the porte, and scour the bridge all along. For the day befor most of the canon shott wer made against one of the corners of the porte, which looked to the south-west, whereby one of the two small watche turretts upon the sydes of the porte, was much shattered in the topp of it, being all hewed stone, as all that bridge is, being," says Gordon grandly, "one of the gallantest in Scottlande, if not the statelyest itselfe." Johnston put his few men "in the roundis of the brig on both sydes, where they could defend themselves with little loss." Afternoon came, and yet there was no sign of victory for the besiegers. Montrose saw to his intense chagrin that—in Spalding's homely language—he "culd cum no speid." Resolving, therefore, to become master of the situation by strategy, he devised a "prettie slicht," to decoy the defenders from their position, by sending a body of his horse up the bank of the river, as if they meant to ford it near Banchory. Loyalist writers, from the time of Gordon down to Mr. Mark Napier, have credited Colonel Gun with the basest treachery at this part of the battle. "The colonel," says Gordon in his most bitter style, "who could espy no occasion before to draw off the horsemen, cries, 'March up the river's side, and stop Montrose's crossing.' It was told him there was no danger, the fords having been lately tried and found impassable. But no assurance could serve his turn, who would not believe that which he knew to be true." Spalding merely says that the feint was "over haistellie believit" by Aboyne, who immediately led off part of the defenders to oppose it. Johnston, with but a mere handful, was left to hold the bridge position. Montrose opened fire on both sections of the divided defenders. He poured his shot on the party that had turned to the river side, and the Royal Standard-bearer, celebrated in ballad lore as "Bonny John Seton" of Pitmedden, was shot dead, "most part of his body above the saddle being carried away and quashed." The ballad is much more minute:—

It fell about the month of June
   On Tuesday temouslie ;
The northern lords hae pitch'd their camps
   Beyond the Brig o' Dee.

They ca'ed him Major Middleton
   That man'd the brig o' Dee ;
They ca'ed him Colonel Henderson
   That gar'd the cannons flee.

Bonny John Seton o' Pitmedden
   A brave baron was he ;
He made his tesment ere he gaed
   And the wiser man was he.

He left his lands unto his heir
   His lady her dowrie ;
Ten thousand crowns to Lady Jane
   Sat on the nourice knee.

Then out it speaks his lady gay
   Oh stay my lord wi' me
For word is come, the cause is won
   Beyond the Brig o' Dee.

He turned him right and round about,
   And a light laugh gae he ;
Says, I woud'na for my lands sae broad
   I stay'd this night wi' thee.

He's taen his sword then by his side
   His buckler by his knee ;
And laid his leg in o'er his horse
   Said, Sodgers, follow me.

So he rade on, and further on
  Till to the third mile corse ;
The Covenanters' cannon balls
  Dang him aff o' his horse.

Up then rides him Craigievar
  Said, Wha's this lying here?
It surely is the Lord o' Aboyne,
  For Huntly was not here.

Then out it speaks a fause Forbes
  Lived up in Druminnor ;
My lord, this is a proud Seton
  The rest will ride the thinner.

Spulzie him, spulzie him, said Craigievar.
  O' spulzie him, presentlie ;
For I could lay my lugs in pawn,
  He had nae gude will at me.

They've taen the shoes frae aff his feet
  The garters frae his knee ;
Likewise the gloves upon his hands—
  They've left him not a flee.

His fingers they were sae sair swell'd
  The rings wuld not come aff ;
They cuttet the grips out o' his ears,
  Took out the gowd signots.

Then they rade on and further on
  Till they cam to the Crabestane ;
And Craigievar he had a mind
  To burn a' Aberdeen.

Out it speaks the gallant Montrose
   (Grace on his fair bodye!)
We winna burn the bonnie burgh
   We'll even lat it be.

Then out it speaks the gallant Montrose
   Your purpose I will break ;
We winna burn the bonnie burgh
   We'll never build its maik.

I see the women and their children
   Climbing the craigs sae hie ;
We'll sleep this nicht in the bonnie burgh
   And even lat it be.

While this blow was being dealt at the river side party, Montrose's men, under Colonel John Middleton, were dealing havoc on the bridge defenders. His men had been growing impatient and discouraged by the death of Captain Andrew Ramsay, brother of the laird of Balquhain, but Middleton rallied them, and led on himself to the attack. The defenders were "cruelie chargit, both with cartow and muskat schot in gryte aboundans, quhilk wes moir feirfullie renewit" the moment Aboyne left the bridge. At last the turret of one of the ports was struck by a shot, and Johnston, who stood all the time where there was most danger, was half buried in the ruins, his leg being "quashed to pieces." The gallant defender was rendered useless. "He haistellie callis for ane horss," says Spalding in one of his vivid outbursts, "and sayes to his soldioaris, 'Gallantis, do for your selffs and haist yow to the toun';

quhairvpone thay all with him self took the flight. Then follouit in certane capitanes, quiklie takis in the brig peceablie, and kest our thair cullouris." The river side party saw their colours flying from the bridge. Gordon, determined to blacken Gun, makes him give the order, " 'Gentlemen, make you for the town, Lieutenant-Colonel Johnston is killed, and the bridge is won,' but his words got slender obedience." He goes on to tell that William Gordon of Arroudale, asked Gun to stand and wait upon the Covenanters' fore-party crossing the bridge, showing him that they yet had the advantage, and, as a final encouragement, reminding him that "it was not the fashion of Huntly's family to leave the field without fighting the enemy. But," he adds, "there was no hearing for it was Gun's fashion always to cry out that, if they would not obey his orders, he would lay down his charge and complain to the King." Aboyne's men, continues Gordon, did not take Gun's refusal to fight well, but began to murmur that he was betraying them, and Arroudale "in a great chafe told him to his face that he was a villain, and an arrant traitor, all which Gun swallowed quietly." The story is far too verbose to have been enacted on the river side at such a critical moment. One is inclined to believe with Spalding, whose royalist tendencies do not lead him to decry his own side—that "the Lord Oboyne, seing thair horssmen stay vpon the vther syd of the water and not coming throw the water, as they seimit to intend and with all seing thair cullouris vpone the brig, takis the flight schamefullie, but straik of suord or ony vther kynd of vassalage."

At all events the bridge was taken about four in the afternoon after nearly two days' fighting. The defenders lost five men, and Montrose but two. Then Montrose marched in triumph into the city " with sound of trumpettis, displayit cullouris, and touking of drumis. As the army merchit, the haill covenanteris wes blyth, and the royallistis alss sorrowfull at this sicht, who for plane feir fled the toun, with thair wyfis and children in thair armes and careit on thair bakis, weiping and mvrning most pitifullie, straying heir and thair not knowing quhair to go. Thus war thay sore distrest for the love they had to the King, and now for following Aboyne." Such is Spalding's wail, and he waxes more mournful as he recounts the subsequent sufferings of the city, how it was rescued from destruction only by a bribe of 7000 merks, and how the citizens suffered gross indignities at the hands of the victors. In a very different vein is the following.

Pasquil made at the Bridge of Dee quhen it was wone from the Ante-Covenanteris of the north:—

God bliss our Covenanters in Fyffe and Lothean,
In Angus and the Mearnis, quho did us first begin
With muskit and with carabin, with money, speare and shield,
To take the toune of Aberdeen and make our Marques yield.

God bliss Montrois, our General,
    The stout Earl of Kinghorne,
That wee may long live and rejoyce
    That euer they were borne.

The man that hes an eiuell wyffe,
    He prayes God to amend her,
That he may live a quiet lyffe,
    And dye a Couenanter.

My Lord Aboyne hes tynt his style
    Vith maney a Northland man,
Quhen couardly they fled away
    For all their craft and can.

Quhen they caroussed at the brigend,
    Drinkand their wyne and beaire,
The Couenanters leuche at theme,
    And drank the watter cleir.

I was a Couenanter,
    Long ere that I came heire,
With my burnish't muskit,
    And my bandeleire.

My 7 yells of Flanders matche,
    And my sheiring suord,
And euery wolly I did shote,
    The limers yeul'd loud.

I purpois to begin,
    I werss for to record,
The commendatioune of our men
    That trusted in the Lord.

Pray for our Couenanters
  Quho still depens one God,
Quho proued treuly to the end
  And marched he south the rod.

The Laird of Banffe is take to sea
  His pilot for the Ruther,
And dars not come to land agane,
  For feare of Muskie's mother.

.

The Prouest's daughter of Aberdeine,
  She is a sore lamenter,
And cursses her father will not be
  Ane honest Couenanter.

The Couenanters of the South,
  They're honest, stout, and trewe,
And they haue woued both saule and lyffe
  To burne fals Aberdeine.

Muskie's mother hes made a wow
  That she will take her wenter,
And thunder throughe (the) brige of Dee,
  Led by a Couenanter.

The Couenanters that ye see
  Come marching alongest the grein,
Wer not for feare of God, they say,
  They vold plounder Aberdeine.

I had a beard as vther men,
   But God reuard the pouder,
He suers he's never cocke hes mathche,
   Nor musket one hes shoulder.

While that the dogs of Aberdeene,
   Which did cast vpe such trinches,
Themselves with speed fill vpe the same,
   To please our Couenanters.

The beaten dogs of Aberdeene,
   Is fled and veighed ther ankers,
They durst not byde into ther toune,
   To feast the Couenanters.

They left ther children and ther wyffes,
   To reed yare reuelit yairne,
And cuckold-lyke fled for their liues,
   Unto the Iyle of Ferne.

There is probably a good deal of truth in this skit. "Musket's mother" had, according to one verse of the pasquil—whose suppression the taste of the day demands,—a disastrous effect on Aboyne himself. Sir Walter Scott touches the same key when he quotes in *Waverley*, from one of the numerous "old ballads" that could sprout from his imagination like mushrooms. "In an old ballad on the Bridge of Dee," he says, these verses occur :—

   The Highlandmen are pretty men
      For handling sword and shield,
   But yet they are but simple men
      To stand a stricken field.

> The Highland men are pretty men
>   For target and claymore,
> But yet they are but naked men,
>   To face the cannon's roar.
>
> For the cannon's roar on a summer's night
>   Like thunder in the air;
> Was never man in Highland garb
>   Would face the cannon fair."

For long the "Brig Raid" was one of the reckoning dates with the citizens.*

This battle was the leading event, but for the next five years the bridge often crops up in the history of the struggle. It was, as Spalding says, a "randevouss" of the parties. Not satisfied with crushing Aberdeen at the Battle of the Bridge, the Covenanters made another campaign to the north; and, on May 26th, 1640, Earl Marischal penned the following epistle from Dunnottar:—

"To my loving friends, the prowest and ballies of Aberdeine. My very loveing freinds, these ar to show zow that I intend (God willing) on Thursday nixt, in the eftirnoone, to be at Abirdeine, quhair I will bring with me generall Maior monro and his regiment, for quhome I pray zow cause prowyd victuallis for the payment, for nothing sall be takin without reddie moneyis, ye alvayes approving zourselffis gude cuntrie men. And with all ye sall be in armes, and meitt ws at the brig of Dee, that

---

* *Spalding Club Miscellany*, V., p. 137.

we may joyne for defense of your toune, and of so many honest men as sall be fund thairin, and for the peace of the cuntrie about. But I wish ze be better conveened nor ze were at last wappin showing. So, not doubting of zour cair and diligence heirin, I rest zouris lowing freinds."

In conformity with the foregoing behest, the citizens, two days after, being "chargit be tovk of drum," marched forth to the bridge. There they met Munro with 40 horse and 800 foot, all in "gude ordour, haveing blew bonnetis on thair heidis, with fedderis vaveling in the wynd." The magistrates had to sign eleven articles, each of which humbled them to the dust. The city, already burdened with nigh twenty thousand pounds of debt, was compelled to support the army; having in 'reddiness, 12,000 pund wecht of good bisket breid, togidder with 1000 gallouns of aill and beir; 1200 pair of schoois, togidder with 3000 elnis of hardin tyking or saill canvess, for making of tentis to saif the souldatista from grite invndatioun of raynes accustomat to fall out wnder this northern climat." For three long months the wretched citizens had to comply with these galling conditions, which had been imposed upon them at the bridge.

By a turn of the tables, however, in 1644, Huntly gained the ascendency, and, in April, marched into the town with 10,000 men. Determined to secure himself against a surprise from the south, he ordered the Town Council to "caus build ane port of timber, with ane wicket, on the south end of the Bridge of Dee," threatening to "cut down ane bow" of the bridge unless his order was complied with. The poor Council, battle-dored and shuttle-cocked from party to party, did so "with diligence;" and, instead of one "saif gaird," two were put, one at each end.

The next occasion when the bridge appears is when Montrose marched north in the Royalist interest. Twice he had punished the town in the Covenanting cause, and now he marched north to inflict the severest blow of all for the opposite side. The citizens mustered some 3000 men; and, determined to meet the Marquis before entering the town, began to guard the Bridge of Dee and build fortifications. It was, as Spalding laments, "to litle effect." The Marquis "miskenis" the bridge and outwitted the citizens, on 11th September, by fording the river at Drum. Two days later, at the Justice Mills, he inflicted the most crushing blow that the city had yet received. The battle itself was not so bloody, but "horribill wes the slauchter in the flight"—a few of the fugitives being slain at the very bridge which they had guarded but forty-eight hours before.

A few weeks later the town was again outwitted by the Marquis, whom Argyle had gone in pursuit of after the battle of the Justice Mills. How the latter out-manœuvred Argyle for weeks is matter of history. But at last word was brought to the city that he was marching through Angus with his hotly pursued army, and Marischal, at once, on October 14th, got together "all, of whatsoeuer aige, sex, or qualitie," who had horse and money, to intercept him in advance by guarding the Bridge of Dee. For three days the citizens kept watch and ward, but the clever strategist once more repeated his trick, by fording the Dee at Drum. Thus, while the citizens were "lying watcheing the brig of Dee foolishlie," the Marquis had his "haill army saif and sound," his men "leiving idlie, destroying the countrie and thair cornes pitfullie." All this but shows that the bridge was losing its importance as a city entrance, and with such a clever general as Montrose to deal with, the old edicts against the plague would have been utterly useless.

In the spring of the next year, 1645, Montrose was again master of the situation. He sent the gallant, but reckless, Nathaniel Gordon into the city, with 100 Irish dragoons. He took 1800 muskets from Torry, and routed Captain Keith, brother of Marischal, at the Bridge of Dee. After Hurry's departure from the city Montrose despatched General M'Donald, with 700 men, to guard the bridge. No sooner had he left, than Hurry once more appeared on the scene; but an engagement there was fortunately averted.

In the course of the last two centuries the bridge has almost been rebuilt. From a very early period in the history of the structure, a special mason was appointed to keep it in repair. The first was Alexander Moneypenny, who, in 1531, was engaged to attend daily " and aduert to oure brig of Dee, bulwarkis and chappell, and reforme all small faltis that sall happin in the said varkis." He was not permitted to "depart nor pass away fra the said wark at anay tyme without speciale lycence." Time, however, wrought many changes, and, notwithstanding the caution exercised by the council in taking over the bridge, and obligations entered into to uphold it "in good order and condition," it had, within seventy years of erection, been allowed to fall into considerable disrepair. In the summons served upon the Town in 1591, at the instance of certain citizens, it is stated that the "provest and counsall hes sufferit, and daylie suffers our bridge of Dee, the most profitable monument within the north pairt of our realme, to decay, and the water bushing and rwning throw the hewin work of the pillars thairof, to the utter wrack alsweill of all our liedges, as of our said burgh, the skaithe, damnage, and expensiss thairof, befoir the samyn be sufficientlie repairit, extending to fyve hundredth merkis." In the middle of the 17th century a rude attempt was made to strengthen it. Most activity in this direction, however, occurred during last century, at various dates. A start was made in 1712, but little actual work was done beyond getting materials together. From 1718 to 1722 great masses of material were purchased for repairs, including rough sandstone from Elgin and Edinburgh, timber from the Duke of Gordon's forests, and, in 1722, a quarry was opened on the Pitfodels' property for stone to the bridge. The first improvement did not take place till 1773, when the port and stone walls at the south end were removed for the convenience of traffic. The original bridge consisted of seven semi-circular groined arches, with a total span of 432 feet, but it was only 16½ feet wide. The great inconvenience of such a narrow roadway was first experienced when the great coach traffic began, and the turnpike to the south was made. But it was not till 1841-2 that the bridge was thoroughly repaired and widened, when 11½ feet were added to the west side, at a cost of £7250, Provost Thomas Blaikie carrying on the work.

The history of the bridge is continued briefly in the inscriptions and coats of arms that adorn the various parts of the structure. The first mention of inscriptions is in 1679, when the Council resolved to "caus heu the tounes armes and Bishop Elphingstounes" on the port of the bridge, and "to caus illuminat the same in decent forme." There are no less than twenty-five such—nine on the east side, and sixteen on the west. There are eight inscriptions, the rest being coats of arms. Dunbar's arms appear eight times—six times on the west side and twice on the east front. Elphinstone's arms appear twice, once on each side. The arms of Scotland appear three times—on the first pier and last buttress of the west front, and on the first buttress of the Aberdeen side. The arms of Bon-Accord and of Provost Thomas Blaikie appear on the second pier of the west side, and the Duke of Albany's on the first pier of the east side. Taking the inscriptions chronologically, the following one in black letter takes the first place :—

   GAUIN . DUBAR . ABERDONEN .
   EPS . IPERII . IACOBI . 5ü SCOTORU .
   REGIS . ANO . DNO . ME . LAPSU .
   REEDIFICARE . FECIT . ORATE . P . EO .

The translation is—As I had fallen into a state of decay, Gavin Dunbar, Bishop of Aberdeen, with the assistance of James V., King of Scotland, caused me to be rebuilt, in the year ——. Pray for him.

The next inscription, also in black letter, is as follows :—

   GAUIN . DUBAR . ABERDONEN .
   POTIFEX . ME . TRAS . DEE . FLUUII . FIERI .
   IUSSIT . ANNO . DNI . QUITO . ET . UINESIO .
   SUPA . MILLE^m . ET . QUIGE^m . ORATE . P . EO .
    ANNO . DOMINI . 1525 .

The translation is—Gavin Dunbar, Bishop of Aberdeen, caused me to be built over the river Dee, A.D. 1525.

The next inscription brings us down to the repairs made in the early years of the eighteenth century. It is on the third pier of the west side :—

> SENATUS ABERDONENSIS, QUI, PER
> INTEGRUM ADMINISTRATIONIS
> CURRICULUM, NE QUID INCURIA SUA
> RESPUBLICA DETRIMENTI CAPERET
> SUMMA OPE NITEBATUR, OMNES
> ARCUS HUIUSCE PONTIS, IAM COL-
> LABASCENTES, EX ÆRE AD PONTEM
> SARTUM TECTUMQUE CONSERVAN-
> DUM DEDICATO, INSTAURANDOS
> CURABAT ANNIS DOMINI 1719,
> 1720, 1721, 1722 ET 1723

The translation, taken from Jervise's *Epitaphs*, runs—"The Town Council of Aberdeen, who, during the whole period of their tenure of office, exerted their utmost efforts to prevent the public interests from sustaining any injury through their negligence, caused, in the years 1719-20-21-22 and 23, the whole of the arches of this bridge, which had fallen into a state of decay, to be rebuilt out of monies set apart for keeping the bridge in repair."

On the parapet over the first four arches, Aberdeen side, of the east front, several modern dates are given—as,

> INSTAURATUS
> A.D.
> 1720

The longest inscription appears on a slab inserted into the second piers of the west front, and reads as follows—

ANNVENTE SVMMO NVMINE,
HICCE PONS
EX BENE ADMINISTRATA PECVNIA AD
EVM CONSERVANDVM LEGATA
TRECENTIS AMPLIVS ANNIS POSTQVAM PRIMVM
EST EXTRVCTVS
MVLTVM DILATATVS PENITVSQVE REFECTVS EST
ANNO M.D.CCC.XXXXI . ET M.D.CCCXXXII
THOMA BLAIKIE CIVITATIS ABERDONENSIS
PRAEFECTO,
GEORGIO HENRY } OPERVM PUBLICORVM DEINCEPS
GVLIELMO FRASER }   CVRATORIBVS.
IOANNE SMITH, ARCHITECTO,
ALEXANDRO MACDONALD } REDEMTORIBVS
GVLIELMO LESLIE   }

The arms and initials of Provost Blaikie are on the opposite side of the pier.

The translation, again according to Jervise, is—" Under the Divine blessing, this bridge, more than 300 years after its first erection, was much widened and thoroughly repaired in the years 1841 and 1842, out of the funds left for its maintenance, Thomas Blaikie being Provost of Aberdeen; George Henry and Thomas Fraser, successive Masters of Kirk and Bridge Works; John Smith, Architect; and Alexander Macdonald and William Leslie, Contractors.

At the approach to the west front of the Kincardineshire end stands an old sun-dial. An iron clamp has destroyed part of the face; but the following letters can still be made out on the top of it—

A. W . M^r O .　．．．　B. W. 1719 .

A stone inserted in the wall on the east front, of the Aberdeen approach, shows how far the famous flood came up—

FLOOD MARK.

6TH AUGUST
1829.

The bridge regained much of its ancient prestige in the end of the last century, when turnpikes were being made with such energy. In the days of the old north and south road, when the coaches sped across its narrow roadway daily, it was something of importance; but since that era ceased it has not figured conspicuously beyond being an excellent country road. Perhaps the only incident worth noting in the century—beyond the improvement already mentioned—is one which, strange to say, adds to the death-roll which has been made on the old bridge. On 20th April, 1818, when two police officers, were conveying James Grant from Stonehaven jail to Aberdeen, to stand his trial before the Circuit Court for sheepstealing at Bridge of Dye, the desperate prisoner broke clear at the Bridge of Dee and threw himself over the parapet. He fractured his skull and died instantly.

DOWNIES.

This is a small fishing village situated in the southeast corner of the parish, on the estate of Clashfarquhar, formerly owned by the Thomsons of Banchory, but now by the University of Aberdeen.

Dr. Morison, in his *Account of the Parish in 1792*, states that only one yaul fished from the village in that year. There are now six boats, employing twenty-seven hands, engaged in the haddock fishing, which is the only industry the inhabitants engage in.

The coast in the neighbourhood is particularly rocky, and many a vessel has been wrecked in the vicinity.

In 1640, when Aberdeen was invested by the Earl Marischal, many of the citizens sought shelter among the rocks along the coast, where they suffered much privation.

ESTATE OF FINDON.

In 1281, this estate was owned by "Philip de Fyndon,"* and on 13th April of that year, he appeared before a Justiciary Court, held on the moor of Nigg, for the settlement of a dispute as to the marches of Nigg and Findon, which had arisen between him and the Monks of Arbroath, superiors of the lands of Nigg, and Thomas, the son of the Thane of Cowie. Alexander Cumyn, Earl of Buchan, acted as president, and there were also present Hugo, Bishop of Aberdeen, Sir Reginald le Chen, the Father, besides several other knights and landed proprietors.† The boundaries were defined, and the dispute amicably arranged. Philip, who seems to have favoured the English party during the struggle which took place under Wallace, did homage to Edward I. at Berwick in 1296.‡

On the accession of Robert the Bruce to the throne, the estate had doubtless been confiscated, for, in 1319, the crown conferred an annual annuity arising from its rents, upon John Crab, a Flemish engineer, who had distinguished himself through his skill and prowess at the siege of Berwick during that year. Tytler says "Crab seems to have been a mercenary, who engaged in the

---

* *View of the Diocese of Aberdeen*, p. 258.
† *Book of Bon-Accord*, p. 378, &c.
‡ *Memorials of Angus and Mearns*. Vol. ii., p. 151.

service of any one who cared to employ him." In 1313, Edward II. "complained of depredations which had been committed by him on some English merchants," but, in 1333, after the loss of Berwick to Scotland, he obtained a pardon from the English, and thereupon entered their service. His descendants owned extensive property around Aberdeen. The large stone still standing in Hardgate at the back of West Craibstone Street, and known as the Crab Stone, formed one of the boundary marks of the estate of Rubislaw, which was at one time in his possession.

Findon was converted into a Barony at an early period, and in 1359 William of Keith, Sheriff of Kincardineshire took credit for the payment of £3 out of the lands. In 1390 they belonged to William de Camera or Chalmers, who was a burgess of Aberdeen, and several times provost between 1392 and 1404. Various theories have been propounded as to the origin of this name, but possibly that of Smibert carries most weight. He says "the name of 'Chambers' appears to be derived from 'de la Chambre' which some prominent attendant on a prince, or peer might have left to his posterity—a John 'of the Chambers' for instance—the French 'Chambres' being merely in the Scottish form of 'Chalmers.' 'De Camera' or 'Camerarius' is a word with the same meaning, and arising from an office of 'Chamberlain.'"* Chalmers was

* Peter's *Baronage of Angus and Mearns*, p. 53.

of the family of Balnacraig in Aboyne, and by a charter dated at Perth on 2nd March, 1392, he secured the annuity which had been held by Paul Crab, burgess of Aberdeen, a descendant of John Crab. Kennedy states that he was the founder of the Chantry of Saint Katharine, "to which he presented a silver gilt chalice, and vestments for the chaplains, with the image of the saint placed over the altar." He was witness to a charter by Hugh Fraser of Lovet and Kynnel, dated at Kynnel on 30th of March, 1407. Chalmers was succeeded in the proprietorship of Findon by his son William, who in 1420, sold to Sir Alexander of Forbes, lord of that Ilk, his right to the ward of the heir of the deceased Adam of Balkarne.*

In 1441 Richard Vaus, a grandson of Chalmers, is designed as proprietor; and in 1459 he granted from the lands of Balquharn an annual annuity of forty shillings to Lawrence Pyot, archdeacon of Aberdeen. He owned extensive property in and about Aberdeen, including the lands of Menie in Belhelvie. In 1469 he granted to the Franciscan, or Grey Friars, the property belonging to him situated on the east side of Gallowgate, as a site for the erection of their Monastery. Keith says that the building was "a fabrick of a great length, having a little steeple the bell in which was constantly rung for conveening the scholars to all publick lessons in the college." At the

* *Antiquities Aberdeen and Banff*, Vol. iv., p. 384.

Reformation it came into the possession of the burgh, and by virtue of the deed of gift it was set in heritable feu, except as much as was necessary for the use and sustenance of the poor.

Shortly afterwards Findon was acquired by the Menzies of Pitfodels, and remained the property of that family for many generations. It would appear that in these times a species of falcon—probably the peregrine falcon, a pair of which still haunt the rocks—built their nests upon the rocks or craigs on the coast, and in 1580 Alexander Menzies, son of the Provost of Aberdeen, was charged with the preservation of a nest for the service of James VI., who, as is well known, was passionately fond of hawking. Advantage was taken of Menzies' visits to the falconry to lay an ambush for his life. On the morning of 9th May of that year, William Forbes of Monymusk and Portlethen, whose cause of animosity is now unknown, concealed himself with some followers behind the Cairn of Loirston, in the parish of Nigg, and on the path leading from Aberdeen. After waiting several hours they perceived their victim approaching unattended. By placing their culverins on rests, they were able to take a steady and sure aim, and at the first discharge he fell, pierced through the heart by two bullets. The assassins instantly rushed forward, and inflicting no fewer than nine stabs on the body, robbed it of sword hanger, and cloak. Thirty years elapsed before the perpetrators of this barbarous deed were brought to trial and sentenced, which was rendered nugatory, however, by a royal pardon.* From Spalding we learn that the feud was unstaunched at the distance of more than half-a-century from the date of this atrocity, and that in 1640 it led to a combat between the grand-nephew of Menzies, and the son of his murderer, in which the blood of the latter was drawn.

In the Autumn of 1654, "Sir Gilbert Menzies of Pitfodels, Knight, Heritable Proprietor of the half Barony Lands of Torrie, Barony of Findon, Lands of Cookston, and Badentoy, on the first part, Sir John Forbes of Monymusk, Heritable Proprietor of the other half of the Barony of Torry, with consent of Robert Forbes of Barns his Tutor, of the second part, and John Forbes, Elder, and William Forbes, Younger of Leslie, Heritors of the Lands of Banchory, considering that there had been controversy and debate anent their meiths and marches, which had occasioned 'many unnecessary jarrs, discontents and troubles to their great hurt and prejudice,' and to settle all former unhappy differences, by advice and pains of their worthy friends chosen and taken to that effect," entered into a formal deed defining the meiths and marches of said lands for all time coming.

Findon proper, which included Wester Cookston, Badentoy, Redmyre, etc., and extended to about 1,500 acres, belonged in the end of last century to Dr. William

---

* Pitcairn's *Criminal Trials*, Vol. iii., pp. 204, 206.

Nicol of Stonehaven, who gave great encouragement to the tenants to reclaim and cultivate the waste land. Full particulars of the method of working followed, and the results of the transformation effected are given in the *Agricultural Survey of Kincardineshire*. The lands were afterwards divided into separate lots, and sold to the highest offerers.

The village of Seaton of Findon stands in a bleak, exposed position, on the ridge of cliffs that are very precipitous at this part of the coast. In striking contrast to this exposed situation, is the sheltered little harbour, some way from the village, which is reached by a long winding footpath. The village has made its name known all over the world, by the excellence of its cured haddocks. Since the time of Dr. Johnson, the "Finnan" haddock has been celebrated in history. Its excellence seems to have arisen from the mode of curing adopted. Whether the special process was instituted in this village or not, is a moot point; but certain it is, that a smoked yellow haddock will always be known as a "Finnan haddie". "A Finnan haddock," wrote Sir Walter Scott, whose knowledge of the geography of the village, like most people's, was not quite exact, "has a relish of a very peculiar and delicate flavour, inimitable on any other coast than that of Aberdeenshire. Some of our Edinburgh philosophers tried to produce their equal in vain. I was one of a party at dinner where the philosophical haddocks were placed in competition with the genuine Finnan fish. These were served round without distinction whence they came; but only one gentleman, out of twelve present, espoused the cause of philosophy." Philosophy has hardly been more successful to-day; for, though "Finnan" no longer holds a monopoly of the article, the process originally adopted there has proved the best, and the modern method of smoking the fish is as unsatisfactory as the "philosophical haddocks" turned out to be at the Edinburgh dinner party. To the great mass of people this minor industry is the most remarkable thing about Findon.

It is a singular coincidence that precisely the same number of hands is now engaged at the fishing as was in 1792. There were then two fishing boats, requiring six hands each, and three yawls, wrought by four men each. There are now four boats, employing twenty-four hands, fishing from the village.

In the end of last century, when less attention was paid to the subject of agriculture than now, it was no unusual circumstance for the crofters around the village to secure a yield of eighty bushels of bere off the English acre in one season. And what may appear more incredible, is the fact that the same land, in some cases, yielded the same crop, without intermission, for several generations.* Of course this arose from the plentiful supply, and specially favourable quality of manure the crofters were able to give the ground.

* *Agricultural Survey of Kincardineshire, p. 90.*

The Earn or Eagles-heugh, on the coast, is remarkable as having been the landing place of seven students from Saint Andrews, who had been drifted about the sea in an open boat for the space of six days. The sad story was commemorated by the father of one of the survivors in a painting and engraving. A copy of the latter (24" by 17") is preserved in the library room of Marischal College, Aberdeen. It represents the landing of the boys; and a portrait of one of them seated, and pointing to the scene, exhibits much ingenuity in its conception. At the foot is a description in Latin of the melancholy occurrence, accompanied by the following translation:—

"On the 19th of August, 1710, this young gentleman, David Bruce, aged 15 years, with six others about the same age, in company (David Rankilour, John Wilson, James Martin, Alexander Mitchell, James Thomson, and James Watson,) went out from the harbour of St. Andrews in a little boat, with a design to recreate themselves. But it happened in their attempt to return they lost one of their oars, and were driven into the ocean. 'Twas late before their parents missed them, and therefore not in their power to afford them any relief till morning, that they despatched some boats in quest of them, but all in vain. Whereupon every body gave them up for lost. Meantime the boys were tossed up and down, without being able by all their endeavours to make any shore, though every day within sight of it. At length by the good providence of God, the wind turning easterly, after six days and six nights continued fasting and labour, they got to shore alive under a steep rock commonly called Hern-heugh (Earn-heugh) four miles south of Aberdeen, and fifty north of Saint Andrews, which two of them climbed up by the direction of an old fisherman who chanced to be near the place. And making known their distress to an honest countryman, John Shepherd, he kindly received them into his house hard by, notifying at the same time so extraordinary and moving an accident to the Magistrates of Aberdeen, who forthwith despatched their Dean of Guild, with Dr. Gregory a physician, and William Gordon a surgeon to attend them, by whose means, under God, all of them were preserved excepting only the two youngest John Wilson, and James Martin, who died some time after they came ashore, and were honourably interred in Aberdeen by the care of the Magistrates. In thankful commemoration of this wonderful event Robert Bruce, goldsmith in Edinburgh, father to the above David, caused this copper plate to be engraved. *Soli Deo Gloria.*"

Kennedy states that a copy of the engraving was presented to the Magistrates of Aberdeen, and that it hung in the council room until "removed by order of one of the baillies, to give place to a catchpenny engraving of one of the heroes in the late war." The engraving in Marischal College is doubtless the one here referred to.

Mr. Bruce presented John Shepherd, with a piece of silver plate in the shape of a boat, now in the possession of his grandson, also named John Shepherd, farmer in Cairnrobin. It is oval-shaped, about four inches long, and thus inscribed :—

> "This silver boat is gifted to John Shepherd by Robert Bruce, goldsmith, for the kindness he showed to his son David Bruce and others, after they were six days and six nights at sea without meat or drink, and by Providence, thrown in at Earn-heugh, near his house, on the 25th August, 1710."*

* Kennedy's *Annals, Stat. Account of Kincardineshire*, and Jervise's *Epitaphs*.

Seal of William de Camera of Findon.
(Mar *Charters*, 1404.)

ESTATE AND VILLAGE OF PORTLETHEN.

This estate, which embraces the village of Portlethen, comprises 720 acres, and was formerly comprehended in the Barony of Findon. It is situated on the coast, south of Findon, from which it is divided by a deep ravine and small rivulet. According to "an old writer," cited in the *Book of Bon-accord*, Portlethen is more correctly "Port-Leviathan, so called, by reason of certain whales that came ashore there."

In the middle of the fifteenth century the lands were owned by David Menzies, burgess of Aberdeen, who is described in Wilson's *Aberdeen* as "a person of great affluence." In 1424 Aberdeen, together with Edinburgh, Perth, and Dundee, became bound as security to the English for the due payment of "forty thousand pounds of good and lawful money of England, to be paid in yearly sums of ten thousand marks till the whole was discharged," as ransom for James I. after his eighteen years confinement in England. Menzies, from his influential position, was selected as one of the hostages for Aberdeen, and as such, it is believed he was for a time resident in England. In 1459, he granted an annual annuity of four pounds payable from these lands to Lawrence Pyot, archdeacon of Aberdeen.

In 1618 Sir William Forbes, of Monymusk and

Banchory, had a charter of Portlethen, in favour of himself and Elizabeth Wishart of Pitarrow, his spouse.

A few years later the estate passed to Robert Buchan, who built the house of Portlethen. He was the son of Gilbert Buchan of Dorbshill, and married Marjorie Patrie, daughter of Hendrie Patrie, burgess of Aberdeen.* During his ownership the struggle of the Covenanters raged with fierceness, and he suffered severely at their hands. Spalding says that "with his second sone efter his houss and ground wes plunderit, he takis the sea, and so ilk man schiftit for himself, pairt by sea and pairt be land as thay thocht best."† In 1677 George Buchan, then resident in Lublin, in the kingdom of Poland, as only surviving son, proved his descent before a Bailie Court in Aberdeen.

The next proprietor was Robert Patrie, who was Provost of Aberdeen on several occasions between 1664 and 1674. He received the honour of knighthood at the hands of Charles II., and married Anna, second daughter of Sir William Forbes, first Baronet of Craigyvar. He is said to have been the representative of the ancient family of Glenavon in Banffshire. His arms were *Azure, a bend between a stag's head, erased, in chief, and three cross crosslets fitchée, in base argent, on a chief of the second, three escallops, gules.* Crest—*An eagle soaring aloft,*

---

* *Birth Brieves, Spalding Club Miscl.*, Vol. v., p. 359.
† Spalding's *Trubles*, Vol. i., p. 267.

looking at the sun in splendour, proper. Motto—*Fidi sed vide (Trust but observe).** Burns says "The lass that made the bed for me" was composed on an amour of Charles II., when skulking in the north about Aberdeen, in the time of the usurpation. He formed *une petite affaire* with a daughter of the house of Portlethen, who was "the lass that made the bed for him."

> "Her hair was like the links o' gowd,
> Her teeth were like the ivorie ;
> Her cheeks like lilies dipt in wine,
> The lass that made the bed for me."

Facsimile of the Signature of Provost Patrie.

Patrie's daughter, Elizabeth, became the wife of Robert Farquhar of Mounie, who received the honour of knighthood at the hands of Charles II. in 1651, whilst his sister, Elizabeth, was married to James Chalmers, second son of William Chalmers, the first legally established minister at Boyndie after the Reformation. He was first, professor of philosophy in Marischal College, afterwards minister of New Machar, thereafter of Cullen, and subsequently of Paisley. It is recorded that during his incumbency at Cullen, and when Cromwell's soldiers

---

* Peter's *Baronage*, p. 274.

were in possession of the town, he one Sunday preached such a fiery and pointed sermon on Jotham's parable—Judges, 9th chapter—that the soldiers who were in church became indignant, and as a revenge carried him prisoner to Elgin, where he was confined for some time. He left two sons—James, who became minister of Kirkpatrick-Fleming; and Charles, who succeeded his uncle, Provost Patrie, in the proprietorship of Portlethen. The latter studied for the law, and passed W.S. in 1704; but not liking the legal profession he gave it up, and joined the Scots Guards. He attained to the rank of captain, but sold his commission in 1714, when he went to reside in Aberdeen. In the following year, on the outbreak of the Stuart rising under the Earl of Mar, he threw in his lot with the insurgents, and joined their army. He took part in the battle of Sheriffmuir, at which he was mortally wounded, his remains being afterwards interred in Dunblane, in the burying-place of Chisholm of Cromlicks, within the church there. He married first, Jean, daughter of Alexander Boog of Burnhouses in Berwickshire, and secondly, Helen, daughter of Bishop Young of Edinburgh, by both of whom he had issue.*

The estate passed by public sale into the possession of Alexander Thomson, advocate and town clerk of Aberdeen. He was married to Helen Gregory, who died in 1711. His daughter, Helen, became the wife of

---

* Nisbet's *Heraldry*.

George Skene of Rubislaw.* In 1751 the estate was owned by James Thomson, advocate in Aberdeen, after which it passed into the hands of the Auldjo family, one of whom was for sometime Provost of Aberdeen.

Facsimile of the Signature of Provost Auldjo.

The estate was afterwards broken up, part being acquired by John Yeats, and part by the family of Gammel. The portion acquired by Yeats afterwards passed to the University of Aberdeen.

It is worth noting that John Burness, the author of the interesting "Thrummy Cap," whilst following the calling of a book canvasser, perished in a snow-storm at a spot near the church of Portlethen, on the night of 12th January, 1824. His body was found four days later by some farm servants, who were casting the road of snow; and it was afterwards interred in the Spital Cemetery, Aberdeen.

Within the last three years, funds were collected towards defraying the cost of erecting a public hall, which is intended to commemorate the Queen's Jubilee, as also

* *Skene of Skene*, p. 135.

to supply a much felt want in the district. On the evening of 12th August, 1889, the foundation stone was formally laid by Mrs. George J. Walker, Hillside House, whose husband designed the building. It is to be 70 feet in length by 35 feet in breadth, and although of plain appearance will be substantial throughout.

A suitable school was erected for the accommodation of the district by Dr. Morison, who also mortified £200 towards the support of the teacher. The Rev. William Paterson, schoolmaster of Nigg, also bequeathed £200 for the same object. There have been several excellent teachers in office including Charles A. Ewen, David Silver, John Watt, and Charles Meston. Mr. Watt, who some time ago had the degree of D.D. conferred upon him, is now minister of Anderston Church, Glasgow.

During the present century the fishing industry has largely extended. In 1792 only three large boats and one yawl fished from the village. There are now fourteen boats employing seventy-six hands constantly engaged.

PORTLETHEN CHURCH.

The history of Portlethen Church dates from the year 1649, at which time "the Presbytery of Aberdeen, taking into account the fact of the people dwelling in the 'remottest pairtis of the parochines of fetresio and netherbanchie fare distant frome their owne paroche kirkis That it is almost impossible to thame, Especiallie in the winter tyme, to repair to their owne paroche kirks for the worship of god and educatioune of their soules The way being deip and almost impossible,'" supplicated Parliament to take into consideration the propriety of erecting a place of worship here. It was stated that the number of communicants amounted at that time to "about 8 or 9 hundredth soules," and the matter was referred to the Committee for "the Plantation of Kirks."* Nothing practical, however, resulted from this application, but the Roman Catholic Chapel of Portlethen, which had been erected by Robert Buchan, proprietor of the estate, about 1635, having fallen into disuse, gradually came to be utilised as a presbyterian place of worship. In the beginning of last century, the parish ministers of Banchory-Devenick held services in the chapel, usually on Sunday afternoons. Regular entries of these preachings were made in the minute books of Session, and although

* *Acta Parl VI.²*, pp. 343-726.

it is stated in Macfarlane's Geographical Collections M.S., written in 1725, that "this present minister preaches once in the fifteen days in the afternoon in the summer time, and once in the twenty days in the winter time," there can be no doubt considerable attention was devoted to the spiritual requirements of the district. On Sunday forenoons the residenters were in the habit of attending at the parish church, where in 1711 a special space was set apart for their accommodation. This system continued for many years, and so jealously had the clerical interests been then guarded, that in 1742, when a Muchalls' clergyman obtruded by preaching in the chapel, the parish minister resolved "to have him prosecuted for so doing."

About two years later, however, a formal arrangement was entered into with Mr. Wilkins, a licentiate of the Church of Scotland, under which he undertook to preach each alternate Sunday here and at the Sod Kirk of Fetteresso, distant about three miles. This "sod kirk" was built in the northern part of Fetteresso. It was for long a wretched erection, but in 1816 exertions were made to procure a better and larger building; and a chapel capable of accommodating 400 sitters was erected at Cookney on the property of Muchalls. It having in time become insufficient for its object, fresh exertions were made, which resulted in the construction of a church, in which 700 are properly accommodated. The district is now converted into the *quoad sacra* parish of Cookney, and thereare at present upwards of 530 communicants on the roll. The Rev. James Taylor, M.A., who was ordained in 1867, is the minister. When the preaching was held at the latter place the people were warned to attend at Banchory. Regarding Mr. Wilkins we are informed that, by means of very low-priced and ill-paid seat rents and poor collections (his only source of income), he obtained the mere necessaries of life in the meanest grade of living. The worthy man had, at the frequent peril of his life, been extremely useful to the royal army in the Jacobite rebellion of 1745-46. For these valuable services the only reward that could be obtained for him from the Government was the offer of what is described in the Session Records as an "Itinerantry in a remote part of the Highlands." But Mr. Wilkins was too conscientious to accept of this, as he did not understand the Gaelic language—preferring poverty and usefulness in this unoccupied field for his ministrations.

After his death the two chapels were practically closed, with the exception of Portlethen Church, which was sometimes occupied by the parish minister, and both occasionally were taken possession of by any strolling and self-licensed preacher; most frequently by a fish-cadger of the name of Carse, who came to the coast in the way of his principal employment.* From 1785, the year that Dr. Morison came to the parish, a duly licensed minister

* *Session Records.*

officiated in it. In the end of last century Mr. Scorgie was the officiating clergyman. A Mr. Pirie also acted as minister for a considerable period, but on his death, in 1827, Mr. William Law, schoolmaster of Maryculter, was appointed to preach in the church each Sunday. His salary was at first £30 per annum, but in 1832 it was at Dr. Morison's instigation increased to £35, and a pony was presented to him so that he might ride over from Maryculter each Sunday. In December, 1834, it was reported to the Presbytery "that the Church having recently undergone extensive additions and alterations, is now seated for the accommodation of about 540 people, and the average amount of seat rents £51 5s. per annum. The average collection for the year is £28 10s." In 1840 Mr. Law was formally ordained minister of Portlethen as a chapel of ease, when a manse and more adequate salary were provided. He then demitted office as schoolmaster of Maryculter, and betook himself exclusively to the work of the ministry. Sixteen years later, he got the whole of the parish of Banchory-Devenick on the south side of the Dee, with the exception of the estates of Banchory and Ardoe, erected into the *quoad sacra* church and parish of Portlethen. Twelve years subsequently, on account of increasing years and failing strength, he was obliged to apply for an assistant and successor. This having been granted by the church courts, he handed over the ministerial charge of the district to the assistant. He died suddenly of apoplexy on the morning of 11th January, 1870, in the 73rd year of his age.

William Bruce, M.A., who had been appointed assistant and successor in 1868, now succeeded to the full charge. He was a native of Sauchentree, in the parish of New Aberdour, where his father for long carried on the business of an ironfounder, and thereafter of a farmer. Previous to his appointment at Portlethen, Mr. Bruce had for many years acted as schoolmaster of Finzean. As a minister he became very popular with the fishing community, to whom he discharged almost the whole functions of a doctor. He also took a keen interest in the educational and parochial matters connected with the parish; but unfortunately his career was blighted through the church courts having to take cognizance of certain indiscretions he had committed, and for which he was for a time placed under suspension. Shortly after he was seized by a paralytic affection, from which he never regained his wonted strength. In the autumn of 1882 the illness assumed an acute form, and he died somewhat suddenly on the 28th November of that year, aged about 45 years. His remains were interred in the burying-ground of Portlethen, where a handsome tombstone has been erected to his memory. He was a widower, but left no family.

The present incumbent is the Reverend Alexander Robertson Grant, M.A., son of Mr. Grant who was long a hotel-keeper in Abernethy, Inverness-shire. He received his early education at the school of Tomintoul, from whence he removed to Aberdeen for the purpose of prosecuting his studies. Matriculating at King's College in 1874, he graduated in 1878; and subsequently passing through the divinity course, was licensed by the Presbytery of Aberdeen in the spring of 1881. Being elected minister of Portlethen, he was ordained in the church in 1883. The communion roll exceeds 650 members, and the duties of minister in such a large and divided fishing district are of a delicate and trying character.

AUCHORTHIES.

These lands which include Auchlee and Bourtreebush extend to about 850 acres, and lie in the south-west corner of the parish. In 1390 they belonged to William de Camera of Findon, who in that year infefted Thomas Kennedy in the ownership. The Kennedys had the hereditary title of "Constable of Aberdeen," given to them under the following peculiar circumstances. The citizens of Aberdeen having taken by storm, during the reign of David II., the fortress which long stood on the Castlehill, "least at any tyme thereafter it should prove a yock upon the tounsmen's necks," razed it to the ground, and "in place thereoff builded a chappell which they dedicated (according to the fashione of the tymes) to St. Niniane; hoping by that meins that the hill, being converted to a holy use, it wold be unlaufull for any to attempt to imploy it againe to a profayne use any more."* "Ther leader, in this atchievement, wes one Kennedy of Kearmuick, for which service his posteritie wer honored with the title and dignity of *Constables of Aberdeen*."

In the beginning of the seventeenth century the estate belonged to the Irvines of Kingcausie, and passed in the end of last century to Claude Boswell, Lord Balmuto, who

---

* Gordon's *Description of Aberdeen*, p. 13.

married the heiress of Kingcausie. The Boswell family claim their descent from Sieur de Bosville, a Frenchman who came to Britain with the Conqueror, holding a command at the battle of Hastings in 1066. His descendant, Claude Boswell, who was born in 1742, passed advocate in 1766, succeeded to the estate of Balmuto, in Fife, on the death of his father, and afterwards became a lord of Session under the title of Lord Balmuto. In 1783 he married Anne Irvine of Kingcausie, who, by the death of her brother and grandfather, became heiress of that estate. This Claude died suddenly on 22nd July, 1824, leaving one son and two daughters. The name of their son was John Irvine Boswell, and his history is told in a well-known monument on the hill of Auchlee, which is one of the landmarks of the district. The monument is a massive circular tower rising from an octagonal base. The following biographical inscription is inserted on one of the sides of the base :—

"In Memory of John Irvine Boswell, of Balmuto and Kingcausie. Born 28th December, 1785. Died, 23rd December, 1860. A man who loved his Saviour, walked steadfast with his God, and whose rule of life was—'Whatsoever ye do in word or deed, do all in the name of the Lord Jesus Christ.' In early life he joined the Coldstream Guards, and carried their colours in the battle of Talavera. Retiring from the army he settled at Kingcausie, and lived to transform the natural barrenness of the estate into luxurious fertility. He will be long remembered in the district for the enlightened zeal he displayed in the introduction of all the improvements of modern agriculture; and he did not confine his attention to his own estates, his knowledge and experience being ever at the service of his neighbours, rich and poor alike. In every position and relation of life, he maintained, with rare fidelity, the character of a Christian gentleman; and he died in peace, trusting simply in the merits of his Saviour for acceptance with his God. His sorrowing widow, Margaret Irvine Boswell, erected this monument as a solace in her bitter bereavement, A.D. M.D.CCC.LXII." This lady was the daughter of James Christie of Durie, and died 18th April, 1875, aged 86 years. Boswell left no issue. He had two sisters, the younger of whom died unmarried; while the elder married Mr. Syme, drawing-master of Dollar Academy, and had issue a son and a daughter. The Boswell estates were divided between these two—the Balmuto property going to the son, and the Kingcausie portion to the daughter, who married Mr. Archer Irvine Fortescue, of Swanbister, in Orkney.

MANNOFIELD.

This district, which has a population of 1022, lies in the north-eastern corner of the Aberdeenshire division of the parish. Within recent years many beautiful villas have been erected, and, as several shops have recently been opened, it is a place of considerable importance. The Aberdeen District Tramways Company have a terminus and stables here, and to the south are the recently laid-out grounds of the Aberdeenshire Cricket Club. To the west are the two large service reservoirs connected with the Aberdeen water-works, used for the purposes of storage, the total capacity of the two reservoirs being not less than eighteen million gallons.

In the centre of the district, and on a most accessible site, a handsome Established Church was erected about ten years ago. The Rev. William Forbes, who was ordained in 1877, is the present incumbent, and he has a communion roll exceeding 271 members. To the north-west there is a small Episcopal Chapel in which service is regularly held.

A market was formerly held here on the second Tuesday of each month, but it has given place latterly to the markets and stock sales which are now regularly held in Aberdeen.

TWO MILE CROSS.

The spot, which formerly went by the title of the Two Mile Cross, was on the Old Deeside Road, west of Kaimhill, and almost directly south of the two reservoirs which have been constructed north of the Deeside Railway. Recent improvements have obliterated the actual cross, but considerable historical interest still hangs round the spot.

A cairn was raised here in commemoration of Sir John Seton of Pitmedden, who was killed at the battle of the Bridge of Dee in 1639,* but it has since been removed.

Montrose, after defeating the Covenanters at Tippermuir on 1st September, 1644, marched northwards and forded the Dee at the Mills of Drum. Ten days later the citizens had marched to the Two Mile Cross, but next day "thay returnit bak to the toune at nicht." Montrose immediately pitched his camp on the spot they had vacated. Two days after, he despatched a commissioner to the magistrates of Aberdeen, bearing a letter which he had written at his tent door on a drum head. This characteristic communication was couched in the following terms :—

" Loveing freindes—Being heir for the maintenance of Religion and liberty and his Mas. Just authority and

---

* *Antiquities, Aberdeen and Banff,* Vol. i., p. 359.

service, thes ar in his Mas. Name to requyre you that Immediatly, upon the sight heirof, you rander and give up yr toune, In the behalf of his Mas., otherwayes, that all old persons, women, and children doe come out and reteire themselfs, and that those who stayes Expect no Quarter.—I am, as you deserve,

(Signed)   MONTROSE."

The magistrates refusing to surrender, the battle of the Justice Mills ensued, when the citizens were completely defeated.

In September, 1645, Major M'Donald encamped his army, consisting of "about 700 Irishes," at the Cross, and partly at the Bridge of Dee. Tradition asserts that a warrior, while riding on a white horse, was here cruelly slain by a ball from a cannon fired from the Covenanters' Faulds on south side of the Bridge of Dee. Doubtless the death of Seton, before described, gave origin to the story.

ESTATE OF PITFODELS.

Any history of the estate of Pitfodels is also a history of the Roman Catholic family of Menzies, once so important in local annals, but now utterly extinct. They held the property for about four hundred years; and its history before their advent is brief, and comparatively unimportant. It was their connection with it that will make it remembered long after the account of its other proprietors shall be forgotten.

The lands were at first divided into three parts—Easter, Wester, and Middle Pitfodels, and it was not till the sixteenth century that they all became joined under one proprietorship.

Early in the fourteenth century, the property, like many other estates, was in the hands of a cadet of the powerful family of Moray,—frequently Murray—who had attained prominence under David I. At that date the lands of Pitfodels embraced the whole of Banchory-Devenick north of the Dee, and east of the Den of Cults. The family of Murray lost their hold of the property in 1389, when Alexander of Murray, then designed as "Lord of Culbyne," granted a deed of wadset in favour of his kinsman, "William Rede," of the lands of "Wester Badfothellis" with the fishings, for £56 13s. 4d. sterling. In the following year sasine was granted in favour of Reid who thus became the owner of Wester Pitfodels.

The next step in the history of the property brings the Menzies into the field. The family—a branch of a stock located in Athol—had long been well known in Aberdeen. In 1424 David Menzies, a burgess—as has already been noticed—was one of the hostages to England for the payment of £40,000, on the release of James I. Their importance evidently had grown to the extent of their acquiring land, and in 1430 a city burgess, Gilbert Menzies, a christian name that remained in the family for centuries, appears on the scene. A precept was then granted to infeft him in the lands of "Wester Badfothel" and half of "Middle Badfothel." He was a younger son of Sir Robert Menzies of Weems, and he employed his patrimony chiefly in securing mortgages over estates in the counties of Aberdeen and Kincardine. He was the first of his family to win the blue ribbonship of the city, the rank of provost, but he was not the last. For over two hundred years—1426-1634—the family held that honour—with "great applause," quoth Parson Gordon—no less than twenty-eight separate times. In 1436 Gilbert was elected to represent the burgh in Parliament at Edinburgh, £16 scots being allowed him for expenses. He was married to Marjory Liddell, probably a member of another well known Aberdeen family of the period. The date of his death is a puzzling point, for though a monument to the memory of him and his wife, which was erected in St. Nicholas Churchyard, Aberdeen—it disappeared in the middle of last century—is known to have borne the date

1439, yet his name is to be met with after that time. It is believed that the date should have been 1459, as he was undoubtedly alive during that year. A pair of stone effigies, now lying on the window sill of the West Church, Aberdeen, represent the couple. When the church became ruinous in 1730, the effigies were removed for safety to the churchyard of Maryculter, where they lay till quite recently. It was he who, in 1448, having previously secured infeftment, granted a premonition to Andrew Reid for the redemption of the lands of " Wester Badfothellis," which had been mortgaged by Alexander of Murray to Reid's grandfather, William, for one hundred merks. Two years later Menzies was granted a charter by Stephen of Balrony, of a Templar land in the barony of " Badfothal," paying therefor four shillings yearly to the brethren of the house of St. John of Jerusalem at Torphichen. The knights of this Order had a foundation near where Arnlee now stands, and till within the last sixty years a croft which stood there went by the name of The Temple.*

* The Order of the Knights of St. John superseded that of the Knights Templars, and inherited the greater part of the extensive property of that rival Order. They had their Scotch headquarters at Torphichen, now a small village in Linlithgow-shire, but then a place of great importance. Keith says that Sir James Sandilands, the last preceptor, at the Reformation resigned all the lands of the Order in Scotland into Queen Mary's hands, and she feued them out again to Sir James for 10,000 crowns, and the yearly annuity of 500 merks. She also erected all the lands into a temporal lordship, in favour of him and his heirs, by a charter under the great seal, dated 24th January, 1563.

In 1457 Andrew Reid, before mentioned, granted a precept to infeft Andrew Menzies in the half of "Middle Badfothalis," given in exchange for the lands of "Wester Badfothalis." Thirteen years later, James III. confirmed to Alexander Menzies the lands of Middleton of Pitfodels, together with the lands of Potartown and Orchardfelde.

In 1488 Alexander Reid, who was then the owner of the greater portion of Pitfodels, got confirmation from James III. of a charter granted by him in favour of Mariot Cullane, his wife, in liferent, of the lands of " Wester Pitfodellis." James IV. confirmed to Reid and his second wife, Margaret Crawford, the lands of Eastertown and Westertown of Pitfodels, with the fishings in the water of Dee. Reid, who was provost of Aberdeen for the years 1492-3 was held in such high estimation by the Town Council and citizens generally, that in 1504 his portrait was ordered to be executed and hung in the session-house of Aberdeen. It remained there till 28th June, 1640, when a very curious incident occurred. "The session wnderstanding

Thereafter, Sir James disponed all the Temple lands lying in the shires of Edinburgh, Linlithgow, Stirling, Kincardine, and Aberdeen, in favour of James Tennent of Lynhouse, and Robert Williamson, writer in Edinburgh, for 10,000 merks, reserving to himself out of the disposition the lands of Torphichen, Liston, Dennie, Thankerton, Balintrodoch, and Maryculter, as also his right to the Churches of Torphichen, Temple, Inchmachan, Maryculter, Aboyne, Tulloch, and Kilbartha, with the teinds belonging to them.

that some capitanes and gentillmen of the regiment of sojours lying in this town, had tein some offence at the portrat as smelling somequhat of poprie, and standing aboue the session hous door, ffor removeing of the quhilk offence, ordaines the said portrat to be tein down and not to be sett wp again."*

Arms of Provost Reid of Pitfodels.

Reid died on 27th May, 1506, and was succeeded by his wife and only daughter, Marion, the latter of whom he had made his heiress. Three of his descendants held in turn the pastorate of Banchory-Ternan after the Reformation. With that foresight characteristic of the Roman Catholic, the widow set aside part of her income to the service of the Church, and for the safety of her husband's soul and that of her own after death, granting, in 1508, "to the Curate and Chaplains of Aberdeen, an annuity of £1 for celebrating an obit, annually, on their anniversaries at the altar of Saint Christopher, on the first Sunday immediately subsequent to the first day of the month of March, with the *Placebo* and the *Dirige* on

* *Ecclesiastical Records of Aberdeen*, p. 114.

the Saturday preceding; a solemn mass on Sunday, and a commemoration for thirty days by the Curate and Chaplains at the weekly masses. The procurator for the time was required on the said Saturday to send through the town a crier with a hand-bell, to invite all and sundry to prayers for the souls of the above named persons; to place a table on the grave stone, which was to be covered with a black cloth, and furnished with wax lights; and the sacristan of the Church was ordered thrice to toll the bells at this part of the service, and thrice while a mass *de requiem* was chanted. The Curate and Chaplains were likewise required to chant and celebrate another solemn mass with other thirty days' commemorative masses, after the death of the granter, at the altar near which she should happen to be interred."*

Alexander Menzies died without issue, and his brother, David, was served heir to him in 1506, while his widow, Elizabeth Leslie, had her terce adjudged to her out of the same lands. David was twice married, first to Margaret Fotheringham, daughter of Thomas Fotheringham of Powrie, by whom he had a son, Gilbert; and secondly to Katherine Wricht, who survived him.

Gilbert was served heir to his father on 3rd October, 1508, his stepmother being found entitled to a terce of the lands. He was known by the sobriquet of *Banison Gib*, and was married to Marjorie Chalmers, daughter of the

---

* Kennedy's *Annals*, Vol. ii., pp. 24, 25.

laird of Murtle, by whom he had several children. Besides being proprietor of Findon, he in July, 1535, acquired from the Knights Templars of Maryculter the lands now known as Blairs. He was provost of Aberdeen for twenty-four years between 1505 and 1536; and was the first to break through the municipal statute that the chief magistrate should be elected for one year only. In 1508 he contributed three barrels of salmon towards the "theiking and decoring" of the kirk of Aberdeen. Ten years later he was appointed to go to the King and Council, and raise Law-burrows against the Lord Forbes, on account of the great oppression and cruel spoil done to the burgh in its fishing and freedom lands. No public service, however, could have been more congenial to his taste than that deputed to him in 1525 by the king, when as sheriffs he and Sir John Rutherford—who was a great favourite at court*—were ordered to search for those who owned the heresies of Luther, or used his books; and that the Act of Parliament thereanent should be published, whereof an extract was sent to all "foundin holding these heresies, or reading these books."† Provost Gilbert and Baillie

* Rutherford, who was proprietor of Tarland, was frequently provost of Aberdeen and one of its representatives in Parliament. On one occasion a complaint was lodged with King James IV., by certain of the burgesses, accusing him as being a masterful oppressor, but the King replied desiring an exact account of the charges against his friend Sir John.—Skene's *Survey;* Munro's *Members of Parl.*, &c.

† Walker's *Deans of Guild.*

Collison were chosen commissioners to represent the burgh in the first parliament of James V., in 1524. They were allowed 6s. 8d. per day for expenses, and "were furnished with eight horsemen to attend in their train, that they might appear at court with a splendour becoming the representatives of the opulent city of Aberdeen."* Menzies lived in a house in the city known as Pitfoddels' Lodgings, which occupied the site now taken up by the Union Bank at the top of Marischal Street, and was the scene of more than one eventful incident in the city's history. The first of these was the murder, on 7th January, 1527, of Alexander Seton laird of Meldrum, by the master of Forbes, who, eleven years later, was executed for attempting to shoot the King with a culverin, as he passed through Aberdeen to hold a justice ayre. Two years later the house was laid in ruins by an accidental fire, when a large new building of stone, with turrets, was erected on the same site. This house was probably the first stone building in Aberdeen. An edifice of such a character was then considered a mark of the greatest opulence, and it is recorded that in 1545, one of the inhabitants defying Menzies said "he did not care for all the power of the provost or his stane house." In 1530 Menzies, along with four of his sons, and certain of the citizens of Aberdeen, was charged before the High Court of Justice with killing a servant of Alexander Forbes, heir-apparent

---

* Thom's *History of Aberdeen*, Vol. i., p. 166.

of Brux; but was, with the others, acquitted through its having been satisfactorily proven that the Forbeses were the aggressors.

Up to this time Pitfodels had been divided between the Reids and the Menzies, the former possessing Eastertown and Westertown, while the latter were the proprietors of Middle Pitfodels. It was not until the families became united by marriage that the two portions were joined. This happened on 12th January, 1520-1, when Thomas, the eldest son of Provost Gilbert, married Marion, the only daughter of the deceased Alexander Reid of Eastertown and Westertown. Thus the whole of Pitfodels passed into the Menzies family, and gave them their designation for the next three centuries. Like his father, Thomas took a leading part in the local, and to some extent in the general history of the period. In 1525 he was elected provost of Aberdeen, holding office for forty years, which is the longest period of one provostship on record. His popularity, and that of his family, was such that Parson Gordon afterwards wrote: "ther [are] not a few of the best of the citizens quho are joynt with that familie by consanguinity and affinitie, and esteemed it ane honor to be so. Nay, and in the yeer 1545, George Gordon, Erle of Huntlie, the most powerfull of any in the north of Scotland, sought to be provost, and wes chosen, not without protestatione against his electione by many, as ane incroachment upon ther liberties; which moved him presentlie to resigne it againe, in favor of Thomas Menzies of Pitfoddells." He was also Marischal Depute of Scotland in 1538, and for several years after 1543 he was Comptroller of the Royal Household. His father, *Banison Gib*, died on 27th September, 1543, when Thomas succeeded to the proprietorship of the whole of Pitfodels, by virtue of his marriage already explained. In the following November* he obtained confirmation of a former grant, erecting these lands into a free barony, with the Castlehill of Middleton of Pitfodels as principal messuage. His wife died 20th September, 1551, and she was buried in Collison's Aisle, Aberdeen, where a well-preserved tombstone still keeps on record their wedded life of nine-and-twenty years.

Arms of Thomas Menzies and Marion Reid, on tombstone in Collison's Aisle, Aberdeen.

* *Reg. Mag. Sig.*, Vol. iii., p. 658.

In the following year he entered into a formal contract with Lord Forbes and John Leslie of Balquhane for the amicable settlement of all their feuds and differences, but its terms were not long in being disregarded. In 1557 he signed the treaty of marriage between Queen Mary and the Dauphin of France.* He himself married for his second wife Elizabeth Forbes, "Lady Towe," and in June, 1571, he granted, in life-rent, to Violet Forbes (natural and lawful daughter of Alexander Forbes of Pitsligo, future wife of George Menzies, his grandson, son of Gilbert, his elder son and heir), the lands of Easter Pitfodels, together with the office of bailliary of the same. The charter was confirmed by James VI., under the great seal, 1576.†

Some idea of the lawless and disturbed state of the country at this time, and the duties of a sheriff of the period, may be gathered from the following incident, in which the heir of Pitfodels figures as a "sheriff of Inverness." "In 1573 Alexander, Earl of Sutherland, complained to King James VI. that, although he was desirous to serve the king's briefs of inquest of the lands in the sheriffdoms of Innerness and Aberdeen, in which his father, Earl John, died vest and seised, he was unable to serve the brief of inquest of the lands in Innerness in the Tolbooth of the burgh, because he could

* *Acts of Parliament*, 1557.
† *Reg. Mag. Sigi. lib.* 35, No. 135.

find no inquest of barons and hereditary proprietors within the sheriffdom for that purpose, by reason that many barons and gentlemen of the sheriffdom—such as : Colin Makkanze of Kintaill ; Hugh, Lord Fraser of Lovet ; Lauchlin Makintosche of Dunnauchtane, Robert Munro of Fowlis, with many other families and men of the country—were at deadly feud among themselves. The king, therefore (30th May), with the consent of George, Earl of Huntly, Sheriff Principal of Innerness and Aberdeen, appointed John Leslie of Buchquham ; Gilbert Menzies, apparent of Pitfodellis ; Patrick Menzies, burgess of Aberdeen ; Master Robert Lummisdane of Clova ; and Master Patrick Rutherfurde, burgess of Aberdeen, sheriffs of Innerness in that part, to serve the said briefs in the Tolbooth of the Burgh of Aberdeen."

Seal of Provost Thomas Menzies.
(Pitfodels Charter, 1573.)

Provost Thomas Menzies died about December, 1576, and was survived by his wife, whose death is recorded under date 22nd January, 1584-5: "Elizabetht Forbes, Lade Towe, and spowse to Thomas Menzis of Petfodellis and prowest, departtit." He had at least two sons—Gilbert, who succeeded him, and James, who qualified for the ministry and was, by James V., presented to the rectory of Dunnet. One daughter, Marjory, married James Gordon of Haddo and Methlick. Another, Katherine, married George Johnston, dean of guild of Aberdeen, who was, in October, 1577, by David Cunningham, first protestant bishop of Aberdeen, inaugurated as one of the elders chosen by the kirk and congregation of the burgh.* In December, 1578, their son, Patrick Johnston, died at Aberdeen from the effects of a gun-shot wound recklessly inflicted by Keith, the young laird of Ludquharne, in Buchan. George Johnston himself died in April, 1579, and his widow in May, 1599. Before passing from the history of Provost Thomas Menzies, it is specially interesting to note that, at an early period, he embraced the tenets of the reformed faith. He is named as one of the six deputies appointed by the General Assembly of the Kirk of Scotland, on 28th May, 1561, to meet the Lords of the Secret Council, and to present to them the supplication and articles "tuitching the suppression of idolatrie". His immediate successors and relatives continued, for the most part, staunch Roman Catholics, and, as will be seen by a

* *Inverurie and Earldom of the Garioch*, p. 456.

perusal of the following pages, suffered much persecution for their adherence to that religion.

He was succeeded by his eldest son, Gilbert. Born 10th June, 1522, he followed the traditions of his house occupying several positions of importance in the country. In 1576 he was created provost of Aberdeen, continuing in office till Michaelmas, 1588. He married Margaret Keith, daughter of the laird of Troup, by whom he had several children. As already noticed a son, Alexander, was murdered in 1580, by William Forbes of Portlethen and Monymusk, at the Loch of Loirston—the Forbes-Menzies feud of the beginning of the century breaking out afresh. In 1588 Menzies and his brother, Thomas Menzies of Durn, became bound, in "manrent and seruice," to George, Earl of Huntly, in consideration of which that nobleman granted, in favour of the Menzies', a "band of protectioune" to "mantein, supplie, and defend them" during all the days of his life. The provost, however, did not long require this protection, for he died within five months of the date of the obligation.

He was succeeded by his son George, before mentioned; who in turn was succeeded by his son Gilbert, commonly called *William of the Cup*. This laird bought the lands of Gilcomston, in 1597, from Sir John Gordon for 7000 merks Scots. He married Margaret Irvine, daughter of the laird of Drum, by whom he had issue. The deadly feud of the Menzies with the Forbeses of

Monymusk was renewed in this laird's lifetime, necessitating the interposition of the powers of the law.

"On 26 November, 1613, William Forbes, Elder of Monymusk; Robert, Johnne, and Mr. James Forbes, his thre sones; Johnne Forbes, callit of Burnegranes; James Geillis and Johnne Farquhar, domestik seruitouris to Monymusk; and George Raitt, in Coiff, Dilaitit for vsurpation of his Maiesties authoritie, in takin of Williame Duguid, seruitour to George Gairdin; committit the 24 of July last, and for contravening the Actis of Parliament, in cutting of certane grene growand coirnes, pertening to Gilbert Menzies of Pitfoddellis, grow and vpone his lands. The Justice, wth advyse of my lord Aduocat, continewis this dyet to the thrid day of the Air (of Aberdeen), or sooner, vpone XV. dayis warning . . . At same diet Margaret Irwing, Lady Pitfoddellis; Gilbert Menzies of Pitfoddellis, hir spous, for his entries; Dauid Knowis, his domestik servand; Johnne Ramsay his greif, Johnne Philp, Williame Daveny, Williame Dougatt, and Johnne Ramsay, dilaitit of airt and pairt of the contravening of our souerane lordis Actes of Parliament in cutting and distroying of coirnes; committit in the moneth of July lastlypast. This case also continued to the same Air." Pitcairn, from whose *Criminal Trials* the extracts of these two cases are taken, says it is obvious that they arose out of the deadly feud which then raged between the families of Monymusk and Pitfodels. No information is afforded as to how the cases ended; but, as they were withdrawn to "the Air,"—the old Scotch law term for justiciary court—it is probable they were compromised through the intervention of mutual friends. Menzies died about 30th November, 1622, being "bureit in the auld Kirk of Aberdeen".*

The next laird of Pitfodels, Gilbert, son of *William of the Cup*, is the most distinguished member of the family. With him the prestige of the family came to an end, and the faith which distinguished the family for two centuries found its greatest martyr. Succeeding his father in 1622, he in the following year married Lady Anne Gordon, daughter of the twelfth Earl of Sutherland. "A woman of excellent beautie"—according to Gordon the enthusiastic historian of her house—she was destined to undergo many afflictions. It would require a second Spalding to recount the "trubles" of the family; for Menzies' royalty spelt ruin.

His "trubles" may be set down as first occurring in January of the momentous year 1639, when he took the Marquis of Huntly into his house. The Marquis, "thinking and taking Merschall still to be on the Kinges syde, as he wes nocht," had applied to his brother nobleman for lodging, and had been refused. Menzies "kyndlie lent him his hous,"—Pitfodels' lodgings—and the Marquis "flitit out of Old Abirdein his haill famelie and goodis and thair took wp houss". Spalding details, with

* *Sum Notabell Things.*

Pepys-like minuteness, how twenty-four gentlemen were told off to wait on the Marquis, and how "thair wes aucht gentilmen appointit to watche his lodging on the night, thair tyme about, and fyre and candill still burning ilk night within the houss." Pitfodels followed the fortunes of his noble guest with enthusiasm during the next month, and in March they resolved to go to England with sixty other fugitives who were determined not to "subscrive" the Covenant. "Vpone the 28th of Marche," says Spalding in a quainter vein than usual, they "hoysis wp saill, and to the King go thay, bot," as he adds, "this flicht did litle good." None of the fugitives suffered more than Menzies, he having laid himself open to greater suspicion by harbouring Huntly. That nobleman was now in the safe keeping of his young brother Marquis, Montrose, and Menzies had not been absent from the city a single day ere the Earl of Kinghorn, who, to Spalding's disgust, had the boldness to call himself governor of Aberdeen, got the keys of Pitfodels' house from Lady Menzies, who had been left behind. A curious incident occurred at this stage, for the lady was delivering up the keys "thair wes ane suddant fray," writes Spalding, "throw occasioun of ane schot rakleslie lettin go in the same houss, quhair the governour and the ladie, with vtheris, war togidder. None knew quhairfra nor how this schot cam, for all the tryell culd be maid. Aluaies, the ladie, in the tumvlt and preass, loist her pvrss, weill plenishit with gold and ryngis, and culd not get the same agane." A few days afterwards an inventory was taken of the "goodis and geir" in the house, "alsweill pertening to the laird himself, as that whiche the Marquess left behind him at his removing thairfra;" after which the keys were restored to the lady.

Not only did the town house of Menzies suffer, but his lands of Pitfodels were also burdened. A few days after these events 500 of Argyle's men were quartered on the lairds of Drum and Pitfodels, where they "leivit lustellie vpone the goodis, nolt, scheip, cornes, and victuall, to the gryte hurt and wrack of the countrie people for thair maisteris causs, being grite ante-covenanteris." These troops—continues Spalding—"wantit not aboundance of beif, mvttoun, and vther good fair, for littill pay," in these snug quarters. It was in this year, according to Gordon's *Scots Affairs*, that Menzies received the honour of knighthood from the sovereign he served so loyally. But this was all that Charles could do for him. Troubles rained thick upon his faithful subject, who was now nothing short of being a fugitive in his own country. In July, 1640, Marischal actually collected the rents on the Pitfodels estate, and in October following, Menzies, who had returned to Aberdeen, fled with his family to England, to come back again in December forced to sign the Covenant—"more foolis nor thay went out, but succour or relief of the King." In fact for some time they were "soundlie wardit and keipit long in waird in Edinburgh and tolbuith thairof." Menzies got into a further peck of troubles in reviving the old family feud with the Forbeses. In October, 1642, he shot John Forbes of Lesly at the memorable Crabstone. "Thair wes, vpone both sydis, schot about ellevin pistollis, and none gat skaith bot Lesly. Thair wes sum old roust betuixt thame; for Leslyis father killit Petfoddellis goodschiris brother vnworthellie."* The wounded gentleman "lay wnder cure quhill Januar, 1643, and then began to walk vpone ane staf feblie, and not soundlie heallit." The most remarkable bearing of this episode is the fact recorded by Spalding, that it "brocht in the beiring and weiring of gvnis, quhilk bred mekill sorrow and mischeif in this land." In December following he fled to France, "feiring the trubles to cum," accompanied by Madame de Gordon, one of the heroines of Father Blakhal's tedious panegyric of his services to "Three Noble Ladyes".

But the penalties of loyalty told on others than on the knight himself. His wife and a son were drowned in 1648, while on one of their many voyages of flight to France. Two years later another heavy blow fell on the unfortunate laird, when his eldest son, Gilbert, was killed while acting as standard-bearer in Montrose's army. At the battle of Invercharron, in Ross-shire, 27th April, 1650, the standard bore the picture of the headless corpse of Charles, with the motto—"Judge and revenge my

---

* *Trubles*, Vol. ii., p. 205.

cause ". It is a matter of history how Montrose's army was put to rout by Colonel Strachan. When all appeared to be lost, Menzies was urged by Montrose and others to save himself by flight, but he refused, and met his untimely fate on the field. The old ballad laments the gallant youth in well-known lines :—

> "Gilbert Menzies of high degree,
>   By the whom the king's banner was borne;
> For a brave cavalier was he,
>   But now to glory he is gone."

The now almost heart-broken laird was again attacked by the church within a few months after this crushing blow. The supercilious kirk-session sent two parsons to confer with the wayward truant. He replied that he "haid nothing to doe with them, and that [he had] given them thair anser long agoe ". The session waxed indignant, and, "all in ane woice," they declared him "contumacious" for failing to answer their charges of his "apostacie and defectioun from the trew protestant religioun." He was set down as a perfect pariah in the district, and it was a mark of suspicion for a man even to visit his house, far less to associate with him. His very servants were the subject of inquisition; but they seemed to ignore the session and their powers. One case is still preserved. "On 14 November, 1653, Alexander Gordoun, servant to Petfoddellis, being sumondit tuys abefoir to compeir befoir the sessioun of Abirdein, to give ane accompt of his professioun, and, being demandit whairfoir he did not compeir sooner, he anserit if it haid not bein to hold in the offiris paines, he had not compeirit now, nor at all; and being demandit if he wes of our professioun, he anserit he cam not to give ane acquittance, and all the wholl tyme he carried himselff vncivillie and wpbraidinglie, thanking God that the tymes wer not as formerlie." On 20th March, thereafter, he was "excommunicat, with the greater sentance for his poperie and apostasie from the true Protestant religioune."*

It would take too long to detail all the troubles of this catholic laird. In 1668 matters had reached such a climax, that he dispatched a detailed narrative of the sufferings he had experienced to Sir Alexander Fraser of Durris, who was private physician to Charles II., and a favourite with that monarch. Fraser had promised to lay the document before the King in the expectation that some sort of recompense might be made. The document, still preserved,† is an excellent summary of his trials.

"To informe his Sacred Majestie of the great losses and sufferings the said Sir Gilbert and his familie have sustained wpon the accompt of his constant adhering to the deceased King's Majestie, of ever blessed memorie, and his present Majestie's interests and service, from the beginning of the trubles, by quarterings extraordinarie

---
* *Ecclesiastical Records of Aberdeen*, pp. 121, 122.
† *Antiquities of Aberdeen and Banff*, Vol. iii., pp. 284-286.

leavies of horse and foot sequestrationes, plunderings, peyment of fynes, and other extraordinarie occasiones; bot most of all by the losse of his lady and children, besyd the hazard of his oune persone severall tymes, both by sea and land.

"First the said Sir Gilbert did engage himself in his Majesties service at the Brigge of Die, in the year 1639, wnder Sir Williame Gunne, generall of his Majesties forces at the tym, having his eldest sone in company with him. And the enemy having prevailed that tym, himselff and his sone wer forced to reteir to the Highlands, wher they lived for a considerable tym in exile, till they wer forced to goe over seas for ther securitie, and shunning the present imminent danger at that tym. Therefter, having stayed abroad for a long tym, the enemy having entered in possessione of his fortune, being advertised hereoff by his freinds, forced to returne home for preventing of his totall ruine, and to submitt himselff to the enemies mercie, who did fyne him in fyve hundredth pundis sterling, whilk he reallie peyed; and having stayed somewhyle in the countrey, the troubles encreasing and being pressed to subscryve the Covenant, he wes againe necessitat, and his sone, to goe over seas, wher, having stayed about eightein moneths, he sent for his lady and children, who, going to France, wer totallie robbed and all taken from them, by the Parliament ships and carried to Ostend, so that the said Sir Gilbert was forced to goe in persone, and his eldest sone, thither for their releiff, to his great charges and expenses, and caried them to France, wher, having stayed for a long tym and not having wherupon to maintaine themselfs, he wes constrained to send his lady home for endeavoring to get some supplie furth of his oune fortune for their aliment at home and abroad. Bot his lady finding the wholl countrey in a combustione, and her husband's wholl fortune exhausted by quarterings, leavies, mantenance, loan moneys, and other publict burdings above exprest, shee having acquaint him therewith, he and his sone wer againe forced, efter four yeirs absence in France (not being supplied in the least by their oune fortune), to returne home. At which tym finding by just accompt that not only the four yeares rent, during the tyme of his absence, wes exhausted, bot that the tennentis were super expended; in the fyrst he wes forced to discharge the same to them, otherwayes to turne the wholl land useless and unprofitable. Efter his returne, having stayed some sex moneths the troubles encreasing daylie more and more, he wes forced, with his lady, and his eldest sone and ane younger, to returne to France. And he and his eldest sone being embarked in one veshel, and his lady and the younger in another, tho' he and the elder by God's providence were preserved, his lady and the younger perished by storme and tempest. And thereafter he and his elder sone, having stayed some six moneths in France, reteired to Holland, wher his present Majestie being for the tym, and having given his commission to the Marquis of Montrose for Scotland, the said

Marquis, at his aryvall there, did confer that honor upon the said Sir Gilbert, his eldest sone, as to carie his Majesties standard, who wes killed under the samen in the yeir 1649. During all which tym the said Sir Gilbert remained abroad in exile, and till the year 1652, that the Usurper did make himself master of most pairt of the kingdome, and having stayed some two or thrie yeares at home, wes again necessitat with his familie to abandon his countrey, being hardlie pressed to subscryve the Tender disclaiming the King's laufull authority, and to returne againe to France, efter they had been taken prisoners at Ostend for the space of sex moneths (as is notourlie known to his present Majestie), wes necessitat before his releasment to pay for his ransome and releiff the soum of three thousand gilders, so that by his losses at sea, his imprisonment at Ostend, and his ransome for his releiff, he was prejudged in above ane thousand pounds sterling before the sequestratione of his fortune during the space of two yeires in the Vsurpers tym.

"By all which occasiones above mentioned, the said Sir Gilbert hath been prejudged in the soum of tuelff thousand pounds sterling and upwards, besyd the great losse of his lady and sones, and hath been forced to dispone and sell a considerable part of his fortune, so that the remainder is now brocht verie low and lyk to ruine, wnlesse his Sacred Majestie of his royall bountie provyd some speidie remeid therfor."

Menzies had a large family. Besides those already

mentioned, a son, Paul, joined the Russian army, in which he died a lieutenant-general in 1694; while a daughter, Elizabeth, married Francis Gordon, who succeeded to the estate of Craig on the death of his father about 1650.

During the eighteenth century the estate passed through several members of the Menzies family. In 1680 the proprietor sold the lands of Gilcomston to the town of Aberdeen for 26,000 merks scots. In 1696 the valuation of the whole of Banchory-Devenick on the north side of the Dee was given up at £951, of which £500 was applicable to this estate. The tenants were George Milne and Alexander Milne in Eastertown, Alexander Troup, David Philp, Alexander Philp, and Agnes Davidson in Westertown; John Lighton and William Troup in Middleton, and Andrew Davidson in Brae. In the memorable '45 Gilbert Menzies, who was then in possession, raised a detachment of twenty-five men to aid the cause of the Pretender. In 1747 the proprietor was William Menzies. He married Mary Urquhart, daughter of John Urquhart of Meldrum. In 1755 John Menzies married Marion, daughter of William Maxwell of Kirkconnell—one of the oldest families in Galloway.

In 1805 John Menzies, his son, then proprietor, exposed the lands of Pitfodels to sale. No purchaser appearing he subsequently feued off several portions, and the balance was ultimately acquired by a joint-stock company, which feued and sold out the whole in lots. This John, who died in Edinburgh, a widower, in 1843, aged 87 years

was the last of his race. Jervise says: "he was a member of the Abbotsford Club, and at his expense the volume entitled *Extracta Variis e Cronicis Scocie* was printed for the members. He was one of the most accomplished gentlemen of his time, and his purse was open to the poor of all denominations. He died, as was to be expected, a true believer in the religion of his forefathers, of his attachment to which he gave proof by making over by deed, dated in 1827, the mansion-house and lands of Blairs for the establishment of a college for young men designed for the Roman Catholic priesthood." The bulk of his fortune was also bequeathed for schemes connected with the Catholic Church. His lands of Charlestown in the south side of the parish, which now yield an annual revenue of upwards of £125, went to the Ursuline Convent of St. Margaret's, Edinburgh.

Arms of John Menzies.

It is sad to contemplate that of this once famous family not one single representative now remains. Their castle, which so long stood like a gray-haired warder overlooking a wide stretch of country from its ground of vantage, is now completely demolished. Indeed, its site can scarcely be pointed out, although it is known to have been at a spot formerly called Castleheugh, and close to the east side of Norwood Hall.

Where formerly there were crofts and farms, magnificent mansion houses and villas have been erected, each having tastefully laid-out grounds adjoining. The principal are Garthdee, the residence of Mr. Alexander Edmond, advocate, Aberdeen; Norwood Hall, the residence of Mr. James Ogston; Drumgarth, belonging to Mrs. George Jamieson; Inchgarth, the residence of Captain George Skene Taylor, R.N.; Southfield, the residence of Mr. T. A. W. A. Youngson; Wellwood, the property of Mr. George Davidson; Cliff House, the residence of Mr. James Catto; Morkeu, the residence of Mr. Alexander Forbes; Craigton, the residence of Mr. William Knox; Woodlands, the residence of Mr. Robert Collie; Woodbank, the residence of Mr. Alexander Davidson, shipowner, Aberdeen; Balnagarth, the residence of Mr. George Collie, advocate, Aberdeen; and Viewbank, the residence of Mr. James Collie, advocate, Aberdeen.

ESTATE OF CULTS.

In 1650 the proprietor of this estate was Alexander Thomson, advocate in Aberdeen, great-grand uncle of the first Alexander Thomson of Banchory. He was twice married, and by his second wife left issue—John, and Alexander, the latter of whom became an advocate in Aberdeen, and proprietor, by purchase, of the estate of Portlethen.

On 7th October, 1674, John Thomson was served as nearest heir of his father "in the lands of Cults, with the mill, mill lands, multures, and pertinents thereof, with the salmon fishing on the water of Dee, adjoining and belonging thereto within the parish of Banchory-Devenick, and sheriffdom of Aberdeen, held in chief of the King and his successors for service of ward and relief." In June, 1679, he sold the estate to Robert Irvine, son of John Irvine of Murtle, who had three years previously acquired the lands of Bieldside.

Irvine was twice married; first to his relative Jeane Irvine, who died on 21st March, 1678, aged 32; and secondly to Margaret Coutts, who died in 1710, aged 45 years. In 1696 he had his valuation of Cults entered in the Poll Book at £286, anent which, and for himself and his lady, he paid £9 12s. of poll. He also paid £2 2s. for the following "childring in familia—Marie, Margrat, Hellen, and Bettie, Robert and James Irwings." One of the daughters became the third wife of " Robert Skene of Ramore, descended of a second brother of the laird of Skene;" whilst another—Issobell—married Dr. James Donaldson, who was professor of medicine in Marischal College, Aberdeen, in 1732. Irvine, who erected a new house on the same site as that of the present one, had his coat of arms painted on his seat in the parish church. He acted as a commissioner of supply for many years, and died 10th April, 1728, aged 89. He was buried in the churchyard of Peterculter beside his two wives.

In 1750 Alexander Livingston, provost of Aberdeen, purchased the estate from the Irvines. He was the only son of Alexander Livingston of Fornet, Skene, who, in 1714, became a member of the Guildry of Aberdeen, dean in 1730, baillie in 1731-32, and died 8th July, 1733, aged 52 years. Provost Livingston, who was born in 1716, was entered in the burgess roll in 1730, and subsequently became a merchant in the city. He was provost for two years, 1750-51. In 1752 he feued the sixth lot of the lands of Gilcomston; and in the same year, in partnership with John Dingwall, William M'Kenzie, Alexander Milne, junior, and Andrew Walker, under the title of the Porthill Company (afterwards Milne, Cruden, & Company), feued part of the Porthill where a linen manufactory was erected. This venture proved unsuccessful, and about eleven years afterwards the company suspended payment—Provost Livingston being pecuniarly involved to a heavy amount. The worthy man sold off his whole belongings—including the lands of Cults, Countesswells, and Loanhead—and with the proceeds satisfied the creditors, who, to mark their appreciation of his conduct, presented him with a handsome dinner service with his arms painted upon them.

Arms of Provost Livingston.

He went over to Rotterdam, where, entering into business as a merchant and banker, he speedily amassed a fortune. He died in 1783 survived by his second wife, Elizabeth, daughter of John Hardie, of Aberdeen, and one son and two daughters.

By disposition, dated 23rd June, 1763, George Chalmers, merchant in Edinburgh, acquired the estate, he having paid £10,500 of purchase price. He did not long continue as proprietor, for in 1774 William Durward was returned as such. The latter during his ownership improved the estate very much; and, according to Dr. Keith, "by cultivating his personal farm, and by giving lime in great quantity to the tenants, trebled its rental in a few years."

In the end of last century the lands, including West Cults and Bieldside, were in the possession of John Burnett of Countesswells, who, in 1804, sold them in separate lots. George Symmers, cloth merchant, Aberdeen, acquired two of these lots, now known as the Estate of Cults. He gave a site for, and substantially aided in the erection of a school at Cults, which is now largely attended and in a high state of efficiency. After his death, which occurred on 22nd December, 1839, and in terms of a deed of entail which had been executed by him, the lands went to George Gibb Shirra, afterwards George Gibb Shirra Gibb, who, by special instrument dated 28th July, 1876, got disentail. Mr. Gibb, who was a son of the Reverend Robert Shirra, minister of the Associate Synod, "Auld Licht," congregation at Yetholm, was born there on 23rd June, 1811. He enlarged and altered the mansion-house, and erected several dwelling-houses on the estate. In 1843 he married Margaret Turnbull, daughter of the Reverend Alexander Turnbull, Glasgow, by whom he had issue three sons and five daughters. Of the sons, Alexander and George died in infancy, and Robert, who qualified as a doctor, is now an extensive sheep farmer on the borders. Of the daughters, Mary married the Reverend James Cameron, minister of the Free Church, Glenbervie, who is now deceased; Elizabeth married the Reverend Edward T. Vernon, minister of the Free Church, Arbirlot; and Lillias Jessie married Mr. J. R. Russell, solicitor, Dunfermline. Mr. Gibb died in Edinburgh, on 5th January, 1880; and the estate is now managed by his trustees, who are rapidly feuing it off.

The lands of West Cults, which lie to the south-west of the Estate of Cults, were for a considerable period in the possession of Dr. Campbell, thereafter of Dr. William Stephen, and some time ago they were sold to Mr. David Allan, upholsterer, Aberdeen.

Bieldside, which lies contiguous to West Cults and Cults properties, although in the parish of Peterculter, was bought in 1805 by the late Mr. William Corbet, supervisor of excise. On his death, in 1841, it passed to his second surviving son, the Reverend Adam Corbet, D.D., minister of Drumoak, who died in 1876, and thereafter to his half-brother, Dr. James Corbet, late of the H.E.I.C.'s Bengal Medical Service.

CULTS FREE CHURCH.

During the memorable Disruption year Mr. Thomson of Banchory, and other influential laymen, aided occasionally by clergymen from Aberdeen, held services in the open air and farm buildings, in various parts of Cults. Although the parish minister, Dr. Morison, with his assistant and successor, Dr. Paul, held fast to the Establishment, a good many parishioners on the north side of the river threw in their lot with the dissenting party. It being found necessary to have a Free Church erected in Cults, Mr. Shirra Gibb, proprietor of the estate, was approached with the view of obtaining a site, which he granted on reasonable terms. The spot selected was a piece of waste ground near the centre of the district, and about three-hundred yards north of the turnpike road. No time was lost over the construction of the building, and the Church was formally opened for divine service early in 1844 by the Rev. W. G. Blaikie, D.D., now professor of Apologetical Theology in the New College, Edinburgh.

For several years thereafter probationers discharged the ministerial duties, under the moderatorship and supervision of the Reverend David F. Arthur of Banchory-Devenick. Some of these licentiates have since taken prominent positions, notably Mr. Macpherson, who is now minister of a Scotch Presbyterian church in Liverpool. As, however, the congregation at Cults gradually increased, it became imperative that a regular ordained minister should be appointed to the charge.

The Presbytery of the bounds readily assented to the change, and the choice of the congregation fell upon the Reverend William Anderson, whose father was minister of the parish of Kippen, in Stirlingshire, at the Disruption, but then resigned his charge, and joined the Free Church party. Mr. Anderson received his education at the Edinburgh Academy, and at the Glasgow University, from the latter of which he went to the New College, Edinburgh, where he attended the Divinity course. He was ordained at Cults in the spring of 1861, and, shortly after, a manse (it has since been enlarged), adjoining the church, was erected for him. He proved a model clergyman and was highly esteemed by the inhabitants of the district, irrespective of denomination. After eighteen years of active duty, and when he expected to be able to overtake the ministerial work with less strain upon himself, he was unfortunately laid aside through failing health. Acting on medical advice, and accompanied by his wife, who was a daughter of the late Mr. George Leslie, shipowner, he proceeded to Bath, in the hope of regaining his wonted strength. His illness, however, increased, and he died there on 5th April, 1879. His remains were brought north and interred in the churchyard adjoining the Free Church of Banchory-Devenick, where a handsome granite monument has been erected to his memory. It bears the following inscription:—

IN MEMORY OF
THE REVEREND WILLIAM ANDERSON,
FOR 18 YEARS MINISTER
OF THE FREE CHURCH, CULTS,
WHO DIED 5TH APRIL, 1879,
AGED 45 YEARS.
AN ABLE MINISTER, A FAITHFUL PASTOR,
AND A GOOD SOLDIER OF THE
LORD JESUS CHRIST.

ERECTED
ALONG WITH A TABLET IN THE CHURCH AT CULTS
BY HIS CONGREGATION AND FRIENDS.

The tablet in the Church, which is of white marble, is thus inscribed:—

IN MEMORY OF
REVEREND WILLIAM ANDERSON,
FIRST MINISTER OF CULTS.
BORN 31ST OCTOBER, 1833.
ORDAINED 16TH APRIL, 1861.
DIED 5TH APRIL, 1879.

BE THOU FAITHFUL UNTO DEATH AND
I WILL GIVE THEE A CROWN OF LIFE.

—*Revelation*, ii. 10.

The Reverend Charles Adamson Salmond, son of Mr. Salmond, an Arbroath manufacturer, was, out of a number of candidates, elected to the vacant charge. His ordination took place in the Church, on 21st August, 1879. For several years previously the Church had been found too small for the requirements of the district, and as Mr. Salmond was an excellent preacher and organizer of Church work generally, the congregation continued to increase. He set himself to the work of enlarging the church and also of providing an adjoining hall. When these alterations were completed he considered himself free to close with a call he had received from the congregation of Free St. Matthew's, Glasgow. The Presbytery, having heard the respective pleas of parties, refused to sanction the translation so soon after ordination; but this judgment was reversed on an appeal to the Synod. Mr. Salmond was accordingly inducted at Free St. Matthew's, on May 12th, 1881.

The Reverend Robert William Barbour, son of the late Mr. George Freeland Barbour of Bonskeid, Perthshire, was unanimously appointed successor, and his ordination took place at Cults, on 13th October, 1881. Mr. Barbour, who was married to a daughter of Sir Robert N. Fowler, M.P., ex-lord mayor of London, was possessed of large means, which enabled him to do many philanthropic acts. He not only took the keenest possible interest in the congregation, but the cause of temperance, and the furtherance of the education of the working people of the district, by evening classes and otherwise, had his close attention. In 1886, owing to the unsatisfactory state of his health, he resigned the charge, to the regret of the inhabitants of Cults, to whom he and his wife had endeared themselves.

The Reverend Hugh Morrison, of the Irish Presbyterian Church, who held a charge at Cumber, near Londonderry, was unanimously appointed Mr. Barbour's successor. His induction took place at Cults, on 6th July, 1887. Mr. Morrison had a distinguished college career, and, as a preacher, is eloquent and earnest. He is very popular with his congregation, now numbering close on 300 communicants.

CULTS MISSION CHURCH.

Owing to the rapid increase in the population of Cults, and the long distance residenters, in the western portion of the parish lying on the north side of the river, had to walk to Banchory-Devenick Parish Church, a desire began to manifest itself during the latter years of Dr. Paul's ministry for the erection of a mission station or chapel of ease at Cults, in which evening service and Sunday school classes connected with the Church of Scotland could be held. Nothing, however, was done in the matter till after the Reverend William Lawrence had been appointed assistant and successor to Dr. Paul in December, 1881. The subject was then taken up heartily, and, with the aid of grants from the Baird Trust, and Home Mission Committee, a fund of over £500 was speedily guaranteed for defraying the cost of erecting a Mission Hall.

The Presbytery of the bounds and Kirk-Session of the parish, on being consulted, gave their approval to the scheme, and the Hall was erected on a convenient site on Gateside Croft, quite close to the turnpike road. The title to the feu, extending to about an acre, was taken from the proprietor of Cults, in favour of trustees "for behoof of the Church of Scotland in all time coming." The building, which is of rough ashlar stone, and slated, is handsome and commodious. It was formally opened for evening service in August, 1883, by Mr. Lawrence, minister of the parish.

The managers of the hall had previously entered into an arrangement with Mr. Lawrence, under which he undertook to preach each alternate Sunday, the services on the other Sundays being provided by them at their own expense. From the outset the services were well attended; as also were the Sunday school classes. Towards the end of 1886 the worshippers, including many residenters in the east end of Peterculter who were distant upwards of two miles from their parish church, approached the trustees and managers with a view to double services being conducted, and a minister of their own selection appointed to the charge. Consequently, in March, 1887, it was resolved by the managers to petition the Presbytery to sanction the "formation of the Cults Mission Hall into a Mission Church to be called the Church of Cults".

With the expected aid of a yearly grant from the Home Mission Committee of the Church, an annual stipend of not less than £100 was guaranteed for the missionary. The district asked to be assigned to the new church was a small part of the east end of Peterculter, and practically the whole of the north side of Banchory-Devenick not already included in the *quoad sacra* parishes of Craigiebuckler and Mannofield. The Kirk-Session of the parish opposed this scheme as premature and calculated to cripple the efficiency of the parish church, but the

Presbytery, after deliberating upon the respective pleas of parties, granted the crave of the petitioners.

The Rev. Charles S. Christie, who had been educated at the University of St. Andrews, at which he graduated in 1880, and who had, for some time after license, acted as assistant to the Rev. Dr. Cowan in New Greyfriars Church, Edinburgh, was unanimously appointed to the charge. Accordingly, since the second Sunday of 1888, double services have been given in the mission church. Continued success has attended the ministerial labours of Mr. Christie, and, as the Presbytery gave him ordination in June, 1888, he is thereby enabled to discharge all the functions of a parish minister. There are upwards of eighty communicants on the roll, and the income for 1888 was £184 4s. 10d., the special collections for the schemes of the church representing £20 15s. 7d. In the autumn of 1889 a lady member of the congregation presented to the church two massive silver cups— each inscribed CULTS—for use at the communion services.

MURTLE.

Murtle, like many of the neighbouring lands, was originally Church property. Malcolm IV., by charter dated at Banff, 15th November, 1163, conveyed to Bishop Matthew Kinninmonth, his "haill Barony of Murchill, [Murtle] with the pertinents and common pasturage in the Forest of Aberdeen." William the Lion confirmed this charter to Bishop Matthew, granting him in addition the lands of Brass, now called Birse, with the forest thereof.

In 1382 the Bishop's tenant was John Crab, from whom the lands were attempted to be reclaimed.* A lawsuit followed—the proceedings under which were peculiar. First, the Bishop held a court for exhibition of charters, from which Crab appealed to the Sheriff, on the ground that it was incompetent for the Bishop to be both judge and party. The civil and common law, together with the laws and constitutions of the kingdom, were referred to. The whole proceedings and pleas, written in Latin, are in the chartulary of Aberdeen.†

In 1388 Bishop Adam, in consideration of a yearly payment of ten merks, granted the barony for life in favour of William de Camera [Chalmers], burgess of Aberdeen, and proprietor of Findon, who was elected

* *Reg. Episc. Aberd.*, i. 143, 155.
† Dalyell's *Remarks*, 39, 40.

alderman of Aberdeen in 1398. This is the earliest minute on record of a municipal election connected with the Scotch burghs.*

In 1402 the assedation was renewed for life, on the same terms to Thomas Chalmers, his son. Thomas became Provost of Aberdeen, and married Elizabeth Blinshell, by whom he had issue. He founded the altar of St. Katherine, in the Church of St. Nicholas, for the repose of his own soul and that of his wife's, endowing it with an annual rent of "four merks." Before the year 1427, Bishop Henry, in consideration of a sum of money paid to the fabric of the Cathedral by Chalmers, and at the request of Alexander Stewart, Earl of Mar, and Alexander of Seton, Lord of Gordon, prolonged the lease for the lifetime of his two successive heirs.†

Alexander Chalmers, son of the foregoing, succeeded, and also became Provost of Aberdeen on two occasions, viz.:—in 1443 and 1446. He died in 1463, and was interred in Saint Nicholas Churchyard, Aberdeen.

In 1488 Alexander Chalmers, then designed of "Quiltis," or Cults, in the parish of Tarland, having renounced his claim to the gift of the barony of Murtle, made in his favour by Bishop Thomas, and his predecessors in the See of Aberdeen, obtained from William, bishop of Aberdeen, a lease for life of the barony, with its

---

Scottish Notes and Queries, i., 196.
† *Antiquities Aberdeen and Banff*, Vol. iii., p. 351.

fishings, at the yearly rent of twelve merks. In the event of his decease before his son Alexander Chalmers, the latter was to have a lease of half of the barony, at the rent of five pounds yearly.*

The pedigree of the Chalmers family, 1669 (father and son), is as follows :—" Alexander Chalmers of Cults, son of the House of Balnacraig, married Agnes Hay, daughter of the Earl of Erroll ; Alexander Chalmers married Janet, daughter of John Leslie; Alexander Chalmers married Elizabeth Douglass of Glenbervie; Thomas Chalmers married Mary Menzies, daughter of the laird of Pitfodels ; Alexander Chalmers married Helen Rait, daughter of the laird of Halgreen; Alexander Chalmers married Janet Lumsden, daughter of the laird of Cushnie ; Gilbert Chalmers married Elizabeth Fraser, daughter of the laird of Durris ; Alexander Chalmers married Janet, daughter of James Irving, brother of the laird of Drum ; Marjory Chalmers, their only child, was mother of Sir John Urrie.†

In 1550 William, bishop of Aberdeen, with consent of the dean and chapter, and in virtue of certain Acts of Parliament, granted a feu charter to Andrew Buk, one of the baillies of Aberdeen, and Matilda Menzies, his spouse, of All and Whole the lands of the Milltoun of Murthill, with the pertinents, for the yearly payment of

* *Reg. Episc. Aberd.*, Vol. i., pp. 319, 320.
† *Earldom of the Garioch*, p. 254.

£3 11s. scots, eight bolls of barley and meal in equal proportions with a peck to each boll of barley, four sheep, and twenty-four well-fed capons. Every heir was to pay double feu-duty, being also taken bound to serve in the army of the kingdom sufficiently armed, under the baillie of the bishop, and to take the oath of fealty to the bishop and his successors. From the general grant was reserved the office of bailliary, which was given to George, Earl of Huntly. This arrangement, however, does not appear to have been carried out, as three years later, 18th July, 1553, a tack was executed between the same parties, for a period of nineteen years, of the Milltoun of Murtle, which is said to extend to eight oxengang. The tack-duty was declared, however, to be the same as that specified in the feu charter. The superiority of the lands and fishings is all that appears to have been left to the bishopric, as Thomas Buk, son of the foregoing Andrew, with consent of Elizabeth Strachan, his spouse, disponed the lands, and fishings subsequently acquired, to William Strachan of Tibbertie, in 1597. The lands were afterwards in the hands of Patrick Cheyne of Ferryhill, in 1599; Thomas Murray, in 1607; and James, his son, in 1620, who, by charter dated 24th March, 1648, disponed them to Dr. William Guild and Katherine Rolland, his spouse.

Guild was the second son of Matthew Guild, armourer, Aberdeen, and was born there in 1586. He was educated at Marischal College, and subsequently received license as a minister. In 1608 he was appointed to the charge of King-Edward, in the Presbytery of Turriff, and two years later he married Katherine Rolland, daughter of John Rolland of Disblair. In 1631 he was appointed, by the magistrates of Aberdeen, to one of the city charges. In 1638, he subscribed the Covenant, under three separate limitations, and in the same year he was appointed one of the commissioners to the General Assembly, which met at Glasgow and abolished Episcopacy in Scotland. In the following year, on the approach of an army to compel an unconditional subscription of the Covenant, he fled to Holland. Returning shortly afterwards, however, he accepted the principalship of King's College, which had become vacant through the deprivation of Dr. William Leslie, and he then signed the Covenant without reservation. He held the appointment till 1651, when he was deposed by Cromwell's military commissioners. He thereafter lived in retirement in Aberdeen, and died in July, 1657, in the 71st year of his age. He was the author of many excellent works, and his charitable bequests to the trades of Aberdeen and otherwise, perpetuate his name as one of Aberdeen's greatest benefactors. His wife, Katherine Rolland, about a fortnight before her death, which occurred in December, 1659, executed a deed of gift, conveying to the magistrates of Aberdeen the lands of Milltoun of Murtle, and the lands of Ardfork and Kilblain, held in wadset from Patrick Urquhart, for the following purposes :—

"For the maintenance of four bursars at Marischal College, and four at the Grammar School, being burgess' sons, the presentees to be of honest parentage, and if possible, well inclyned in theire owne natures and given to learning." For the clothing of six poor scholars receiving free education at any school, £48 scots was directed to be expended yearly, and 24 bolls of meal to be given among six widows of decayed burgesses, while 20 bolls were to be given among the common poor. In satisfaction of a legacy of 1000 merks left to the poor of King-Edward by her husband, she provided that they should receive 18 bolls of meal annually for distribution.*

Shortly after this the lands of Murtle passed into the hands of the Irvine family. The progenitor of this branch, and that of Cults, was Gilbert Irvine of Colairlie, fourth son of Alexander Irvine of Drum, who was killed at the battle of Pinkie in 1547. Alexander Irvine, eldest son of Sir Alexander Irvine of Drum, who was sheriff-principal of Aberdeen in 1634, married, for his first wife, Lady Mary Gordon, fourth daughter of the Marquis of Huntly, by whom he had issue three sons—Alexander, Robert, and Charles—and four daughters, of whom Margaret, married Gilbert Menzies of Pitfodels; and Jean, Alexander Irvine of Murtle. On his succeeding to Drum, the king renewed to him the offer which had been made to his father, of the Earldom of Aberdeen,

* *Scottish Notes and Queries*, ii., p. 139.

but he declined accepting it. About twenty years later the king, in granting a charter containing a novodamus of "Drum's whole estates, holding of the crown, took occasion to express in it the deep sense which he had of the family's loyalty, and their services and sufferings in the royal cause."* Irvine in 1687, while upon his deathbed, tailzied his estate, failing heirs male of his own body, to the Irvines of Murtle, Artamford, and Cults, and their heirs male in order.† His eldest son Alexander, who succeeded, died in 1695 without issue, and to him, therefore, in terms of the Deed of Tailzie, Alexander of Murtle became successor. The latter thereupon sold Murtle, and the estate of Strachan, which were not included in the entail.

Mains of Murtle, Oldfold, Stonegavel, Binghill, and Newtown of Murtle were purchased by the master of mortifications of Aberdeen from Irvine in 1695, for the benefit of Sir Thomas Crombie's mortification, at the purchase price of £9,463 6s. 8d. scots. The Town let out the lands to tacksmen till 1758-9, when the estate was divided into the following lots, for feuing at the feu-duties undernoted :—

I. Binghill, -   £7 15 0 stg. and 12 bolls of meal
II. Auldfold, - 11 10 0   do.   16   do.
III. Mains, -   18   0 0   do.   16   do.
IV. Newton, -   16   0 0   do.   11   do.

* Anderson's *Scottish Nation*, ii., 538.
†Nisbet's *Heraldry*. ii., 67-8.

As illustrating the great rise in the value of land, it may be mentioned that part of these lands, burdened with the feu-duty as above specified, was sold in 1773 for £1,500, in 1808 it changed hands at £4000, and the large sum of £12,000 was paid for the property in 1880.

In the beginning of the present century the lands of Murtle were in the possession of Mr. John Gordon, who, by his last will and testament dated 11th August, 1815, left large sums for charitable and religious objects. His trustees pay annually ten pounds to each of the Kirk-Sessions of Banchory-Devenick and Peterculter, as remuneration to Sunday school teachers; as also fifty pounds sterling yearly for the purpose of establishing "Lectures on Practical Religion and the Evidences of Religion," in the University of Aberdeen. These lectures are delivered by the three Theological Professors in turn yearly.

In 1821 the lands were purchased from Mr. Gordon's executors, by Mr. John Thurburn who had amassed a fortune abroad. He was a native of Keith, and married the only daughter of the Reverend Mr. Findlater of Cairnie, by whom he had issue. One daughter, Barbara Anderson, died on 5th October, 1858, aged 32. Mr. Thurburn had a fine new mansion-house, in the Grecian style of architecture, erected on a site which overlooks the river Dee. The old house of Murtle was thereupon converted into stables, coach-houses, &c. He expended large sums in beautifying and improving the property, which became one of the most choice residences on

Deeside. He died on 31st January, 1861, aged 80, and his remains were laid beside those of his daughter in the churchyard of Peterculter. His wife, who survived him, was the founder of the Thurburn Cooking Depôt in Aberdeen for the benefit of working men. She died at Murtle on the 24th December, 1872.

Mr. Thurburn's only surviving daughter, Anna—who in September, 1848, had the honour of presenting Her Majesty Queen Victoria with a floral bouquet on the occasion of Her Majesty's first passing up to Balmoral—succeeded. She married Mr. William Osborne Maclaine, who is an extensive proprietor in Gloucestershire, and they, had issue two sons and one daughter. The eldest son, Hector, joined the Royal Horse Artillery, in which he held the rank of lieutenant. With his regiment he served under General Sir Frederick Roberts in the late Afghan War. At the battle of Maiwand, fought on 27th July, 1880, he distinguished himself by his firmness and bravery. During the retreat which followed, he was taken prisoner, and on 1st September following, his lifeless and mangled body was found in the camp of Ayoub Khan, outside Candahar. Mrs. Maclaine died on 10th October, 1882.

Mr. Thurburn Maclaine the surviving son succeeded. He was born on 2nd July, 1853, and married Miss Rachel Hay, daughter of the Reverend Patrick Leslie Miller, grandson of Mr. Miller of Dalswinton, Dumfriesshire, the inventor of steamboats.

CURIOUS
CRIMINAL AND ECCLESIASTICAL TRIALS

Some curious criminal and ecclesiastical cases have occurred in the history of the parish. Two cases of theft, about 1698, show the fearful retribution then inflicted for petty pilfering. One, William Spence, was "apprehendit with the fang, incarcerate at Stonehyve and afterwards confessed that he did steal a hen and three chickens from the Laird of Ardoch's henhouse. Banished the shire, and his goods escheat. Janet Forbes and James Ross convict of stealing two pecks of malt out of a kiln in Banchory-Devenick, ordered to be scourged through the town and banished the shire for ever."*

A debt case occurs as early as 1562, when " Loke Traill, duelland in Petfoddellis grantit and confessit him awand to Alex. Robertson, and Johnne Robertson, his Brother, the soume of aucht pound 13s. 4d. vsuall money of Scotland, quhilk he obleist him to pay to the saidis personis . . . for the quhilk the said Alexander for himself and all vtheris, his kyn, and freyndis remittis and forgiffis the said Loke and all vtheris, his kyn, freyndis, assisteris, complicis, faueraris, and part takaris of the bluid drawing of him, and art and parte thairof; and als of the slauchter of vmquhill Besse Chalmer, his spouse, allegit, committit be the said Loke of suddentie , . ."†

* *Black Book of Kincardineshire.*
† *Burgh Records.*

A case of slander appears in 1598 which the Presbytery dealt with. A woman, Barbara Baddie, had an action "aganis hir nichtboris, vyftelling maney, efter tryell baith afoir thair particular sessione of Banchorie-Devenick, and sic lyk heir." The Presbytery "findis that the said Elinge haid committit offence aganis the said Barbara Baddie, yit be the consent of the said pairtie offendit var reconsilit afoir the presbitrie, be the said Ellinge teallinge hir pardone upone hir kneis, and baith var admonesit to keip guid concord in tym cuminge, under penalty of ten lib, and to mak thair publick repentance upone the stuill, within thair awin paroche kirk, that utheris may tak exempill theirby." On the same occasion "Mathow Hill, being convict afoir his awin sessione for the sclanderinge of his nichtbor, Thomas Philpe, in Pitfoddell, calling him commond theiff and cuttar of fenss and siclyk, be his awin confessione, vas ordenit heirfoir to pey tua merkis, and to aske the pairtie quhome he hes offendit forgeveness; and in caice he dissobey this, the ordinance of the presbiterie to the persone of Banchorrie to proceid aganis him, aie and quhill he satisffie this act in all pointtis."*

An extraordinary case of assault occurred at the kirk of Banchorie for which Alexander Cruickshank, in Little Banchorie, Robert and James Cruickshank, his children, "were summondit before the Sheriff at Stonehyve to underly the law for beating, blooding, and dragging Jean

* *Eccles. Records of Aberd.*, p. 166.

Darg in Little Banchorrie through the gutter, and threatening to put her in the joggis. And at last, taking her prisoner, carrying her to the kirk of Banchorie and there tying her and locking her within the same, affrighting her out of her wits. Cruickshank convict and mulct in £50 scots of penalty, and £4 of damage to the party injured, as also to pay ilk ane of the witnesses."

It is a remarkable coincidence that in the five cases of murder and murderous assault that occurred in the annals of the district, the perpetrators in each case got off unpunished. It will be remembered that in 1580 Forbes of Portlethen cruelly murdered Alexander Menzies at the Cairn of Loirston; that in 1642 Menzies of Pitfodels attacked Forbes of Leslie, and that two years later Forbes, the young laird of Banchory, killed Irvine of Kingcausie. The lairds of the lands escaped, and their subjects were no less fortunate. In 1788 Robert Walker, residing at Findon, was tried at the spring Circuit Court on a charge of murder. Proof having been led, the jury returned a verdict of "not guilty," when the accused was dismissed from the bar. The other case has become famous in the annals of local crime. In it, Francis Forbes—it is noticeable that some one of the name Forbes appears in four of the important cases cited—was tried at the High Court of Justiciary held in Edinburgh in November, 1854, charged with the murder of Ann Harvey at Cults, on the morning of Sunday, 7th May of that year. Harvey, who was a young woman engaged at the paper mills at Peterculter, had gone to Aberdeen on the evening of Saturday, 6th May, with a view to purchasing a supply of provisions. After making several calls in the city, she left intending to proceed to Peterculter. It was alleged that Forbes, who was considered as a sweetheart of Harvey, accompanied her on the journey, but the movements of the pair were not clearly traced. Next morning, however, two young men, on their way to Aberdeen, and whilst passing a spot on the public road a little to the east of Cults House avenue, saw a quantity of blood and a shawl lying close to the left wall. The lads were surprised at the sight, and on looking over the wall beheld the corpse of Harvey in a ghastly condition. On the deceased were found two shillings and several letters, one of them being a love epistle, with some verses, bearing the address of "Francis Forbes, East Middleton, Banchory-Devenick." Suspicion at once fell upon this man, and, as blood was found on his clothes when examined, the authorities had him arrested and lodged in gaol on the capital charge. A large amount of evidence was adduced at the trial, which strongly pointed to the accused as guilty, but it failed to satisfy the jury, who brought in a verdict of "not proven." The prisoner was thereupon discharged.

A single case of witchcraft trial appears in 1607, when the Presbytery visited Banchorie and tried Isabell Smith for this offence :—" Accused grantit that James Bryanis wyff, haiffing hir dochter seik, callit Janet Mellit, causit the said Elspet tak a threid and a slew of the said Jonettis and put a threid about hir, to sie giff the seikness was the feweris or not." Several witnesses were examined on oath, one of whom deponit that Elspet "causit hir tak a wolne thred and a slewof, and put the threid about hir bodie and the slewoff, and then commandit hir to gang anes about, in the name of the Father, the Sone, and the Halie Gaist." The case was continued indefinitely.

The remaining cases are all ecclesiastical.

In May, 1605, the kirk-session of Aberdeen appointed an officer to "nott the persones that passis ovr the watter to Dunie, and absentis thameselffis fra the sermone at efternone, and ordainis him to giwe vp thair names, that they may be puneist for thair brak and prophanatioun of the Lordis Saboth." In 1696 a number of persons were tried before the kirk-session of Aberdeen, and censured for celebrating May-day morning. One of them "acknowledged his offence on the first morning of May, but denyed it to be any offence to be a precentor to Mr. James Gordon," minister of Banchory-Devenick. On the 11th October, 1678, "the Bishop and Synod, considering that Mr. James Gordon at Banchorie, and Mr. Alexander Leask, had uttered some unbesseeming and passionat expressions yesternight, the one against the other, in face of the synod, therefor, both the said bretheren wer rebuiked publickly for the same."

ANTIQUITIES.

The most remarkable piece of antiquity in the parish besides the old Bridge of Dee is a "Druidical Temple," situated on an eminence about a mile and a half from the coast, which was till within these few years remarkably perfect. It consisted of three circles of stone within each other. The outer circle, which was about forty-five feet in diameter, consisted of twelve large stones placed on end. The inner circles were composed of smaller ones placed in the same manner, and between the two outermost, upon the east side, there was a stone chest, sunk in the earth, about three feet long and one-and-a-half wide, which having been accidentally uncovered by a countryman, disclosed an urn in which nothing but a little dust or ashes was found. A little farther down the hill towards the south-east there is another erection of the same kind. It consists of one circle of pretty large stones.

Druidical Stones at Portlethen.

An exploring party consisting of Mr. Dyce Nicol of Ballogie, Mr. C. S. Dalrymple of Westhall, Mr. Nicolson of Glenbervie, Captain Burnett, yr. of Monboddo, the Rev. Mr. Stewart of Oathlaw, and Mr. Thomson of Banchory, carefully inspected these circles, and the latter specially reported on them to the Society of Antiquaries of Scotland. The conclusion arrived at was, that one use of them was as a place of burial, but whether the persons buried had been sacrificed on the spot as victims of a cruel superstition, or were heroes in whose honour the stones had been set up, they could not determine. They found no trace of sculpture, or inscriptions, nor of flint knives or weapons.* "A gentleman writing in beginning of the present century, observes that a workman having cut one of these druidical stones, which had fallen from its upright situation, produced out of it a millstone and forty feet of pavement. Close to the principal circle there are two fields of extraordinary fertility, although much encumbered with large quantities of stone interspersed through them.

The soil of these fields has been long remarked for its productiveness; and the tradition of the country is, that in the time of the Picts, soil had been brought to these fields, all the way from Findon, a distance of two miles, and that this was done by ranging a line of men along the whole distance, who handed the earth from the one to the other."†

* Smeaton's *Life of Thomson*, pp. 493, 494.
† *Agricultural Survey*, p. 84.

Near Cults House were three stone cairns, all of remarkable size, where it is stated that at an early age a battle was fought between the Scots and Picts. Whether these had been intended to mark the scene of the battle or the resting place of certain warrior chiefs who had fallen in the fray, remains a mystery. Latterly two of the cairns have been greatly diminished in size, and the third has been entirely removed by the withdrawal of the stones for building purposes. In the removed cairn were discovered arrow heads, and a sword, but the latter was of quite modern manufacture.

Nearly four hundred years ago an important find was made near Findon, which consisted, as quaintly described by Bellenden, "of ane ancient sepulture in quhilk wer ii lame piggis craftely maid with letteris ingrauit, full of brynt powder, quhilkis sone efter that they wer handillit fel in dros."*

A few stone coffins have been found in various parts of the parish at different times. In August, 1817, one was discovered in repairing a road on the farm of Clasfarquhar, at a spot about a quarter of a mile from the sea, and on the top of a bank of gravel. "The coffin was composed of eight stones, two at each side, one at each end and two forming the cover; and contained the remains of a human skeleton, and two vases or urns. The skeleton, although considerably decayed, appeared from

---

* Jervise's *Epitaphs*, ii., p. 282.

the jaws to be that of an adult. The larger of the vases, which was accidentally broken by the labourers, must have been about ten inches in diameter, and five in height. The smaller was six-and-a-half inches high, and five across the mouth. They appear to have been made of pounded granite and mica slate, commonly found in the vicinity, and covered with a coating of clay, ornamented with small patterns executed with considerable care. The vases were round as if turned in a lathe, and appeared to have been dried in the sun. At what period this deposit was made must be purely matter of conjecture." Two other stone coffins were found in 1850, a little to the north of Cults mansion-house. They contained skulls, bones, and other remembrances of mortality. A curious feature of this find was a row or circle of stones enclosing an area of almost eighteen feet in diameter. Another stone coffin was found in forming that part of the turnpike road which passes through the estate of Ardoe. No tool appeared to have been employed to carve it out. It was bedded in the shingle (not sand) was only two-and-a-half feet long by two broad, and contained an urn, within which was a human skull of a small size, but apparently that of an adult.

Stone cists were discovered on the estate of Banchory in 1823, and again in 1847. Two of these were in a gravel hillock, and each contained an urn of baked clay, in addition to which there was a gold ring in one of them. Unfortunately one of the urns got broken, but the other, which was shaped somewhat like the head of a thistle and richly ornamented, has been carefully preserved.*

Among the varied objects in the collection of the Society of Antiquaries of Scotland is a skull found in an ancient cist on Clashfarquhar in 1822. " It is that of a young man, of small size, imperfect, and extremely fragile, owing to the loss of most of its animal matter. On the crown of the head is a hole, nearly circular, and rather more than an inch in diameter, caused, it may be presumed, by the blow of a stone axe, which had abruptly terminated the earthly career of its owner. In form and cerebral development it corresponds to a class of skulls found in the earliest Scottish cairns and barrows; and, as already said, it is not difficult to conceive of the wound having been inflicted by the narrow end of a stone celt. In each corner of the cist, from which the skull was taken, lay a few flint flakes carefully piled up into a heap, the sole evidence of the rude arts of the period to which it pertained. Mr. Thomson of Banchory remarked of them, in a letter which accompanied the donation of the skull:— 'They are very proper for being made into arrow heads, but none of them appear to have been wrought'."†

About sixteen years ago, owing to the flooding of the river Dee, a landslip took place on the south Deeside turnpike road, at a point due north of the Mansion House of Ardoe. A large quantity of material being required

* Jervise's *Epitaphs*, ii., p. 282.
† Wilson's *Prehistoric Scot.*, i., 176-7, 257.

to fill up the gap which had been made, Mr. Ogston gave permission to the Road Trustees to remove a gravel knoll in a field east of his stables. During the progress of the operations, the workmen came upon several ancient graves, in which at least one complete skeleton, bones, three urns, and part of an old lamp were found. The skeleton was presented to the Museum of Marischal College, and one of the urns to the late Dr. John Stuart, whilst the two remaining ones are preserved in the house of Ardoe.

Urns found at Ardoe.

Of these two, the larger one measures fully two feet in height, whilst the smaller one, which unfortunately got somewhat broken by the workmen, is eight-and-three-fourth inches high. The latter is richly ornamented, and seems to be of a quality and shape entirely different from the larger one. At what time the interments had taken place it is difficult to estimate, although antiquaries generally believe it was shortly after the Romans had left the country.

Within recent years an axe head, and flints of two distinct colours, have been unearthed, close to a running stream in the grounds of Lynwood, Deebank, belonging to Mr. George D. Rutherford.

Axe Head found at Lynwood.

The axe head measures eight-and-a-half inches in length, by about three inches in breadth, and weighs close on two pounds. It is believed that the natives had an encampment at Deebank during the stone age.

About twenty years ago a splendid specimen of the ancient *quern*, or hand-mill, was dug out of a piece of mossy ground in the hollow below West Cults. It belonged to the late Mr. Alexander Hepburn, Birchfield, and is now in the custody of the author, with a view to being handed over to the Public Museum in Aberdeen when such is instituted. The lower stone measures eighteen-and-a-half inches in diameter, by about three inches in thickness, and the upper one is slightly less. Each has a hole bored through the centre to admit of being fastened to the ground, the upper one, of course, having an opening sufficiently large to allow of its being easily turned round, and the corn at the sametime allowed to run in. It has, in addition, a small hole near the upper edge for holding a handle with which to drive it. The smooth surfaces are cut with a downward inclination towards the outside, so as to let the flour or meal run out more easily.

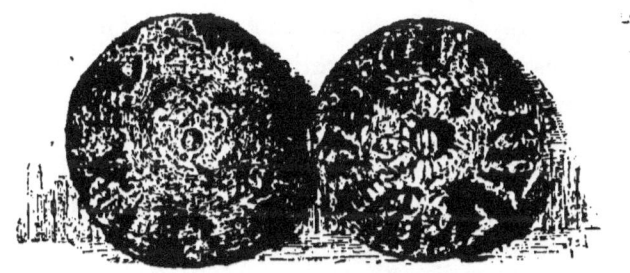

Quern found below West Cults.

EXTRACTS FROM THE SESSION RECORDS.

The Session Records of Banchory-Devenick have not hitherto been published, although they contain some curious entries. They extend to seven large volumes, commencing on 4th January, 1708, and—with the exception of a hiatus from 12th December, 1714, to 1st March, 1716; another from 7th June, 1724, to 23rd October, 1726; another from 16th August to 8th November, 1747; and another from 12th August to 3rd November, 1757—go on uninterruptedly down to the present time. Two older volumes had unfortunately been destroyed by fire during the ministry of the Rev. James Gordon, which extended from November, 1667, to December, 1714. The following are the more interesting particulars from the existing records, which have been arranged according to subject for greater convenience.

PAROCHIAL BOARD AND RELIEF OF THE POOR.

From the earliest times the subject of affording relief to the poor, and those on whom affliction had suddenly fallen, formed matter of concern to governments, magistrates, and public bodies generally. In Banchory-Devenick it is abundantly manifest that during severe seasons considerable poverty and distress existed among the lower orders. Charity, however, was liberally extended by the better to do class of the population.

As early as the year 1620, a system of relieving was organized by the Heritors and Kirk-Session, under which the latter body became sole administrators. A perusal of the Extracts will give a slight insight into what was done from 1708 onwards. In that year there were over twenty regularly enrolled poor, who received £10 6s. 8d. amongst them quarterly, besides which many supplicant poor from other parishes were from time to time temporarily relieved. School fees of children were frequently paid, perquisites provided, and subscriptions given to the most peculiar objects conceivable. This practice of promiscuous giving, however, led to a large increase in the number of beggars who roamed over the country, and of whom it was no unusual circumstance to find as many as forty waiting to be relieved at the church door when service ended. So many able-bodied men and women found the begging profession a profitable one, that they became a nuisance to society, so much so that the legislature was compelled to pass measures of repression. In consequence the Kirk-Session, in the end of 1737, found it necessary to give badges, or tickets, to their own poor, and to concert a method for effectually getting rid of all other vagrants not belonging to the parish. A payment of twelve shillings was accordingly made for tickets to the privileged poor; and, a year later, special collections were made to defray the expense of "apprehending and prosecuting beggars and vagabonds."

In some districts a "scourger" was employed, at a

fixed salary, to keep out beggars not provided with the requisite badge. With regard to the expedients adopted to excite pity, these were, in many instances, most ingenious. One was to profess blindness and helpless lameness, necessitating the pretender's being carried in a sort of hand-barrow. As recently as 1840 it was not uncommon, in one day, for several of these hand-barrows to be set down at the door of a dwelling-house. To get clear of such unwelcome visitors, the only course available to the inmates was to administer relief, and get sufficient hands together to carry the burden to the next door. So many beggars were sent into Banchory in this way from the parish of Fetteresso, that the Kirk-Session had to send a special injunction against the continuance of the practice.

On 15th April, 1739, it was agreed that three shillings and fourpence sterling should be paid for making the poor's coffins, two carpenters having agreed to supply them at that figure. It was appointed by the Session that "the haill effects" of such poor as should be buried by them should fall to the remaining poor. It was also ordained that one of the poor should attend the others when sick, and should be paid per day by the Session for so doing; and in case of refusal "their names to be cancelled out of the roll." The sum paid at this time for digging the graves of the poor was sixpence each.

In November, 1751, it was enacted that all poor,

before being placed on the Charity Roll of the parish, should subscribe a disposition making over to the collector of the Session and his successors in office "their whole goods, gear, debts, and effects that shall be due and belonged to them at the time of decease."

When any famine or special calamity overtook the country it was customary for the Government to vote a sum in relief. In 1783, owing to the complete failure of the previous year's crop, a sum of £10,000 was appointed to be paid out of the Royal Exchequer to assist the poor in the Highlands and northern parts of Scotland. Returns were called for from all parishes, the one from Banchory-Devenick showing that, on 3rd July of that year, there were thirty recognized poor, besides other thirty-four families, representing 256 souls, requiring assistance. One hundred and twenty-eight bolls of meal were asked; but, owing to more crying demands from other districts, only a small proportion was sent.

In the latter years of the Session's management of the Poor's Fund, they distributed to the higher class on the roll ten shillings, and to the lower eight shillings each, a quarter. What was further required for their support, Dr. Paul says, "was partially supplied by the earnings of the females, in knitting stockings and spinning, but principally through the benevolence of kind neighbours, whose liberality and sympathy were greatly diminished after the introduction of the poor's rates. In the year 1845 the whole sum distributed among the poor amounted to £253 14 3d. There were no expenses of management."

By the passing of the Poor Law Act, however, the whole system of relieving underwent a sweeping change. A Parochial Board, with duly qualified medical officer and inspector, nominated and voted for by the ratepayers from whom the taxes were made exigible, fell to be appointed by each parish. If this Board has not accomplished all that was expected by its votaries, it has at least been the means of reducing vagrancy to a minimum, and making those on whom alimentary legal responsibility rests discharge their obligations.

At present the business of the Parochial Board is managed by seventeen of a committee, with Lieutenant-Colonel Joyner * as chairman. The sum raised in 1888,

---

* Lieut.-Col. Joyner has had a most distinguished career. Born at Lonmay, he joined the 93rd (Sutherland) Highlanders as a private, in February, 1840. He served for two years at Fort-George and Aberdeen, when he embarked with his regiment for Canada. After serving alternately in Toronto, Kingston, Montreal, and Quebec (at the latter town he was slightly frost bitten) he returned home, after an absence of six years. On the outbreak of the Crimean War, however, the 93rd were ordered to proceed for active service, arriving in the Crimea in September '54. During the next two years he shared in all the hardships and difficulties of that memorable campaign. He was present at, and took part in, the battles of Alma, on 20th September, '54; Balaklava ("thin red line"), 25th October, '54; Kertch and Yenikale, 16th May, '55; and Sebastapol, 8th September and 18th June (in one of these engagements he was slightly wounded by the bursting of a shell). Peace being

in the shape of poor's assessment, was £624 15s., of which amount £124 4s. 10d. was expended on alimenting fifteen poor in the parish, and about £100 in relieving ten poor resident in other parishes; besides about £240 in supporting twelve lunatic poor in various asylums. The following extracts illustrate these remarks :—

restored, he returned to Britain in June, '56, when his bravery was acknowledged by the presentation of *the Crimean Medal and three clasps, for Alma, Balaklava, and Sebastopol; The Turkish Medal and the French War Medal for valour and discipline.* In addition he had received his commission as Quartermaster whilst in the Crimea. In June, '57, the regiment embarked for China; but, the Indian Mutiny having broken out in the interim, they were, whilst passing through the Bay of Bengal, signalled by the Governor-General to land at Calcutta. This being done, active operations were at once commenced to quell the mutineers. Space will not admit of details being given of the forced marches, privations, and difficulties encountered for the next few years. Suffice it to say that the subject of our memoir took part in the following ordeal :—Relief of women and children, Lucknow, 14th to 25th November, '57; Defeat of Gwalior Force at Cawnpore; Battles of Serai Ghât, Kaleh Nuddee; Lucknow Siege, 2nd to 21st March, '58; Allygunge, Bareilly, 5th May, '58; Posgaon, 19th October, '58; Russelpore, 25th October, '58; and afterwards the Storming of Fort Mithoulie. For the signal achievements at Lucknow he was presented with *the Indian Mutiny Medal and two clasps.* In March, '70, he returned with the regiment to Aberdeen, and for the next ten years discharged the duties of Paymaster, to which position he had been promoted six years previously. He retired from the army as a Staff-Paymaster, in October, 1880, after a service exceeding forty years. The gallant soldier, now promoted to the rank of Lieutenant-Colonel, resides in Cults, and takes a lively interest in every work tending to the welfare of the parish.

DISBURSEMENTS, BEQUESTS, &c.

1708 Jan 4—Quarter's college fee (13/4d.) of Student paid. Given to stranger supplicant impoverished by piracie, 7/-.

Mar. 28—Given to a poor travelling stranger, 6/-.

May 16—Given to a paralytick Schoolmaster in Buchan, 20/-

Sep. 5—Four punds scots ordered to be given to help to pay the curing of a poor boy in Aberdeen, who was grievously wounded in the forehead by the stroak of a horse foot.

1709 May 22—Given to a poor old minister, 12 lb.

1710 Jan. 29—To a Mary ffrazer, ane epileptick lass, to buy a plade and shirt to her, 3 lb.

Dec. 31—Payed to the fishers of fody, for salvage of the ferry boat, which was caryed away by a violent swaling water, £4 10/-.

1712 Feb. 10—Andrew Donald, being old and impoverished by the death of a cow in bringing furth a monstruous calf with two heads, ordered to receive 6 lib to help to buy another cow.

June 22—Given to a poor boy to help to pay his apprentice ffee with a view to his learning a trade, £6 13s. 4d.

1713 Nov. 22—Given to two orphans in Nigg, 20/-.

Nov. 29—Given to supplicant with a cancer in his face, 6/8.

1714 Oct. 10—Alexander Leslie being reduced to poverty, ordered to receive the price of a firlot of meal.

1716 June 10—Given out of the collection 3 lib for a coffin to a poor woman, who must otherwise have been laid down in her grave without one.

1716 Aug. 19—Collection of £6 8s. 2d. made for the encouragement of learning, and the supporting of Charity Schools in the Highlands.

Oct. 7—Minister from Pulpit intimated to the congregation that, whereas upon the representation made to him by some honest men in the North side of the Parish, a beggar boy who went about leading his mother—ane old blind woman—the foresaid boy in his folly had fallen off a dike, and haveing a sharp pointed knife in his pocket it had struck into his belly, and that thereupon they had taken up the youth, who was near dead, and carried him in to the Chirurgions att Aberdeen, and that he would need something for his support as long as he lived, and therefore he urged the people to extend their charity next-Sabbath for the effect foresaid.

Oct. 14—The wounded boy for whom the collection was intimated was dead, and buried last week, as severall members of the congregation reported.

Given to the Kirk Officer 8/-, for carrying a poor distressed supplicant on horseback first to Aberdeen, and then to Causey Port.

1717 March 24—Six shillings given to a poor supplicant, who had lost all his worldly substance in the late horrid rebellion.

Nov. 3—13/4d. given to Alex. Wilson, who has a sone dying in the Cruells, and can doe nothing for himself, and the father a very poor man with many children.

Dec. 16—Given 6/- to a seaman cast away on the North coast, and 2/- scots more to some poor people about the kirk door.

1718 June 29—£1 6s. 8d. given out of the collection, for behoof of the child who suffered by fire.

1718 Nov. 16—Collected this day for the distressed Protestants of Lithuania £5 14s. 8d.

1719 Dec. 20—Collected £2 17s. 6d. for the kirk at Cairstoun (Stromness) in Orkney.

1720 Nov. 27—Collected £3 3s. for the following special objects, relieving the distressed Protestants in Saxonie, for erecting a new kirk in Orkney, for building another at Zetland, for building a bridge on the water of Anachie, for another bridge in the parish of Bourtie, for another on the water of Tarlan, as also for a charitable contribution to Ann Urquhart and John Henderson, taylor in the Cannongate and for the distressed protestants belonging to Inverness taken by the Galy men.

1721 Aug. 18—Collected £3 19s. for Charles Erskine, and 3 men in Old Meldrum all sufferers by fire.

1722 May 6—Twenty shilling given for takeing the children over water the winter quarter for their education at school.

Dec. 16—£3 paid for takeing the ferry boat out of the sea, being carried thither with the violence of spait water.

1728 March 3—This day John Mowat, at Mill of Finnan, gave in to the box £6 13s. 4d. scots, for the priviledge of burying his mother in the Church, according to custome in this place. This day, also, Alexander Milne gave in £3 scots, the marriage pledge of William Marshall in the Parish of Peterculter, forfeited for non-performance of his contract with a woman in this parish.

1729 July 27—Generall contribution intimated for building a harbour at St. Andrews, and congregation advised to give liberally.

£3 scots was subsequently handed over for the foregoing object.

1729 Oct. 19—Irish Presbytery Bursar's discharge for payment of £2 scots handed over by the minister.

1730 Oct. 18—Given for making the sackcloth, 6/-.

1731 April 11—Two pounds scots given out to one James Anderson a poor man in Maryculter, whose wife had brought forth three children at one birth.

Oct, 24—Collected £15 scots for the sufferers by fire in Monimusk.

1732 June 7—This day the Session, considering the great disorder occasioned by the multitude of dogs in time of worship, did agree to employ Alexander Couts to keep them out, and allow him three pence every Lord's Day out of the collection for the same.

Dec. 10—14/- Scots given to Alexander Couts for an iron instrument wherewith to keep out the dogs.

1733 Oct. 14—£7 10s. 6d. of bad half-pence to be disposed of to best advantage.

1734 April 7—Given for a hand-bell, to be employed at burials along with the mortcloth, £4 12s. scots, of which £1 4s. was deducted anent the bad half-pence.

1735 Sep. 28—Four merks Scots given to Alexander Couts, who holds out the dogs, to buy a new coat to him.

Dec. 14—The day being short and very cold the Minister lectured only. Given to 3 Bluegowns 3s. scots.

1738 Feb. 5—Collected £11 3s. scots for an Hospital to be built in Edinburgh for curing sick people.

March 5—Given to the man who holds out the dogs, 5/-.

Oct. 29—Collected £14 2s. for Blind Davidson's support. Minister intimated that he was appointed to go to Edinburgh anent the demolishing the Church of Kinnernie, and annexing that Parish to Midmar and Clunie.

1750 Dec. 2—Collection intimated for the building of a Church and School at Breslau.

1755 June 8—Given to a poor man who was robbed near the Causey moss, £1 4s.

Sep. 21—Collected £8 for building of a new college at Jersey.

Dec. 7—Given for burying a murdered child, by Jean Steven now in prison, which was found above Hilldountree, £2 8s. To the officer for ringing the bell longer than ordinary for the salmon fishers, £1 10s.

1756 Feb. 6—£14 of a fine received from the Procurator-Fiscal at Stonehaven, said sum having been recovered from one of the Ardoe salmon fishers.

Sept. 18—Given to James Farquhar, a poor man in the parish of Fetteresso, whose wife had born 3 children at one birth, £2 8s.

1759 April 8—Given in for the fines of the Brewers, £27 12s.

April 29—Given to the Officer for carrying a cripple man to Aberdeen upon his horse, 6/-.

1761 July 12—Collected £11 2s. for building a place of worship at Curgarf.

1766 Given £10 10s. as taxation to the Old Town College.

1769 Given to help to make the church road on Cranhill, £12 scots.

Nov. 19—Collected £21 12s. for building the new church of Gilcomston.

1770 March 4—Monies now calculated at sterling or British value.

June 10—Given to George Lessly in Kinnellar, whose farm yard was wilfully set on fire by two miscreants, 10/-.

1772 July 5—One of the Elders reporting that a poor herd boy in Easter Ardoch had been accidentally drowned, Session agreed to pay the funeral expenses.

1775 Oct. 22—Given to buy a surt-coat to Annie Buchan, 4/5½.
Nov. 15—£5 6s. 10d. of bad copper ordered to be sold.
„ 19—18/6 received for the bad copper which weighed 37 lbs.

1777 Feb. 16—Given to a poor man in Drumoak, whose wife lately died of the bite of a mad dog, two shillings.
Sept. 28—Compeared William Milne in Kirktown, and Robert Anderson in Tullohill, constables. They represented that they had last week taken up Ann Fraser, a poor delirious woman, who had been happily prevented from drowning herself in the River Dee, and got her with difficulty forwarded safely to Maryculter. They received 2/- for their trouble.

1780 Jan. 16—The day being remarkably bad collected only 9d.

1781 May 6—Male child laid down at a Parishioner's door this morning, taken charge of by the Session, who offered a reward of five guineas for discovery of the mother.
Entries afterwards occur of cost of wearing apparel and board of the child.

1782 April 25—£100 bequeathed for behoof of the Poor, by Mr George Martin, Shipmaster in Aberdeen.

1787 March 11—Collected £41 3s. 8¾d. for assisting in the relief of the families of three fishermen accidentally drowned at Cove.

1790 June 27—Collected £5 10s. 5d. for behoof of the widows and 26 children of 6 Fishermen drowned at Cove on 17th May last.

1798 Nov. 10—£45 collected throughout the Parish for the defence of the country against the threatened invasion.

1801 Dec. 20—£500 handed over to the Kirk-Session by James Calder, wine merchant in Aberdeen, the interest whereof to be applied annually for the relief of the poor.

> Mr. Calder's daughter, Mrs. Emslie, in 1836, devoted £26,000 towards the erection and endowment of an hospital in Aberdeen for orphan and destitute children.

1804 Sep. 9—£1 given to a Farmer who had his horse stolen out of his stable.

1805 Dec. 5—Collected £9 7s. for the Trafalgar relief fund.

1807 Feb. 26—Collected £9 5s. for the relatives of 37 Fishermen who lost their lives by the destruction of 6 fishing boats during a severe storm in the Moray Firth on 25th December last.

1815 Oct. 1—Collected for the Waterloo Fund, £7 2s. 1d.

1825 June 26—Intimation received from the Trustees of the late Mr. John Gordon of Murtle of an annual legacy of £10 bequeathed by Mr. Gordon for the teaching of Sunday Schools throughout the Parish.

Oct. 23—Intimation received from the Trustees of the late Mr. James Gammel of Countesswells of a Legacy of £100 on behalf of the poor of the parish.

1828 Jan. 26—Salary of Precentor at this time, £3 a year.

1829 Dec. 27—Body of a female found on Tuesday last, not having been indentified buried at expense of Session.

Dec. 29—Collection which had been made on behalf of the Highlands not being required for that purpose to be handed over to the Royal Infirmary, Aberdeen.

1853 Aug. 27—Legacy of £200 bequeathed by the late Rev. William Paterson, Schoolmaster of Nigg, received. The terms of the bequest were :—To the Kirk-Session of Banchory-Devenick, two hundred pounds as a fund, the interest of which is to be paid to a Schoolmaster whose schoolhouse shall be situated conveniently for the fishing villages of Findon and Portlethen, and house adjacent to the turnpike road. He must also be qualified to teach reading, writing, arithmetic, and navigation, and if Latin so much the better ; be patronized by the Proprietors of Portlethen, Findon, Lands adjacent to the Turnpike, and the Minister of the Parish ; and teach gratis scholars of name of Paterson and Merser, whose parents are poor, and these failing a few poor scholars recommended by the Kirk-Session.

1863 March 1—£17 11s. 3d. collected throughout the parish on behalf of the Lancashire Operatives.

1867 Nov. 17—Intimation made of a legacy of £500 being left to the Session by the late Alexander Calder, son of James Calder, who, on 20th December, 1801, handed over a like sum for behoof of the poor of the parish.

CHURCH LAWS, &c.

1712 Aug. 3—Enacted that all pariochiners placing gravestones in the churchyard should pay ten marks scots. Outsiders and strangers to pay eight punds scots for the same priviledge.

1719 July 26—Act for preventing the running of goods was read, and the people suitablie exhorted.

Aug. 9—Act to prevent the running of goods specially read at Portlethen, where the practice was most to be feared.

1722 July 15—Act read against prophaneness, &c. Intimation also made to the salmon fishers that there were spys to be sett on them, and that, in case of prophaneing the Sabbath day by fishing, they would be proceeded against by Sessions, Presbyteries, and the Civil Judge.

1727 May 21—This day, at the desire of the Elders, it was intimated from Pulpit that no persons whatsomever should reside in this Parish without being clothed with sufficient certificates from the parishes they come from.

1728 June 2—Intimation made that no contract of marriage or publick sessioning should be held on Saturdays, and that, conform to an old practice in this parish, and resolution of Session anent it, those who contract on the Sabbath days morning privately shall pay one pound scots to the poor's box besides the usuall dues.

1729 July 13—Congregation advertised to beware of meeting in crowds on the Sabbath day, particularily upon the waterside, and likewise to beware of fishing late upon Saturday's night. Also to avoid drinking on the Sabbath day to excess, and in great companies, and of going in throngs to the seaside for diversion: with certification, &c.

1730 March 22—New Parish boat being required, contract entered into for its construction. 2/6 scots required from each tenant, and 2/- from each other person within the respective families on the North Side. Due intimation made of this act, that so the recusants, if any should be, may be prosecute before the Judge competent.

1731 March 7—Warning given to young persons in the parish to beware of night meetings in their neighbours houses, under pretence of mirth and drawing of valentines.

1799 Oct. 6—Former resolution against allowing marriages on Saturdays rescinded, on the Bridegroom giving an undertaking that the whole marriage company should be dismissed by 11 o'clock at night at farthest. No penny weddings to be permitted within the Parish on Saturdays, nor any other marriage at which money is received for either meat or drink.

1805 Nov. 3—As various bad consequences flow from Raffles, all intimations of such meetings either by the public crier or otherwise, at the Parish Church and Church of Portlethen, prohibited.

1827 Nov. 11—The holding of raffles within the Parish strictly prohibited in all time coming.

1839 Sep. 27—Shooting at marriages forbidden.

1859 Jan. 23—The crying of public roups and other intimations in the Churchyard after divine service strictly prohibited ; the beadle in future to attach such notices to the pillar at the gate.

ANCIENT FORM OF OATH.

"By the Great and Dreadful God, the searcher of all hearts, and the just and Righteous Judge of all the world, from whose all-seeing eye nothing can be hid, and who will bring to light all those who swear falsely.

By His name, and as I shall answer to Him in the great day of judgment, and as I would wish to escape the visible judgments of God in this world, and His eternal judgments in the world to come. And as I would wish God to prosper me, and not blast all that I take in hand through the rest of my life and as I would wish to die a comfortable death under the sense of God's favour, and not in the rage of an awakened and tormenting conscience, I shall declare the truth." . . . .

OFFENCES AGAINST THE CHURCH, &c.

1710 July 16—Dilation given in by the Minister, who did himself, the Last Lord's Day, see the salmon fishers in the garth of Pitfoddels prophaning the Lord's Day by their scandalous fishing before sun sett. The whole of these Fishermen ordered to be summoned for next Lord's Day. Compearing then they all denied, but, being unable to purge themselves, were amerciat in ten pounds scots of penalty each

1711 Jan. 28—Andrew Troup convicted of prophaning the Lord's Day, in carrying a burden of ale, in a barrow, from the Bridge of Dee to his own house after sunrising, mulcted in ten punds scots, and to appear before the Pulpit next Lord's Day, in the sight of the congregation and profess sorrow for the scandal.

Aug. 19—John Knolls having confessed guilt of horrid and abominable swearing, ordered to go and ask his master's pardon, thereafter to pay a monetary penalty and appear before the congregation as a penitent.

1712 Feb. 24—Penalty for antenuptial fornication, five punds scots, with sundry appearances in pillory.

1713 May 31—Agnas ffrazer and Agnas Cowly ordained to appear before the congregation for scolding and beating one another.

1714 July 10—Magdalen Walker guilty of trelapse in fornication ordained by the Session to appear befor the congregation nine Lord's days in sackcloath, being befor amerciat in the sum of thirty pounds scots money.

Sep. 12—Two parties, against whom a *fama* had been lodged, compeared before the Session and denied guilt, offering to take the oath of purgation in face of the congation. As the minister reported he had known persons stand as firmly resolved to purge themselves of what they afterwards were found guilty, it was ordained that they should appear on the pillory one Lord's Day, to see if their conscience might be awaked. Session being informed that Elspet Craig is still keeping house with Robert Stuart, notwithstanding she had been told by the officer to remove, ordained that she should be again warned to remove, with this caveat—that, if they do not separat against next Session day, the Session would take care they may be put into the hands of the Justices of peace, to be punished as scandalous and profane persons.

1716 July 1—Intimation made of the deposition of Mr. Gilbert Ramsay, late Incumbent att Dyce; Mr. Alex. Gray, late Incumbent att Footie; and Mr. Richard Maitland, late Incumbent att Nigg, for their being accessary to, goeing along with, and haveing a hand in, the late horrid rebellion raised by the Earle of Marr and his adherents, and parishioners exhorted no more to look upon them as ministers, they haveing shamefully and scandalously deserted the Protestant Cause.

July 8—Deposition of other 3 ministers intimated.

1717 Sep. 29—Minister read list of excommunicated persons within the bounds of the Synod of Aberdeen, which embraced 12 for habitual adultery, 2 for uncleanness, and 4 for apostacie to popery and contumacie. These parties were subsequently prayed for and people exhorted.

1718 April 6—Robert Stuart and Elspet Craig, who had previously confessed guilt of ante-nuptial fornication and ordered to appear upon the pillory, reported to be of very ill agreement, the said Robert striking and beating the said

Elspet. Session judging their further appearance in publick would be to no edification, appointed them to lie under the scandal for some time, the Minister to deal with their consciences in private, and the Elder of the bounds to have a narrow eye over them.

1718 June 1—John Craig and Alexander Main being summoned to this diet, confessed themselves guilty of scolding and using bitter words on the Sabbath day some weeks before. After being severely rebuked and admonished they were dismissed.

1719 June 7—Four Salmon Fishers confessing to their prophanation of the Lord's Day, by fishing in the afternoon, were severely rebuked and admonished.

Aug. 16—John Mitchell rebuked in public, and compearing before the Session, his knowledge was found weak and he also appeared very stupid. Dismissed till he gets more knowledge.

1720 July 31—Three salmon fishers publickly rebuked for fishing about sunset on the Sabbath Day.

Dec. 25—Intimation made that one Elizabeth Chrystie is fugitive from the discipline of Old Machar, and people exhorted to give notice if they knew of her.

1723 Dec. 1—Five farmers summoned to this dyet compeared, and being interrogat whether they were in John Mill's house drinking, on the Sabbath day some time agoe. Answered they were, but that they neither stayed or drank to give any offence, that they went straight from the kirk on purpose to take a refreshment and congratulat the said John Mill, who had his daughter married the week before ; that they went sober there, having gone out of the kirk, and came as sober away as a sober man would doe if upon the road or at home refreshing himself; whereupon they were rebuked, and charged at least with the appearance of evil and misspending precious time sett apart for another use. . . . . They appeared again on a subsequent Sunday, when they were again rebuked and seriously exhorted, and they engaged to be more watchfull and circumspect for the future.

1728 April 14—Janet Coly, in Milltoun of Finnan, dilated for scolding at the Church gate when the congregation was dismissing, and thereby giving great scandall. The Session, considering the same, did judge her highly censurable and ordered her to be summoned.

Apr. 28—According to resolution arrived at last Lord's Day the said Janet Coly appeared this day before the congregation and was rebuked.

1729 Nov. 30—Complaint having been given in against five parties for going to a tavern to drink on Sabbath afternoon, they are ordered to be summoned.

Dec. 7—These parties compeared, and acknowleged they had gone home with a servant newly entered to service in that house, a practice that had obtained hitherto in this place; but declared they had not been guilty of any extravagance, and, if they had known it would have given offence, they would have forborne it, promising wt'all to forbear the like practice in time to come; whereupon the Session considering their youth, and that their reputation hitherto had been entire, they judged it proper to deal as tenderly with them as could consist with edification, and agreed to sist in a sessional rebuke, with certification, &c.; and to intimate the same from the Pulpit, in order to discourage the like practices for the future. Accordingly they were sharply admonished and dismissed.

1730 Aug. 16—The Session being informed that some of Pittfodles Tennents had yoked their horses on Sabbath evening last, and being likewise informed that they were in a manner forced to do so, did agree that they be rebuked from Pulpit, and advertised in general, to guard against such practices in time to come, with certification, &c.

Aug. 23—This day the Minister did give the Sabbath Breakers a generall admonition.

Dec. 20—Minister exhorted the congregation not to give in bad money by way of collection.

1731 March 28—An adulterer, having appeared twice before the Presbytery and nine times before the congregation in sackcloth, was to-day absolved.

May 16—Minister intimated the sentence of greater excommunication against Alexander Leiper, in the Parish of Nig, for blasphemy.

Oct. 3—It was reported that a great many were in yoke with horses upon the windy Sabbath night before it was dark. The Session, considering the multitude of those that were guilty, and the great temptation they were under, judged it most for edification that the minister give them a general Rebuke some Sabbath from Pulpit, and sharply admonish them to beware of such practices in time coming: with certification, &c.

Oct. 17—This day the Minister did, conform to Session's appointment, sharply admonish those who had been guilty of leading corn on Sabbath's evening.

1732 Aug, 27—James Williamson and William Malcom, who had been guilty of an abuse at a marriage in this Church, by fyring Pistols in time of worship, called before the Session, sharply rebuked and promising to amend their behaviour were dismissed.

1734 Nov. 17—The Minister from pulpit admonished the inhabitants on the North side of the Dee, especially the younger sort, to behave more gravely and decently in going in and out of the boat.

1736 July 4—It was reported that Jas. Coly was now returned, who had some time ago gone away in company with one Margaret Fraser and had left his wife and children in a starving condition. The Session considering this as a grievous scandall appointed him to be summoned to the next diet.

July 25—James Coly was called but compeared not. Elizabeth Dove his wife craving access to the Session declared that her husband had been some time in the South country, and at his return stayed with her 8 or 10 days, but upon his being summoned to the Session had again fled, she knows not to where. . . . .

1737 Nov. 20—John Ellis and Elizabeth Freeman, both residing in Cookstown, compeared, and being interrogate anent their strife and scurrilous language to each other, they were exhorted to forgive each other and live in peace together in time coming, and to appear at next diet in order to receive a rebuke.

1738 Jan. 8—Three men and two boys in Nigg dilated for Sabbath breaking in drawing a fishing coble from Legart up to the water of Auchunies upon Sabbath last, and that about the time of the people convening to Church after the ringing of the second bell.

They were afterwards rebuked before the congregation.

1738 Jan. 22—A White Fisher in Findon acknowledged his rashness in scandalizing some of the Elders, but declaring his grief was allowed off with a rebuke.

March 19—Minister again exhorted the congregation to the faithful observation of the Sabbath day; and especially the Salmon Fishers, and advertised them that he himself, together with some of the Session, according to a former appointment, were to watch this night at the water until twelve o'clock to see if any would be so wicked as to fish before that time.

April 2—Nine members of the Session watched at the several salmon fishings till 12 o'clock at night.

April 16—Elders and Deacons again appointed to watch, the Minister himself agreeing to watch the Garth of Pitfoddells and Castleheugh.

April 23—Two of the Elders reported that when watching at the Bridge of Dee, Alexander Main and Isabel Pirie had given them abusive language. The Minister appointed to write the Minister of Nigg to prosecute them before his Session.

May 7—For the last two months process proceeded against salmon fishers for Sabbath breaking by commencing fishing operations before 12 o'clock at night. Being found guilty they were ordered to compear before the congregation on the penitential seat, but failing to do so the Presbytery resolved to excommunicate them.

1739 Jan. 14—Names of the following persons who had been excommunicated by their respective Presbyteries read from Pulpit, viz.:—Robertson, in the Presbytery of Kirkcudbright; Strang, in Edinburgh; and Dog, in Aberbrothick, and the people suitably exhorted.

1739 May 6—The Minister intimated that he was obliged to wait upon the General Assembly to meet this week, and therefore hoped the people would behave themselves decently in his absence and carefully keep the Sabbath day.

1740 June 29—Dilation given in against Alexander Mill, one of the Deacons, that, upon last Sabbath, he had his mill at work before ten o'clock at night, and that four witnesses saw the same. The said Alexander alleged that his boy that guides the mill had set her on too soon, without his direction, and that he was sorry that it was done at all but that he should take care that the like should not happen again in time coming. The Session taking above into consideration and finding that he had given scandal by such behaviour, and especially that it had given occasion to the Salmon Fishers to make a handle of it to justify their wicked practice of fishing on the Sabbath day, delayed any further procedure against him till further, in order to be ripely advised thereanent.

Sept. 7—The Minister intimated that Alexander Mill, formerly a Deacon, was now deposed from that office. This day also he was sharply rebuked before the congregation.

1742 Jan. 3—Elizabeth Kemp, who had given birth to an illegitimate child at the burnside of Murtle, being in a dying state her deposition taken by the Session, who exhorted the poor wretch and set a guard over her till the sheriff be acquainted.

Dec. 26—The Minister represented that in regard Mr. Troup, *non jurant* Minister at Muchalls, had made an encroachment into this Parish by preaching at the Chapel of Portlethen, he was resolved to prosecute him for the same, and that in the meantime he was to lay the affair before the Presbytery of Aberdeen.

1743 May 29—Delinquent being resident in Aberdeen the Clerk was ordered to go there and get him to come out. The man promised to accompany, but under pretence of going for his hat and wig had absconded himself, whereupon the Clerk took a letter to the Provost, who promised to secure him if ever he appeared again.

1745 May 26—A female exposed child, found by two gentlemen on horseback, taken charge of by the Session, given out by them to nurse, and baptised "Joanna Carolina Marykirk" in respect to the gentlemen who had been the means of preserving her life.

> Entries of the aliment paid for the support of the child regularly occur in the subsequent years.

1750 Feb. 18—Hugh Ross in Kemhill appointed and chosen collector for uplifting the fines of Sabbath Breakers, and the Officer appointed to ring the bell every Sabbath night at twelve o'clock at night for letting the salmon fishers know when to begin to work. Intimation made to congregation accordingly.

Sep. 2—The Minister represented that a *fama* had been spread in the neighbourhood that several gentlemen had come out from Aberdeen, upon Sunday, 29th July, before sermon, and after spending a great part of the day there, without repairing to any publick place of worship, and in their return home, about 7 or 8 o'clock at night, were guilty of several indecencies and gross profanation of the Lord's Day, at different places in the Parish and upon the Highway; such as behaving uncivilly to several women, throwing one another over among the corns, pulling a woman off her horse, beating and striking a young man on the road to the effusion of his blood, whereby they gave great evidence either of being taken with liquor, or of an abominable and wicked turn of mind, in openly disdaining to pay that religious regard to the Holy Sabbath which is due to it, both by the laws of God and man, and that he is informed that their names are [names of one clerk and six merchants in Aberdeen are here given]; and further if the said Gentlemen should deny their being art or part in one or either of the said crimes, that some of them were so publickly committed, that there would be no penury of witnesses to prove the same. The Session taking the above into consideration agreed that a letter should be written and sent to the Kirk Session of Aberdeen to cause summon them to compear before this Session Sunday next and to return a regular execution of their summonds seasonably.

The Gentlemen subsequently compeared and paying a substantial penalty each were allowed off with a sessional rebuke.

1752 April 5—Clandestine marriages strictly prohibited and act read against them.

1767 Dec. 13—Minister warned the people not to bring their dogs to the Church.

1800 July 21—Certain Farmers who permitted horses to be yoked on their Farms last Fast Day ordered to be written warning them of their danger—the Session being determined to enforce the strict observance of such Fast Days.

1806 April 27—Fornication case investigated when witnesses gave evidence as to the proceedings which had taken place at a "Like" held on two consecutive nights on the death of a Farmer's wife.

1834 May 4—A disorderly meeting having been held in a Tavern on Sunday last the keeper of the same ordered to be summoned. He and his wife as also the young men who had taken part in the disorder debarred from admission to ensuing communion.

1834 July 13—Farmer having yoked his cart last Sunday to convey some Travellers on their way to Stonehaven the Session unanimously agreed that such a desecration of the Lord's Day could not be passed over, and therefore ordered the Farmer to be summoned before them.

> Subsequently compearing and expressing regret he was exhorted and dismissed with a sessional rebuke.

1837 March 5—A residenter in Cults having fallen into a state of habitual drunkenness, giving great scandal in the neighbourhood, Minister instructed not to baptize his child until he shall appear and answer to the said *fama*.

> He afterwards appeared and satisfied.

1839 March 31—Session had under consideration the behaviour of George . . . and resolved that application be made to the Fiscal to secure the Peace of Society and prevent the desecration of the Sabbath as regards the said George . . .

1840 Dec. 6—A family of suspicious character having arrived in the Parish, Officer ordered to cite the man to give an account of himself.

1851 May 4—Six communicants ordered to be written that reasons for their irregularity in attendance on ordinances must be furnished before admission to the communion.

Oct. 25—A Whitefisher in Findon was accused of invading one of the Elder's houses whilst in a state of intoxication, and of using blasphemous language, and laying hands on some of the Elder's family.

> Case deferred.

SPECIAL SERVICES AND INTIMATIONS.

1708 April 2—Said day being the anniversary of the Passion of the Sone of God special Passion sermon preached.

Aug. 26—Fast observed for the victory over the ffrench at Audenard, on 11th July, by Prince Eugene and the Duke of Marlborough.

1709 Jan. 30—This being the dismal anniversary day of the Barbarous Murder of the Royal Martyr, King Charles 1st, of ever blessed memory, sermon suitable to the occasion preached.

Feb. 17—Fast observed for reduction of Ghent and Bruges, &c.

1710 May 28—This being the anniversary day of the descent of the Holy Ghost, called Pentecost or Whytsunday, Mr. Robert Jamieson preached a sermon suitable to this ffeastivall.

Nov. 5—To-day being the anniversary of the mornfull deliverance from the gunpowder plott by the detection thereof, special sermon preached.

1714 March 21—Intimation made that ffriday next being the anniversary day of the dolorous passion of the son of God it is ordained to be religiously observed and all servil work discharged, and the people exhorted to repair to the publick worship of God and to hear a Passion sermon preached.

1716 June 7—This being the day appointed for solemn and publick thanksgiving to Almighty God for suppressing the unnatural rebellion begun by the Earle of Marr and his adherents, the minister lectured and preached suitably to the occasion, on psal. 127 : 1 : 2 & 3 vrs'.

1716 Nov. 11—All the people in Hilldontree, Mains of Banchorie, and Kirktown desired to attend catechising att the ordinary time of meeting on the Sabbath day, and att the ringing of the bell, the one half of them on tuesday and the other half on thursday.

Dec. 2—Minister preached. There was no lecture, the day being far spent before the people could meet, it having cost many men much work before they could water the boat and break the ice.

1717 March 24—Day of humiliation intimated because of abounding sin, the illness of the season, and a feared invasion from Sweden.

April 28—There was no sermon, the Minister falling suddenly ill of a fitt of the Gravell on the Sabbath morning.

Nov. 17—The Minister by appointment of the Presbyterie preached att ffootie in the afternoon, but, beginning early, preached here in the morning. This day Mr. Farquhar, Minister att Nigg, preached att Portlethen to supplie the Minister's place there.

> Mr. Farquhar, who was formerly Minister of Tyrie, succeeded Mr. Richard Maitland as minister of Nigg, and died 23rd December, 1756, in his ninety-first year. In his younger days he possessed herculean strength, on account of which he was frequently employed in preaching churches vacant, which had been in possession of the Episcopalians. "On one occasion of this kind the only Presbyterian gentleman in the parish dissuaded him from doing so, as it might cost him his life. He ordered the bell to be rung, as it stopped he sallied forth, and found two fellows pommelling the bellman, on which he seized the assailants, knocked their heads

together, and, having done so, stood alongside till the bell was rung out. He then invited the onlookers to follow him into the church, where he had a message for them, ' such as they had never heard before.' And tradition adds, they were so pleased with his services that they crowded round at his departure, inquiring when he would return again."— (Woodrow's *Corresp.* and Scott's *Fasti.*)

1717 Dec. 1—Visitation of families not observed because the water could not be crossed.

1718 Jan. 26—Weather so stormy that the people have now crossed the water three Sabbath days on the ice.

1720 June 23—This day being appointed for the visitation the Presbytrie mett at this place. Lect. ordinary, Heb. 10-38. The visitation was gone about in common form and the Minister approven.

> At these Presbyterial visitations the Minister was put upon trial, his Elders and parishioners being questioned whether they had fault to find with his life, doctrine and manner of discharging his pastoral duties, and "whether he was a dancer, carder, or dicer." The interrogatories proceeded :— Is he proud or vain glorious? Is he greedy, worldly, or an usurer? Is he contentious, a brawler or fighter, and saw ye him ever drink healths? (Abridged from Steuart of Pardovan's *Collections*). If the answers were satisfactory the Minister was approven, but if the reverse a libel invariably followed.

Dec. 16—Fast observed because of the plague in a near and neighbour nation. The Officer got a collection for burying the poor according to appointment of the Session on extraordinary days.

1722 April 15—This being the seedtime there is ane intermission of examination.

1722 June 21—Fast observed on account of the plot against the King, the illness of the weather and abounding sin.

> This fast refers to the discovery of a Jacobite Plot against George I., for complicity in which Atterbury, Bishop of Rochester, was banished for life.

Aug. 4—The Minister did not lectur att Banchorie, the water being so great that none could pass, and the burns in the month impassable except on horseback, so that no people either from the south or the north part were present. No session for want of Elders.

Dec. 23—Minister preached but did not lecture, there being only about 40 persons in all the congregation, because no passage through the water, nor any travelling in the mount. The storm was such and the deepness of snow so great that, as the people affirmed, the like had not been seen for twenty years past.

1724 Jan. 5—Minister preached at Banchorie but did not lecture. The convention was so thin, the wind being great, that none could cross the water in the boat. And essaying to goe to Portlethen after sermon, in order to preach there, afternoon, he (the minister) took horse, and the rather there was a child to baptise there, but, after he had rode a piece of ground, was forced to alight, not being able to sitt on horseback, and returned home.

May 24—Intimation made of examination of the families of Easter and Middle Ardoe this evening at 4 o'clock at the ringing of the bell, they being hard by and near the kirk.

1727 Jan. 1.—No sermon by reason of the Minister's sickness. March 26—The Minister (Mr. John Maitland) being called by death, Mr. Alexander Shank, Minister at Drumoak, preached.

1728 Sep. 1—No sermon this afternoon by reason public worship had been delayed longer than ordinary upon the account of a burial.

1730 Nov. 26—Fast observed upon account of the progress of popery and abounding of immorality and atheism.

1736 July 11—Intimation made to the congregation that as the Holy Sacrament could not be conveniently administered here this season such as feel inclined may repair to Maryculter.

1737 Aug. 7—Minister read from pulpit Act of Parliament anent discovering and bringing to Justice the murderers of Captain Porteous, who had been forcibly taken out of Edinburgh Prison and hanged on a dyer's pole by a lawless mob.

1739 July 8—Minister told them he was a mind to give the sacrament once this year, but could not as yet fix upon the day.

Oct. 28—This being Communion Sunday the services commenced at 9 o'clock.

1740 Oct. 5—Minister lectured only before noon, Luke 18, 31-35, and intermitted a little by singing, and discoursed again from the said verses. Afternoon, no sermon by reason of the coldness of the day.

1746 March 2—Proclamation of His Royal Highness the Duke of Cumberland read from pulpit, warning all persons who had any arms belonging to the Rebels, or concealed any of the Rebels, to deliver them up to a Magistrate or Minister of this Church.

June 26—Thanksgiving observed for the victory obtained at Culloden against the rebells.

July 6—Minister warned, by order of my Lord Ancrum, all

in this Parish who had any arms to deliver them up to him or Ancrum to-morrow's morning.

1746 July 20—Minister intimated that he was very soon to visit the Parish, and that such as had lately come to the parish provide certificates within eight days, not only of their being free of Church censure, but also of their behaviour in time of the late rebellion.

1756 Feb. 1—Fast intimated upon account of sin abounding in the land, and the judgments inflicted on a nation allied to this Kingdom, by an Earthquake some strokes whereof had been felt in this nation as well as in other parts.

> This refers to the great Earthquake of 1755 which overthrew the greater part of Lisbon—the capital and principal seaport of Portugal—and destroyed over 30,000 of its inhabitants.

1767 June 7—No sermon the Minister being sick.

June 28—Minister not being fully recovered there was no sermon, only singing of Psalms, and prayers, baptizing a child.

1773 Nov. 9—Arrangements made for celebrating communion on 13th inst. Given out to buy candles, and ropes to hang them on in the Church on Sunday, £1 4s.

1775 April 16—This day by reason of the very tempestuous day no person came to Church.

1776 Dec. 12—Fast observed for imploring the assistance of Heaven in our war with the rebellious Americans.

1783 June 11—Fast observed on account of the failure of last crop.

1793 April 18—Fast observed on account of the war with France.

1798 Nov. 25—Public Thanksgiving intimated on account of the recent victory obtained at sea, and also for the deliverance of Ireland from invasion and intestine commotions.

> This refers to the victory obtained by Nelson over the French fleet on 1st August, 1798. The action took place in the Bay of Aboukir, and resulted in the blowing up of the French flag-ship, *L'Orient*, with its admiral and crew of 1000 men. Of thirteen French men-of-war nine were captured, and of four frigates only two escaped. For several years previously an organization had been going on in Ireland for the purpose of securing separation from England. Napoleon Buonaparte promised his aid to the insurgents, who, in 1798, broke into open rebellion. Several of the ringleaders were captured, and in the battle of Vinegar Hill the rebel army was routed. A French force of 900 under Humbert, which had landed in Killala Bay in Mayo, was compelled to surrender a month later at Carrick-on-Shannon.

1805 Dec. 5—Public Thanksgiving observed on account of Lord Nelson's victory over the French and Spanish fleets at Trafalgar.

1838 Feb. 25—Congregation assembled in the Schoolhouse, it being almost impracticable to get to the Church in consequence of the snow.

1848 July 9—Day of Humiliation intimated on account of state of the country.

> In England many serious riots took place by a faction calling themselves "Chartists," who, on 10th April, 1848, assembled in thousands on Kennington Common for the purpose of escorting Feargus O'Connor to Parliament with a Petition embodying their demands. Two hundred thousand special constables who had been sworn in, however, held the mob at bay. In Ireland a rising took place under O'Brien, but it was speedily suppressed.

1849 Oct. 18—Day of Humiliation observed on account of the ravages of cholera, and for thanksgiving on account of the late abundant harvest.

Nov. 15—Fast and thanksgiving observed on account of the almost total disappearance of the cholera from the country.

1854 April 26—Day of Humiliation observed on account of the Russian War.

Nov. 26—Intimation given that next Lord's Day would be a day of thankfulness and humiliation before Almighty God—thankfulness for the opportune abundance of the late harvest, humiliation for the sins which have brought upon the nation the calamities of pestilence and war.

1866 March 29—Day of humiliation observed on account of the Cattle Plague.

CHURCH AND PARISH PROPERTY.

1708 Nov. 14—Wm. King to be payed his annual agreement of £3 10s. for maintaining Church watertight in the roof.

1711 July 1—Resolution passed for additional loft being constructed with a view to accommodating the parishioners, who have become so numerous that many have to abide in the Churchyard.

Aug. 26—Loft being now completed, at expense of £300 scots, arrangements made for farming it out for the payment of a crown, or three lib. scots, yearly for every box therein. Anyone sitting therein and not paying this sum to be considered guilty of sacrilege by wronging the poor.

1716 Oct. 21—Given out of the collections 4 libs. scots (6/8 stg.) to Jas. Sutherland for acting as Precentor of Portlethen Chapel from Whitsunday to Candlemas.

1717 Nov. 24—Collector instructed to pay 4 lib. 4s. for a wire guarded window, and the Minister instructed to recover the same from Govell, factor for the lands of Banchorie.

1718 Jan. 5—10/- scots given out of the collection at the chappell of Portlethen for broads to collect with.

Feb. 16—Paid Andrew Walker, Kirk Officer, according to fashion, to buy shoes 16/-.

1721 Jan. 1—£4 4s. given for divoting the roof of the kirk, and the breaches in it made by the great winds so that it was uninhabitable. This work took up 2 men 2 days in casting and 8 horse for leading and also for laying them one the roof, meat and wages.

1728 June 16—Minister reported that the part of the church lying a cove the pulpit being very ruinous insomuch that last Sabbath day the rain poured down upon him in the pulpit, which was not only very uneasy to him but likewise tended to rot the timber of the pulpit, that he understood that it had been usual to repair that small piece of the roof out of the public money, and that accordingly he had procured it to be repaired since their last meeting, and had advanced the money accordingly. The Minister produced the Slater's discharged account of £3 17s. 6d. scots, which was approved and sustained.

June 23—Session considering the most proper way for making an effectual contribution for repairing the kirk-boat did agree that the Schoolmaster and Officer shall go to the severall towns on the North side of the water who are only concerned to support the P'boat and gather up twenty shill from each plough. And what should be wanting to be made up out of the box till the workman be satisfied.

1728 Nov. 3—Paid Alexander Donald, Mason, for five days' work in repairing the kirkyard dykes, at ten shillings per day, £2 10/- scots.

Nov. 10—To a man for snedding the trees in the church-yard 12/-.

1730 Feb. 15—Given to the Officer three shillings scots for bringing loam from Aberdeen to help a hole in the Church.

1736 Aug. 29—Session considering that the Church Laders are very much abused by their being lent and keept a long time away, and, therefore, in order to prevent this abuse and to recover the money laid out upon them, it was agreed that whoever borrows them in time coming shall pay a penny a day for each of them.

1738 Aug. 13—Paid for a stair to the penitential seat, £1 16/-.

1742 Nov. 14—Given to the Officer for casting and leading Divots to mend holes in the Church 16/-.

1752 Oct. 22—Trees growing in the Churchyard sold for £5 16/- stg.

1760 April 6—Session met before sermon, when found that the School had been broken up last night and the Church box stollen out of it. They appointed the Clerk to go to Aberdeen and get a warrant from the Justices of Peace in order to recover it. £24 scots of reward also offered.

April 13—It was found that the box had been got on Tuesday last, upon the leys opposite to Kirktown's Park, and £2 8/- in farthings therein, with all the papers.

1762 April 4—Presbytery meeting intimated for settling the Minister's moss.

1773 July 8—Given for repairing the midwifes' seat in Church 3/-

1831 Dec. 11—An evil disposed person having pierced the bottom of the Church boat in various places with a gimlet, the Session offer a reward of Two guineas for information so as to convict the delinquent.

1832 March 11—New Church boat procured at cost of £9 10s.

1837 Feb. 26—During the past week Church forcibly entered and many books stolen, 35 of which were afterwards recovered.

Lower Pond
Banchory House.

APPENDIX.

ESTATE OF BANCHORY.

See pp. 17 and 30.

Since the chapter on the lands of Banchory was printed off, Mr. David Stewart, the present proprietor, has been unanimously elected Lord Provost of the city of Aberdeen. At the election of Councillors, which took place on Tuesday, 5th November, 1889, he was returned for the Ferryhill Ward, and it is worthy of note that he polled the largest number of votes of any of the seventeen candidates in the five contested wards. At the Council meeting which took place on the following Friday he was formally installed in office.

This is the second occasion on which the estate of Banchory has provided the city with its chief magistrate—Mr. Robert Cruickshank having, as already noticed, held the appointment for four successive years, beginning in 1693.

Facsimile of the Signature of Provost Cruickshank.

Translation of Charter by King Alexander II., conveying the lands of Banchory-Devenick to the Abbot and Convent of Arbroath (A.D. 1244)—See p. 3.

Alexander, by the Grace of God, king of the Scots, to all upright men of his whole land, safety. Those now living and those to be may know that we have given up forever, to the Abbot and Convent of Arbroath, our land of Banchory-Devenick, to be held and had by the same monks from us and our successors forever within its legal boundaries. By returning an annuity of 100/- (etc.), and by performing the forinsecal service which pertains to the same lands. We also give up to the aforesaid Abbot and Convent the aforesaid land, that they may hold it for all time to come. The attesting witnesses are :—William, Abbot of Cupar; Malcolm, Count of Fyfe; William of Brechin; Robert of Montealtus; Gilbert of Haya; Eustacius of Balliol. At Inverleith, 5th of April, in the 30th year of our king.

Translation of Charter of Banchory-Devenick lands granted to Lord Alan Hostiarius (A.D. 1256)—See page 3.

To all the faithful of Christ, seeing or hearing of the present charter, Walter, by the Grace of God, Abbot of Aberbrothock, and convent of same place, eternal salvation in our Lord. Know all of you, that we have given (etc.) to Lord Alan Hostiarius, Justiciary, our land of Banchory-Devenick, within its legal boundaries and with all its just pertinents. To be held and to be had by the same Alan, and his heirs, or assignees, in return for his homage and service (etc.), as we hold the same land from our lord, the king, for confirming his claim more peacefully, more freely, and more honourably. He and his heirs (etc.) paying to our successors 3 marks of silver, and giving to our lord, the king, such forinsecal service as pertains in all things to the said land. In proof of which circumstance we have caused to be appended the authentic seal of our Chapter, our Chapter being witness. In the year of Grace 1256, on 20th April, at Aberbrothock.

Translation of Charter of Banchory-Devenick to William of Melgdrum (A.D. 1333)—See pp. 4, 5.

In the year of Grace 1333, on the day of Venus, next after the feast of St. Martin in the winter, at the monastery of Aberbrothock, it was thus agreed among the religious men :—Dompnus Galfridus, by the grace of God Abbot of the said monastery and convent of the same, on the one part, and William of Melgdrum, son of the late John of Melgdrum, on the other part; that the Abbot and Convent of said monastery, with unanimous consent, agreed to give over, to be held in feu, to the said William and his heirs, in return for his homage and service, their whole land of Banchory-Devenick, with pertinents. To be held and to be had by the said William and his heirs from the same Abbot and convent and their successors to be held in feu forever, with all liberties (etc.). And the said William, during the whole period of his life, shall pay to the same religious men yearly for the same land 6 marks stg. (etc.). But the heirs of the said William shall pay yearly to the Abbot and convent of the aforesaid monastery for the time being, for the afore-mentioned land, 40/- stg. (etc.). And over and above, both the same William and his heirs shall be held bound to pay to our lord, the king, 100/- yearly for the said land. And shall make payment in the neighbouring court of Aberdeen for the same, and shall render the other services and burdens which are incumbent, or in future may be incumbent, on the said land. But the said William or his heirs shall in nowise sell, impignorate, assign, or give over to be held in feu, or alienate the said land in any way whatever without the special licence of the said religious men ; that, if they do so, they shall lose all claim to the said land *ipso facto*. In proof of which circumstance a copy of the present writing remains in the custody of the said William and his heirs, and to it has been appended the common seal of the Chapter of said religious men. But the other copy remains in the custody of the same religious men, consigned under the seal of the said William.

Translation of the Charter of William of Meigdrum (A.D. 1346)—See p. 5.

To all who may see or hear of this indentatum writing, Galfridus, by Divine permission Abbot of Aberbrothock and convent of the same place, wishes eternal salvation in our Lord. Since our predecessors, weighing the advantage to the monastery by feu and tailzie, infefted a noble man, the late Lord Alan Hostiarius, for himself and his heirs begotten of his body, in the whole of our land of Banchory-Devenick, with the pertinents, under the vice-countship of Aberdeen into a free barony, so that the late Lord Alan and his heirs should pay from it yearly to our lord, the king, 100/- stg., and the Abbot and convent of Aberbrothock such other valuation as is contained in his infeftment. And the said late Alan, to our prejudice and contrary to the tenor of his infeftment, has conceded and alienated to other persons the said land with its pertinents without consent of the Abbot and convent aforesaid, contrary to his rights; the said injury and grievance being brought upon our convent to its prejudice having been conceived and understood by our predecessors and by us; the said land, with its pertinents, as it belongs to us by the whole remedies of right, we hold confiscated so far as concerns it with its pertinents, so we rightfully reclaim it by escheat. Which land indeed, with its pertinents, being reclaimed by our good advice, weighing well that we cannot immediately remove the holders, and at the same time the masters, from the same land at present, and weighing with competent deliberation and solemn attention the advantage of our monastery, considering also the faithful service, advice, and assistance of our beloved and faithful William of Melgdrum, son of the late John of Melgdrum, master of the same often-paid and to be paid to us and our said monastery, by the unanimous consent of our whole chapter we have given, granted, and by the present writing confirmed, to the aforesaid William of Melgdrum in return for his homage and service our whole land of Banchory-Devenick, with its pertinents. To be held and had by the same William and his heirs begotten and lawfully to be begotten of his body. Thus freely (etc.). Then also the said William and his heirs rendering to our foresaid lord, the king, the service due and usual for such land, and also paying yearly to our lord, the king 100/- stg.; and to us and our successors in name of confirming his right 20/- stg. (etc.), and over and above paying to our successors homage and service. But the said William and his heirs shall in noways sell the said land. In proof of all which we have caused the common seal of our chapter to be publicly affixed to one copy of the present duplicate writing to remain in the possessions of the said William and his heirs, but the other copy, with the seal of the said William, remains consigned to us and our monastery. Done and given in the same Chapter, on the 17th day of the month of October, in the year of grace 1346, the said Chapter being witness.

Description of Lands in Mr. Thomson's Deed of Entail— See p. 23.

"All and whole the Lands and Barony of Banchory, comprehending the Towns Lands and Mains of Banchory, Manour place of Banchory. The Town and Lands of Little Banchory-Devenick, with the houses, biggings, yards, parts, pendicles, and pertinents of the same, as also all and whole The Towns and Lands of Tollohill, Tillyhouses, Broadgreens, over and neither Brandsmyres, and Bridges of Brandsmyres: The Town and Lands of Hilldowntree, Pyketillam, with the houses and pertinents of the said Town and Lands of Stonedykes, upper and neither half thereof, with these parts and portions of the saids Lands, formerly called Banchory, Haughhead, and Berryhillock, comprehending also the crofts called Braeside and Bowbutts, together with the Mill of Banchory, adjacent to the said Lands of Hilldowntree, with two other mills, built upon the said Lands by the deceast Robert Cruickshank of Banchory, sometime Provost of Aberdeen, called the old and new Mills of Banchory,*

---

* In the *Macfarlane MSS.*, written in 1725, it is stated that "the laird of Banchory has the only milne which is on the whole water of the Dee."

with the mill Lands, multures, Suchen Sequels, and knaveships of the same, and privileges and pertinents thereof, to which the said Robert Cruickshank, or his Predecessors, or Successors had right, all lying within the Parish of Banchory-Devenick, Diocie of Aberdeen, and Sheriffdom of Kincardine, together with the whole houses, biggings, yards, mosses, muirs, Meadows, Lofts, Crofts, Parts, pendicles, and pertinents of the said haill Lands, Mills, Mill Lands, and others above specified, together also with the whole Salmon Fishings upon the water of Dee belonging to the said haill Lands, and with the fishing from the mouth of the Burn of Leggart, to the tenements sometime possest by James Brands, afterwards by Alexander Donald, and now by John Calder, conform to use and wont, with the Liberty of Drawing Netts and Labouring the same in manner used and wont. Together with the Teinds, included of the saids whole lands and others above written, and with the privilege of a Dam called the Banchory Dam, competent to the said deceast Robert Cruickshank, or his authors, and with all other privileges whatsomever used . . . . . As also All and Whole the said East Division of the Town and Lands of Balquharn, with the houses, Biggings, Yards, Lofts, Crofts, Mosses, Muirs, Meadows, and whole privileges and pertinents thereof, with the Multures, and Teinds of the same, lying to the East of the King's Highway, being part of the Barony of Portlethen within the Parish of Banchory-Devenick, or Nether Banchory, and Sheriffdom of Kincardine " . . . . .

PARISH CHURCH.

See pp. 38-41.

Additional Particulars Concerning the Old Fabric.

" The present kirk is apparently very old, and is erected on a small mount or rising ground on the south bank of the river. There is a clear spring well close by. On the east end is a weather cock, probably for the satisfaction of the seafaring part of the Congregation. The east gable to the height of the side walls is of the same thickness, but is then bevelled off with a well wrought water table of freestone. The length of the building, outside measure, is 69 feet by 27 feet 7 inches. About 20 years since [1819], the pews were renewed and repaired. A few of the old seats yet remain, much altered. The pulpit, fixed to the south wall, has cut in front I $\overset{M}{}$ G. The Baptismal Basin attached to it is of 1712 pewter, and inscribed 'For the Church of Bachrie.' The pulpit is hung with green cloth.

The fronts of the galleries are now painted white, but appear to have been formerly numbered, the figures being yet visible. In front of the Laird's loft, or in more intelligible language, Thomson of Banchory's Gallery, is painted his coat of arms."*

Arms of Alex. Thomson of Banchory.

* James Logan's *MS. Notes on Churches*, Advocates' Library, Aberdeen.

The following is the State of the Pariochin of Banchory-Davenick with reference to the Church, and the concernes thereof, at 1st January, 1708.

The Stipend payed yearly to the Minister from the Rexive Lands, is as followes, the money being payable at Martimmass, and the victual at the ordinary time of payment of farmes :—   Victual.

	lb.	s.	d.	Bolls	ffl.	pks.	Bls.	f.	peck
Milltoun of Murthil -	13	17	08 meal	1	0	0	0	1	..bere
Newtoun - - -	22	16	08	1	2	0	1	0	..
Bieldside and Cults -	33	06	04	3	3	0	1	1	..
Pitfoddels and Kairnrobin	60	05	08	4	2	0	2	0	..
Banchory - - -	53	00	00	5	0	0	2	2	.
Ardoe - - -	25	10	00	1	3	2	0	3	..
Cookstoun and ffinnon	42	17	08	17	0	2	11	0	..
Portlethen - - -	53	05	00	4	0	0	2	0	..
Achorthies - - -	20	13	04	3	0	0	1	2	..
Glasterberry - -	05	04	02	0	1	1	0	0	..
	330	16	06	42	0	1	23	0	..

The viccarage, or smal Tiends, are valued at 500 merks yearly, but they are not better than 400 merks.

There Belongs to the Church four silver cups made out of the publick Money to serve at the Holy Communion, all of ym weighting fourty seven unces and thirteen drops at 3 lbs 4 shgs. per unce   is £ 153 00 00

For workmanship at 12 shillings per unce -   -   - 28 16 00

In all   £ 181 16 00

The cups are thus inscribed:—"THIS CUP WITH ITS THREE FELLOWES BELONGS TO THE CHURCH OF BANCHORY-DAVENICK, MADE UNDER THE MINISTRY OF MR. IAMES GORDON. ANNO 1704.

It: Yr belongs to the Church, two peuter Basons for serving at the Holy Communion, weighting 7 lbs. and 12 oz. It: a Litle Bason for holding the water when children are baptized. It: a Table Cloath of fine cotton, gifted by the Ministers wife for covering the Table at the Holy Communion: It: a Kirk Bible in 4to. upon wch the Reader officiats.

It: yr is a Mortcloath made upon the publick moe at the beginning of January, 1705 of Black Plush velvet, consisting of seven and a half ells of velvet, at 4 lbs. 10 shillings per ell, wch wt. 18 lbs for 20 unces of black silk for a fringe and lining, and oyr necessaries amounted to seventy punds scots. ffor payment qrof it was ordained yt every person for whose ffunerals it should be employed having lived in the parish, shal pay two merks and if they wer not pariochiners three merks, so long as it could be useful."

What follows has been subsequently added.

Tokens still in use for admission to the communion tables, made of lead, square shaped, and stamped K. N. B. 1739, 1794, and 1835 respectively.

Baptismal Basin and Bracket of brass, presented by Mr. John Blaikie, plumber in Aberdeen, in July, 1838. The Session caused the former to be thus inscribed—

> PRESENTED TO THE CHURCH OF BANCHORY-DEVENICK BY JOHN BLAIKIE, ESQR., WHO, DURING FOUR YEARS RESIDENCE AT ARDOE, HAS TAKEN A LIVELY INTEREST IN EVERY THING THAT CONCERNS THE WELFARE OF THE PARISH.

Two magnificent silver salvers, presented in the autumn of 1845, by the trustees of the deceased Rev. Dr. Morison, in terms of his last Will and Testament, "for the purpose of holding the Sacrament Bread at the Communions."

Large silver wine jug presented by Mrs. Dr. Paul.

The detailed cost of the new Church built in 1822 was as follows:—

James Fraser for mason work,	£240	0 0
John Gowan for wright work, &c.,	429	9 4
Wm. McIntyre for plaster work,	52	15 0
Angus Sutherland for slater work,	42	13 0
George Lamont, Jr., for painting	20	10 0
John Lyon for plans, &c., and superintendence,	27	10 0
	£812	17 4

Tablets in Church.

On south wall there are two handsome marble tablets which are thus inscribed :—

(1.) TO THE MEMORY OF AGNESS FORDYCE OF ARDOE, ONLY DAUGHTER OF THE LATE JOHN FORDYCE, ESQR., WHO DIED ON THE 20th DAY OF NOVEMBER, 1834, AGED 76.

ERECTED BY THE REPRESENTATIVES AND IN COMPLIANCE WITH THE WISH OF THE LATE ANDREW WATSON FORDYCE OF ARDOE, ADVOCATE IN ABERDEEN, WHO DIED ON THE 4th APRIL, 1837, IN THE 26th YEAR OF HIS AGE.

(2.) SACRED TO THE MEMORY OF MARGARET FORBES, WIFE OF MICHIE FORBES ANDERSON, ESQR. OF DEEBANK, WHO DIED OF CHOLERA, AT MADURA IN THE EAST INDIES, ON THE 10th DECEMBER, 1843, IN THE 21st YEAR OF HER AGE.

Letter by James Calder, Merchant, Aberdeen, intimating Bequest of £500 to the Poor of the Parish—See page 238.

ABERDEEN,
5th November, 1801.

Dear Sir,

In a late Interview I had with you I mentioned the outlines of a matter which has long lain near my heart, and which from my earliest years I have had it in view to put in execution whenever Providence should enable me to do so, to wit a Desire to make some effectual and permanent provision for the Poor of the Parish of Banchory-Devenick; a Parish to which I have long felt myself warmly attached. It was there I received the Rudiments of my Education, and there I spent a large portion of innocent and happy days.

APPENDIX.

With Reverence I adore, and with Thankfulness acknowledge the kindness of that Supreme Being who has hitherto not only amply provided for me and my numerous Family, but has so uniformly favoured with success the Mercantile Transactions in which I have been engaged as to enable me at this period of my Life, without inconvenience to my Business, or Injury to those of whom he has committed to me the Charge, to realize what has so long been my ardent wish, to evince my Gratitude to my Creator for his constant Goodness to me, and to discharge one of the most important Duties I owe to that Society of which I am a Member, by setting apart a portion of the Property which he has been pleased to bestow on me, for the Support and Relief of the indigent and distressed of my Fellow Creatures.

With this view, and impressed with these Sentiments, it is my intention to establish a Fund for the benefit of the Poor of the Parish of Banchory-Devenick to the extent of Five Hundred Pounds Sterling, to be settled for them in the name and under the management of its Kirk-Session, as sole and Perpetual Trustees for the Administration thereof. The Money will be ready against next Term, the 20th December, therefore I think it proper to give them this early Intimation that they may be looking out for good and sufficient Security on which to place it. If the Town of Aberdeen would take it I think the Money could not be in better hands, the security is unexceptionable, and being allotted for a charitable purpose its magistrates might be induced to keep it, and allow the legal Interest of the Country, even in times when Money may not be so scarce as at present; but I do not mean to dictate to the Kirk-Session, they will, I doubt not, settle this Donation in a safe and judicious manner, and when so done it will serve as a permanent Fund in all time coming, applicable to the following purpose, and unalienable to any other, that is to say:—The Interest or annual Produce of it to be divided among the Poor belonging to and residing in the Parish of Banchory-Devenick. Under this description I include all such as the Minister and other Members of Session from their knowledge of them consider as deserving or entitled to aid from the Parish Funds, without regard to Age, to Sex, or to Religious Persuasions.

Permit me here to observe, without recommending any one description of Poor in preference to another, that, in Parishes where there is such an extent of Sea Coast, melancholy opportunities for the exercise of Sympathy and Benevolence frequently occur. When such occasions present themselves, I venture to hope that those whom I have appointed administrators of this Charity will not overlook the Widows and young Children of that useful Class of Men. I mean the Fishers, who daily hazard and sometimes lose their lives in the prosecution of their lawful Employment, which, although it procures the Necessaries and also the Luxuries of Life to Society in general, seldom renders its Followers independent or even easy.

The payment of the Interest of this Fund will probably be annual, and in order to give the least possible trouble to all concerned, the division of the produce of it may be so also. About the end of the year and during the inclemency of Winter, the necessities of the Poor press hardest upon them and their Wants are then most severely felt. I should think Christmas, or as early a Period as convenient immediately after, a very seasonable time for the Distribution; and as Charity when divided and sub-divided too much, does not answer the purpose of effectually relieving those who are objects of it, I could wish in the Distribution of this sum, which I have been enabled to bestow in aid of the Poor, that not less than Twenty Shillings per Annum should be given to any Individual; and where there is a Family of young Children, not less than Forty Shillings per Annum.

What I have said regarding the time of Distribution, and the Sums to be given to each, is not to be considered as binding upon the Members of the Kirk-Session, being only hinted as matter of opinion, or rather expressive of a Wish. It is by no means my Intention to confine them to any particular period or mode of division, their own Judgment will direct them according to the situation of times, and existing circumstances. Having appointed them sole and perpetual

Trustees of this my Donation, I have the fullest confidence in them that they will manage it with Fidelity and Discretion, so as to render it as generally useful in the Parish as the nature and extent of it will admit. If so the Will and the Intention of the Donor will be most completely answered.

That the Almighty may be pleased to favour you, the Members of your Session, and the people of whom you have the charge, with abundance of temporal Prosperity, and afterwards with Eternal Felicity, is the fervent Wish of,

Dear Sir,
Your affectionate Friend,
(Signed) JAMES CALDER.

THE REVEREND GEORGE MORISON,
Minister of Banchory-Devenick.

Disposition of Saint Devenick's Bridge, Cults, in favour of the Kirk-Session of Banchory-Devenick for behoof of the Parish (1846)—See pp. 56-7.

"We the Reverend Doctor Duncan Mearns, Professor of Divinity in the University and King's College of Aberdeen, and Francis Edmond, Esquire, Advocate in Aberdeen, the only Trustees and Executors of the deceased Reverend George Morison, D.D., late Minister of the Gospel at Banchory-Devenick, under his Trust Disposition and Deed of Settlement, dated the fifth day of July, Eighteen hundred and thirty seven, and recorded in the Books of Council and Session, the twenty-fourth day of July, Eighteen hundred and forty-five, Considering that the said Doctor George Morison, by his said Trust Disposition, Gave, Granted, Alienated, Assigned and Disponed from him, his heirs, executors and Successors, to, and in favour of us, or to such of us as should accept, and to the Survivor of us and to such other person or persons, as we or the acceptor or survivor should assume, and to the heirs of the last survivor of the said Trustees, named or to be assumed, but in Trust only, for the uses, ends and purposes specified and contained, or to be specified and contained in any writing or writings under his hand, the whole heritable and moveable property, subjects, estate and effects, which then belonged to him, the said Doctor George Morison, or which should happen to pertain, and belong, or be due and owing to him at the time of his death. Farther considering that the said Doctor George Morison, by his Deed of Settlement dated the nineteenth day of November, Eighteen hundred and forty, and recorded in the Books of Council and Session the twenty-fourth day of July, Eighteen hundred and forty-five, ordained and appointed that his Trustees should as soon as convenient after his death, make over to the Kirk-Session of the Parish of Banchory-Devenick, the Bridge erected by him for the accommodation of the Parish called Saint Devenick's Bridge, requesting them, as he thereby requested them the said Kirk-Session, that they would as far as in them lay preserve it from injury and keep it in repair. And seeing that the said Doctor George Morison died on the thirteenth day of July last, and that we are now fully vested in his whole heritable and moveable estate, Therefore we do hereby Dispone, Assign, and Make over to and in favour of the Reverend William Paul, Minister of the said Parish of Banchory-Devenick, George Shepherd, Farmer at Cairnrobin, James Keith, Farmer at Causie Port, George Barclay, Builder at Cults, Charles Alexander Ewen, Schoolmaster at Portlethen, James Duncan, Farmer at Tilly-hows, Alexander Hatt, Farmer at Haughton of Bieldside, John Baird, Farmer at Aquhorthies, and James Shepherd, Farmer at Barclay-hill, being the whole present members of the Kirk-Session of the said Parish, and to their successors in office, the foresaid Bridge erected by the said Doctor George Morison over the River Dee in the said Parish, with the whole privileges and pertinents thereto belonging; and with all right, title and interest which the said Doctor George Morison, or which we as his Trustees had, have or can pretend to the same. With Power to the said Kirk-Session to enter to the possession thereof, and to use and dispose of the same in conformity with the destination thereof by the said Reverend Doctor George Morison. Which Disposition we bind and oblige ourselves, to warrant from our own facts and deeds only. And we consent to the registration hereof, in the Books of Council and Session or others competent for preservation and execution, as effeirs and thereto Constitute, ... our Procurators, &c., In witness whereof.

Subscribed at Old Aberdeen the nineteenth day of June, Eighteen hundred and forty-six.

Arms of the Rev. Dr. Morison.

BRIDGE OF DEE.

See page 130.

Arms of Bishops Elphinstone and Dunbar.

BOUNDARIES OF FINDON AS SETTLED IN 1654.
See page 140.

"Beginning at the east, from a great craig stone on the sea bank, now called the Eastmost March of the said Lands of Torry and Findon, and from the said stone westward to an cairn, now called Elsick's Cairn, lying midway betwixt the Burn of Dynie and the Burn of Coldseas. And from the said cairn westward by an straight line to a pot at the side of the great moss, lying betwixt the Barony of Torry and Barony of Findon, commonly called the Moss of Groundlessmyres, which pot is now called Cairnrobins Pot; and from the said pot in a straight line westward through the said Moss of Groundlessmyres to a cairn on the south-east corner of the Hill of Drumforskie, now and in all time coming to be designed Knockquharney's Cairn. Betwixt the said Knockquharney's Cairn and Cairnrobins Pot there are three lesser pots within the said great moss, which run in an straight line from the said Cairnrobins Pot to Knockquharney's Cairn; and from the said Knockquharney's Cairn westward to a pot within the moss at the foot of the Hill of Drumforskie, now designed Kinaldie's Pot; and from the said designed Kinaldie's Pot to an Cairn on an hard hillock side, within the said moss, now designed Scotstoun Cairn; and from the said cairn westward to a Cairn on a knowhead, now designed Dyce's Cairn; and from the said Dyce Cairn westward to an Cairn, now designed the Cow Cairn; and from the said Cow Cairn to an great Stone at the northmost end of the long caussway, commonly called the Stone of Ardo, or James Mowat's Stone. Which haill meiths and marches, from the said Knockquharney's Cairn to the said Stone of Ardo, run in a straight line. And from the foresaid great stone on the sea bank, the eastmost march of the said haill lands, to the said Stone of Ardo, keeping the marches lying betwixt them above specified. The lands, mosses, muirs, and others, lying south of the said marches, with universal consent and assent of the partys foresaids, and their friends, are hereby declared to be, and in all time coming to remain the property of the foresaid Barony of Findon, lands of Cookston and Badentoy; and that the Laird of Pitfoddles, present Heritor of the said Barony, nor his successors, neither has nor shall crave any property or commonty benorth any of the said meiths or marches, in relation to the said lands of Findon, Cookston, and Badentoy; And Siclike, with consent foresaid, it is hereby declared that the mosses, muirs, and others, lying north of the foresaid marches, Are and Do belong in property to the respective Heritors of the lands of Torry and Banchory; and that, besouth any of the saids marches, none of the foresaid Heritors or their successors, vizt.:—Lairds of Pitfoddles, Monymusk, nor Leslie, neither has nor can crave either commonty or property, in relation to the lands of Torrie and Banchory; and for farther clearing the marches of these parts of the Barony of Torrie, belonging to the Lairds of Pitfoddles and Monymusk, from the lands of Banchory, belonging to the Laird of Leslie, they are as follows :— Beginning at the Burn mouth of Brandsmyres, which fall in the Burn of Hildountree, and so westward, keeping the water draught of the said burn, to an Cairn fornent the eastmost house door of Brandsmyres, now possessed by Henry Herd. The north side of the said Brandsmyres burn belongs in property to the lands of Banchory; and the lands on the south side thereof, to the said cairn, belongs to the lands of Torrie. And from the said Cairn, fornent the said eastmost house door of Brandsmyres, the marches goes southward to a cairn on the north side of the Hill of Drumforskie, now designed Udny's Cairn; and from the said Udny's Cairn southward to a cairn, now called Corsinday's Cairn; and from the said Corsinday's Cairn to an Cairn at the foot of the Hill of Drumforskie and side of the moss, now designed Echt's Cairn. From the Cairn fornent Henry Herd's house door to Echt's Cairn the marches run in a straight line, and the lands, mosses, and others, lying west the said marches, are hereby, with consent foresaid, declared to belong in property to the lands of Banchory, . . . and the lands, mosses, muirs, and others, east of the saids marches, are hereby, with the like consent, declared to belong in property to that part of the Barony of Torrie which pertains to the lands of Pitfoddles and Monymusk." . .

PITFODELS:

Versified Legend of the Baron of Petfoddils quha was Wirriet by his awin cat.

The braif ald Baron is layd in graif,
Jesu be praisit that his saul beis saif!
Na haly priest leint our his hede,
To schrive his sinnis on ane dying bed,
Na beids were tauld, na bell was rung,
Na haly messe was our him sung,
Bot Sanct Devenick heard the piercing prayir
That he raisit to hevin in his bitter despayr,
And gained it ane blissit welcum thair.

The Baron was ane stalwart Knicht
As was evir in armour schene bedicht ;
In mony ane battail he had bene,
And mony ane bluidy deth had sene,
In civill strife, and on forraign strand,
Quhen striving to free the Haly land,
And to plant the banner of the Haly Ruid
Quhair the Cross of Christ on Calvary stuid.
In youthe he was of temper myld,
Thoch that he was ane favorite chyld ;
Bot in manhuidis prime his heart was seired,
By the grieffs that he felt and the dome that he feired.
His ladye was torne frae his syde,
Quhen fuirding the river quhair it was deep and wide ;
And evir thairafter her drouning cry
Stuid the Baron instead of ane lullaby,
As he cursit himselff, on his sleiples bedde,
For refusing to listen to the Laydis redde.

Few yeirs had gone by quhen his onlie sone,
The ymage of hir quha was deid and gone,
Fell deidlie seik and witherit away,
Quhill he passit to the realm of eternall day.—
As the worthlesse weid is evir fund
To cling maist clossely to the grund,
Sa the flouir of fayrest hue and forme,
Is the first upruited by the storme.

For mony ane lang day the Baron did seem
Like ane man that strugglis with ane feirful dreim;
To few he spak, and on fewer he lukit,
And frae nane ane word of denyall he bruikit.
The sone shone bricht, but he culd nocht see
The joy that it lichtit in the puir man's ee;
The flouris put furth thair levis gay,
But thair bewtie for him hed passit away;
The birdis carollit their sweetist sang,
As they sailit the hevin's blue arch alang.—
Na sicht could he see, nor sound could he hear,
Bot was lost on his deidenit ee and ear.
    *   *   *   *   *

O, quha is this that with sic speid
Is rydand on ane fierie steid?
Down, down he comes to the river's syde,
And now he plonges in its tide.
"Arouse ye, Petfoddils, arouse and see
Ane royall herauld quha cums to thee.
To all that it is our kingis command
To tell that it is nobill and guid in the land,
To muster against the reiving Dane,
And drive him back to his schippis again."
    *   *   *   *   *

* * * * *

The Baron sits in his Castill ha',
And his hair is als quhyte as the virgin snaw,
His ene erst sa bright are glasst and dim,
And the strength has fled fra ilk manly limb;
Borne down by age, and toyll, and care,
With na leif heart his greiffs to share,
He livit alane amang living men,
Nor socht their favour nor feud to gain.
The countrie round had cause to bless
The hand that relievit the puir in distress,
And his castell yett stuid wide and free
To all that thair socht herberye;
But frae nane of all that his bountie fed,
Or that under his ruif was sheltered,
Wald the Baron tak heid to ane blessing sincere,
Or to words of thanks or of prayse give ear.
Thoch his deids were guid his words were stern—
Bot for ane living thing ye micht discern
That kindness still sum place of rest
Did hald within his lanely breast;
For frae morning till even on the tabill their satt
Besides him ane grim bot ane favorite catt.

It happenit ance on ane winteris nicht,
Quhen na mone nor starre shed any ray of licht,
That ane ancient man of stalwart forme
Socht shelter frae the cuming storme.
The Pilgrim's scrip and staff he bore,
And the hat decorit with schellis he wore
In eastern land he had travelled far,
And tydings he brocht of the Haly war.

He tauld quhat ladyis of hie degree
Thair livit with the knichts in lemanrie;
He tauld quhat seis of heathen bluid
War shed by the soldiours of the Haly Ruid,
And quhat sangis of joy war raisit quhen
The sepulchre was rescuit frae the Saracen.
Bot quhen that blessit name he spak,
That savit the warld fra sin and wrak,
The Baronis catt raisit ane awsum yell,
That soundit als loud as ane sacring bell;
And the fyir flew fast frae her feirfull ene
Als fierce and als bricht as the levin schene.
The Palmer raisit his staff on hie,
And he strak at the cat with that trustie tree;
Bot scho fled fra the ha' with ane cry of despayr,
And shelter scho socht but na man could tell quhair.
The Palmer exultandlie turnit to the licht,
Bot the brow of the Baron grew black as the nicht.
"Quhat ho! thair my vassals how stand ye aluif?
Is it sa that regaird for your master ye pruif?
Ga, see that vile stroller ance mair on his way—
He will speid on his road ere the dawning of day!
The sky was sa black that the eird seemit all
Wrappit round in ane dismall funerall pall,
The wind blew loud, and the choking drift
Drave fiercely alang throcht the troublit lift.
Quhen the agit man with tryalls besett
Was turnit away fra the castill yett.

He lookit around, but na meith culd he see,
To guide quhair he wald have lykit to be,
Till he fand the path fra the Carlin den,
And hope for ane breiff space upliftit him then,

For ane lemand licht schone befoir him sa cleir,
That he thocht he wald sune enjoy the cheir,
Quhilk belated wicht, quhither laird or loun,
Ay receaves fra the foulk at the Westertoun.
Bot the licht that he saw was fra na mortal flame
To guide him alang to ane earthly hame,
Sune it dancit before him with flickering ray,
And then in the darkness it meltit away.
The Palmer still strugglit against the gale,
But quhen at the last his strength did fail,
He offerit up ane fervent prayir
To Him quha can othir stryke or spair,
Till he swunit away in the sleep of dethe—
And beneath ane snaw wreath closit his brethe.
But befoir he sunk to his peacefull rest
He crossit his arms upon his breist,
Sa that they quha fand him micht eithlie see
That ane faythfull Christian man was he.
The morning dawned als clear and fayr
As gif storme had nevir vexit the air.
The Baron's vassals, then socht to trace
The Palmer to his resting-place.
And they fand him there als pale and chill
As the winding-scheit he was swaithit intill.
Quhen the Baron was tauld that the Palmer was dead,
Quhatevir he thocht, na word he said,
Bot, "Hie ye hence with your picks and shuils,
Ane bury him deip at Sanct Devenick's muils,"

They diggit ane graif, and laid him thair,
Without haly psalme or voice of prayir;
And his resting-place may still be seen,
For thair the grass growis rank and green.

Twice seven days had cum ane gane,
And the Baron walkit furth alane,
And he passed the furd of Auchinzell
As he heard the jow of the vesper bell,
Quhen his favorite catt gaed fleeing by,
Nor heidit the Baronis kindlie cry.
He marvellit sair how this culd be,
For the lyik befoir he did never see.

At nicht as the Baron lanesum satt,
Hame cam his grim and gruesome catt,
Scho jumpit up to hir customed place.
And grimly glowerit in the Baronis face.
He frownit on her with upliftit hand,
And bade hir to tell at his command
How it was that he saw her skirring the moss
That lyis at the fute of the Twa-mile-Cross,
Then out spak the catt with ane feirfull rair,
"Quhair ye saw me ance ye sall see me na mair!"
Syne she fixed on his craig like ane Fure fra hell,
And doun the agit Baron fell.
His servants heard his despayring cry,
And speedily to his help did hie,
Bot befoir they enterit the Baron was dead,
And furth his cruell catt had fled.
But how scho escapit, or quhair scho had flawin,
Was nevir to mortal creature knawin.

Ye quha this dulsome tale shall heir,
Be warnit by it what ye haif to feir,
Gif on earthly thingis ye fix your luve,
And nocht on the blessit thingis abuve;
For our pleasures here are bot sendyll true,
And aften they leave us cause to rue,

And aft, when men think they are sure of a friend,
They bot nurse in their breastis ane disguisit feynd—
Had Petfoddils but duly thocht on that,
He had never been wirrit be ane catt.

NOTE.

"The foregoing story has no other foundation than a tradition which sets forth that an old Laird of Pitfodels had a favourite cat—that on one occasion he saw his cat scampering through the Clash, a piece of boggie ground behind the north-east shoulder of the Two-mile cross—that when the cat afterwards jumped up on his table, as was her custom, he asked what she had been about where he had seen her—and that the cat answered 'Whare ye saw me ance ye sall see me na mair,' and forthwith worried him to death.—Tradition points out a solitary grave beside Daveny's Meels, not far from the site of the old Castle of Pitfoddels. Its tenant, however, was no holy Palmer, but a fellow who used to endeavour to make a lie pass current by praying that he might be buried out of sight of kirk or kirkyard if his tale was untrue. When his funeral arrived at the place alluded to, his corpse became so heavy that the mourners were forced to bury it there, and thus was his oft-repeated prayer complied with. At the present day his grave is beyond the reach of church superintendence, although it made a narrow escape from the tower of the recently erected Kirk of Nigg."—*Deeside Guide.*

Contract between the Lord Forbes Johne Leslie of Balquhane and Thomas Menzes of Pittfoddelis.[1]—*(A.D. 1552.)*—See page 174.

At Grantulie the xxvii. day of Februar the yeir of God ane thousand five hundred and fifty ane yeris in presens of ane potent and nobel lord George erll of Huntlie luftennent of the north it is . . . contractit and faithfullie oblegit betwixt Williame lord Forbes and Johne Leslie of Balquhane for thameselffis kyn frendis seruandis assisstiris pairttakkeris on that ane pairt and James Gordoun of Methlyk in name and behalf of Thomas Menzes of Pittfoddilis he oblesand for him himselff his kyn freindis seruandis assisstiris and pairttakkeris on that vther pairt eueschuing

---
[1] Antiquities *Aberdeen and Banff*, iii. 277-9.

all eilestis offencis displesure . . . standand betwixt thame and in special of the slauchteris happenit betwixt Maister Thomas Dauedson Maister Walter Leslie and otheris ther complices and pairttakkeris baitht of the slauchteris mutilatioun gif ony be hurting blude drauing and woundis and otheris whatsomeuer . . . to the effect following that is to say for till euischew griter inconvenience and commond weill of the haill cuntreth the saydis Lord Forbes for his kyn freindis seruandis and all personis perteining to him that it is offended to hes oblesit him for thame and in likwayiss the sayd Johnn Leslie of Balquhane oblesand him for himself his kyn friendis seruandis and all personis perteining to him that it is offended to and als the sayd James Gordoun of Methlyk in name of the sayd Thomas Menzes for his kyn freindis seruandis and all other personis perteining to him that it is offended to hes submittit the decisioun of all the premises to my sayd Lord Luftennent Williame Lord Forbes and Johnn Leslie of Balquhane all three coniunctly in ane voce as gugis arbitrateris and amicable componituris quha sal convein God willing in the cathedrall kirk of Aberdene on Monunday the ellevint day of April . . . followand the date of ther presentis at nyne hours befor nowne and sal deliuer thair finall sentence and amicable compositioun within xxiiii. houris thairefter and as thai deleuer the saydis partiis sal fulfill and for securitie and guid rewile to be had in the mydtyme and that Thomas Menzeis of Pitfoddellis Gilbert Menzeis Mr. Thomas Menzeis Alexander Menzeis Robert Menzeis and William Menzeis sonis to the sayd Thomas Menzeis Dauid Menzeis and Gilbert Menzeis brether to the sayd Thomas Thomas Menzeis his brothers sone Patrik Menzeis Gilbert Menzeis and Gilbert Menzies seruandis to the said Patrik / Maister George Johnstoun Alexander Waus younger lard of Mane Thomas Nicholsoun Dauid Mar bailyie Alexander Knowis Maister Andro Herwy Williame Herwy his brother James Litster Patrik Malisoun Jhone Crawfurd son to Andro Crawfurd / James spens Robert Middiltoun Patrik Middiltoun seruandis to the sayd Thomas Menzeis / Jaspart Bard Alexander Kempt Thomas Burrol Jhone Boyd Andro Beney Henrie Laying William Jamesoun masoun Thomas Shand and Coling Pertaweill sal be harmless and skaithless of all bodelie harme to Sonday callit *Dominica in Albis* inclusiue the said William lord Forbes and Johnn Leslie of Balquhane obleiss thame for thameselffis kyn freindis seruandis assisteris or pairttakkeris respectiue ilk ane for thair awn sae mony as the sayd Thomas betwix this and Twysday nixt cummes deleueris in bill subscriuit with his hand to Mr. Robert Lumisden and otheris quhom thai ma lat that the foresaydis Thomas Menzeis of Pitfoddellis and personis forsaydis sal be harmless and skaithless to the said Sonday under the pane of periure infame and inhabilite and refound to our Souerane Lady hir tutor and thesaurar the soume of ane thousand lib. Scottis money *tanquam interesse habentium* in case the sayd Thomas or ony of the forsaydis personis get or incur ony bodelie harme or skaitht in thair personis be ony way as sayd is and to euischew all sic eilestis my Lord Luftennent forsayd ordainis quhat tyme my Lord Forbes the Lard of Balquhane his sone the Lard of Wardderis or his sone Arthure Forbes or Maister Duncan Forbes happynis to be in Aberdene the Prouest beyng adwertesit he sal cause his sone and seruandis that was present at the forsayd displesure as is allegit that is to say Robert Menzeis Mr. George Johnstoun young Lard Mane Mr. Andro Herwy John Crauford Robert Middiltoun Patre Middiltoun Jaspert Bard Alexander Kempt youngar Tom Burrol Jhone Boyd Gilbert Menzeis Hewbrand Menzeis Alexander Gibbert to euischow frae all oppin conventioun or passing upoun the get induring the tyme forsayd and als the sayd Thomas Menzeis sal gif to Mr. Duncan Forbes his brether freindis seruandis assisteris and pairttakkeris ane sufficient assurance for sae mony personis as he vill gif in bill to the sayd Sonday *in Albis* ilk person under the panis forsaydis quhilk assurance shall be deliuerit to Mr. Duncan Forbes betwix this and Twysday nixt he requirand the same and the saydis Prouest to assure for the Middiltounis as well as for his awn seruandis induring the forsayd tyme In witness of the quhilks my saydis Lord Luftennent Lord Forbes and Johne Leslie of Balquhane hes subscriuit thir presentis with thair handis day and place forsayd and sic like quhen the Middiltounis happenys to be in the toune or thair special freindis the said Maister Duncan beyng adwertesit he sal cause Johne Tullidaf Williame Jak to euischow frae all oppin conventioun or passing upoun the get induring the tyme forsayd.

(Signed)   George erll off Huntlie.   (Signed)   Jon Leslie of Balquhane.
(„   )   William lord Forbes.   („   )   James Gordoune.

Band of protectioune Huntlie to Pitfoddellis.[1]—*(A.D. 1588.)*— See page 177.

Be it kend till all men be thir present lettiris we George erll Huntlie lord Gordoun and Baidzenochtt to be bound and oblist . . . to our louittis Gilbert Menzeis of Pitfoddellis prouest of Abirdene Maister Thomas Menzeis of Durne his brothir thair sonis kyn and freindis Forsameekill as the said Gilbert and Maister Thomas for themselffis and takand the burding on thame for thair kyn and freindis are bound in manrent and seruice to ws during . . . the lyf tyme of the langest lewar of thame twa as thairlettar of manrent thairupoun beiris heirfore we sal mantein supplie and defend the sayd Gilbert Mengzeis Mr. Thomas Mengzeis thair sonis kyn and freindis and tak afauld and [trew pairt with thame] . . . and sal do to thame and for thame in all thair adois honest and leifull as we sal do for ony of our awn kyn and that for all the dayis of our lyf . . . In witness of the quhilk thing to thir our letteris of manteinance subscriueit with our hand our sell is hungin at Pertht the nynt day of June the year of God M v^c fourscoir and aucht yearis befor thir witness Prouiding that the said Gilbert and Mr. Thomas with thair kyn and freindis remitt to my desicioun all eilestis past or that may fall furtht betwix thaeme and ony of myne and this to be extendit in sae mony as will not submitt thair causis unto me and nae other befor thir vitness Mr. Franzeis Cheyne Johnne Gordoun of Petlurge Thomas Gordoun of Sedyden and Capiten Thomas Ker.

(Signed)   George erlle of Huntlye.

[1] Antiquities *Aberdeen and Banff*, III. pp. 279, 80.

MURTLE.

Charter by Malcolm IV. in favour of the Bishop of Aberdeen, (1163)—See page 204.

"Malcolm, by the Grace of God, King of Scots, to all the honourable men in his haill dominions, Clergy and Laity, sendeth greeting; Know all men, both present and to come, Me to have given, and, by this Charter, confirmed to God and the Blessed Mary, St. Machar, and Matthew, Bishop of Aberdeen, my haill Barony of Murchill [Murtle] with the pertinents; and pasture in my Forest of Aberdeen, as he pleases, any one forest of the four, lying as above mentioned, to chuse, or have for a perpetual Barony, he always serving me, and making oath of fidelity, as other Barons of my kingdom do; excepting to himself the dignity of a Bishop, and the liberty belonging to the clergy; but beyond these bounds, neither he nor his successors must by any means pass; As witness my hand at Banff, the 15th day of November, and 11th year of my reign.

SAVINGS BANKS.

Banchory-Devenick.—In the end of last century, with a view to encourage habits of thrift, and well-doing amongst the parishioners, Dr. Morison organized a parish Savings Bank, under the rules of which a fixed rate of interest was to be allowed on all deposits. The schoolmaster of the parish acted as Treasurer, and, to give additional stability to the scheme, the heritors along with the minister agreed to act as trustees.

Success attended the venture, there being at one time over £3,000 in the bank at credit of depositors. This enabled the capital funds to be laid out to advantage, and, as the expenses of management were practically *nil*, a considerable profit gradually accrued. On the opening of the "National Security Savings Bank of Aberdeen," however, it was resolved to wind up the parish Savings Bank, and transfer the depositors accounts there. This was done in legal form, and when all claims were settled and accounts adjusted, it was found that a surplus of over £200 of profit remained. Dr. Paul, who had succeeded Dr. Morison as chief trustee, arranged "for the annual interest of this sum, being applied in the shape of an annual Bursary of seven pounds, to assist in the education of a deserving youth a native of the parish." Unfortunately the profit fund had been allowed to lie in the Bank of Scotland, Aberdeen, at a low rate of interest, which necessitated slight annual inroads being made into the capital to make up the Bursary. After Dr. Paul's demise, however, the Kirk-Session approached the heritors, who readily in February, 1887, sanctioned the full control of the fund, then reduced to £184 18s. 6d. being handed over to them, the Session undertaking "to invest the amount on good heritable security, the annual interest to be applied towards assisting the University education of a deserving youth a native of the parish, it being understood that when there is a vacancy, the vacant interest shall be added to the principal sum, and that the nomination by the Session shall be from year to year, but not to be held by any individual Bursar for a longer period than four consecutive years." It must be matter of satisfaction to those interested, to know that the sum placed under charge of the Kirk-Session as above, is now invested on a Bond and Disposition in security over valuable house property in Aberdeen, at such a rate of interest as will warrant the original Bursary of Seven Pounds being paid annually.

Cults.—About twelve years ago through the influence and exertions of Mr. T. A. W. A. Youngson, Southfield House, "a Penny Bank" was started for this rapidly rising district. Its primary object was the fostering of habits of economy amongst scholars and other young people. Mr. Youngson acts as chief trustee, and there is a duly qualified treasurer. The bank is open for the transaction of business each alternate Saturday afternoon in Cults school. The rate of interest allowed on deposits is fixed at three per cent. per annum. There are now over seventy depositors, with an aggregate sum at credit exceeding £95.

Portlethen.—Quite recently a public meeting, largely representative of the fishing population, was held in the public school, at which it was unanimously resolved "that a Penny Savings Bank" should be instituted for the district. Arrangements were made for the constitution of the bank, of which Mr. George J. Walker, Hillside House, and the Rev. A. R. Grant were elected trustees.

AGRICULTURE.

Dr. Morison, writing in 1792, says "a spirit for agriculture has begun within these few years to make its appearance in some parts of this parish. Still, however, it is with a few exceptions, confined to those farms which lie near the river, particularly on the north side. On that side the soil and exposure are good, and the heritor, Mr. Menzies of Pitfodels, has wisely granted leases of 19 years and a life, with an obligation to take off houses and fences to a certain extent, at the expiry of the lease. The change which this has effected on that part of his estate, within these five years is astonishing. On this side there is not the same encouragement, and less, consequently, is done. Besides, in all the parish south of the river, there is a vast quantity of moss, and being in the vicinity of Aberdeen, the tenants who pay upwards of a £1 an acre for small bits of land, depend for a livelihood upon driving peats to town, where they find a ready market for them. This is one cause, why the cultivation of the land is very much neglected. Another bar to agriculture is the high price of labour. A day labourer, if a good hand, earns a 1/- a day for nine months of the year, and 9d. the other three; and the wages of a capable farm servant, who has his victuals found, are seldom under £6, and sometimes as high as £9 sterling a year. And a third cause of the uncultivated state of our fields, is the poverty of the people, which renders many of them unable either to stock or manage their farms to advantage. I must, however, for the honour of spirit and exertion relate one instance of the increased value of land, which is remarkable. I allude to Mr. Fordyce who purchased the estate of Ardoe in 1744. When he took possession he found the mansion house, such as it was, with the garden, and about 40 acres of land adjoining, in the hands of a tenant, who paid about £3 6s. 8d. sterling of rent annually. Having it in contemplation at that time to go abroad again, he asked the man if he would renew his lease, which was expired, at the annual rent of £5 sterling. His answer was 'na by my faith, God has gein me mair wit.' Mr. Fordyce settled and employed himself in improving the land, which is now in a good state of cultivation, and would rent at £1 5s. an acre."

The Agricultural Survey gives the following statistics in reference to the soil on the south side of the parish in 1807.

In Wheat	3 acres.
Bere	382 ,,
Oats	992 ,,
Peas	41 ,,
Turnips	307 ,,
Potatoes	62 ,,
Flax	2 ,,
Gardens	30 ,,
Sown Grass	658 ,,
Fallow	16 ,,
Cultivated	2493 ,,
Wood	204 ,,
Improvable by tillage	1594 ,,
Hill, &c., unfit for tillage	3104 ,,

The same authority gives the live stock as follows :—

Calves reared	248
Milch Cows	289
Draught Oxen	26
Other Cattle	587
Total Cattle	1150

Riding Horses	3
Horses in husbandry	100
Foals reared	6
Sheep	256
Swine	6

Leases are invariably granted for a period of 19 years, and the rotation of cropping is generally that of the fifth course, viz:—1st oats, or barley, sown with grass seed, after turnips or other green crop; 2nd, 1st grass; 3rd, 2nd year's grass; 4th oats, and 5th turnips. In some instances the sixth course is followed, which means the taking of a third year's grass crop. Little attention is now paid to the rearing of cattle, as the farmers find it more profitable to sell the milk and other dairy produce in Aberdeen, where good prices are readily obtained. The average rental may be estimated at £2 10s. per acre, although as much as £5 an acre is sometimes paid.

Very little of the parish is now lying waste, every acre which could possibly be expected to yield a crop having been carefully reclaimed.

POPULATION STATISTICS.

Year	Kincardineshire.	Abdnsii.	Total.
1755	1736	...	...
1774	1980	...	...
1792	1340	...	...
1801	1465	...	...
1811	...	...	1867
1821	...	...	2232
1831	1905	683	2588
1841	...	...	2736
1851	...	...	3078
1861	...	...	2919
1871	2230	822	3052
1881	2095	1222	3317

INSCRIPTIONS ON TOMBSTONES IN PARISH CHURCHYARD.

Quaint.

Respecting the Churchyard, James Logan, in his MS. *Notes on Churches, 1819*, now in the Advocates' Library, Aberdeen, states:—"The oldest inscribed gravestone is of the date 1712. There is another of 1733. On one we see two hearts, with the memento that 'death parts the dearest hearts.' Upon a slabstone, in memory of Alexander Murray, who died in 1765, at the age of 81, is inscribed—

> Farewell vain world, I had eneugh of thee,
> And now I'm careless what you say to me,
> Thy smiles I court not, nor thy frowns I fear,
> My days are past; my head lies quiet here.
> What ill you've seen in me, take care to shun,
> And look at home, eneugh there's to be done."

The first stone referred to is doubtless the one initialed:—
"1712. R. G. : IM."

And the second:—
"1733. W M^y MS^o. HER LYES MA : Murk . . .

(1) In memory of Elizabeth Sivewright, wife of William Hunter, Salmon Fisher, Aberdeen, who died 15th May, 1842, aged 29 years.

> God my Redeemer lives,
> And ever from the skies
> Looks down and watches all my dust
> Till he shall bid it rise.

(2) Here lies ye Body of John Allen, late Tenant in Mill of Elsick, who died ye 29th of May, 1744, aged 49. And Margaret Murray, his Spouse, who died ye 13th day of March, 1771, aged 69 years.

(3) Here lys the body of George Ross, also his spowes, Isobel Mideltoun, also theer dawghter, Agnes Ross.

(4) Here lies George Brown, who died 19th November, 1793, aged 26 mn^{s}.

(5) This stone is erected to the memory of John Westland, who officiated as an Elder of this Parish upwards of 40 years, and who died on the 11th day of January, 1826. He possessed great strength of mind and independence of character, and till the day of his death, although in his 88th year, he supplied his daily wants by his daily labour. He survived his wife, Isobel Leich, and a family of four sons and one daughter.

(6) This stone is erected by John Martin, Flesher in Middletoun of Pitfodels, in memory of his beloved wife, Elspet Martin, who departed this life 1st May, 1812, aged 63 years; also the foresaid John Martin, who departed this life on the 30th December, 1819, aged 85 years. Also Helen Martin, spouse to John Frost, Feuar, Hardgate, Abdn., who died 25th Jan, 1828, aged 79 years. And I heard a voice from Heaven saying unto me, Write, Blessed are the dead which die in the Lord, from henceforth; Yea, saith the Spirit, that they may rest from their labours; and their works do follow them.

(7) To the memory of Margaret Innes, spouse to James Ross, Shipmaster, Aberdeen, who died on the 4th Jany., 1801, aged 19 years. Immediately on the North side of this stone lie the remains of the said James Ross, who died on 6th September, 1803, aged 58 years. From a sense of filial duty, not more the dictate of nature than the tribute of willing gratitude, this stone is erected by their only son, James Ross, Merchant, Aberdeen.

(8) In memory of James Reid, Mason in Aberdeen, who died the 16th of March, 1800, aged 52. Also his wife, Elizabeth Rhind, who died the 1st of November, 1791, aged 39. Likewise their two children, James and Helen, who died in infancy.

> They rest in Hope, exempt from Pain,
> They liv'd to Christ, their Deaths are Gain,
> And now those Friends together meet,
> In Christ their Joys are full compleat.

APPENDIX.

(9) J. R.   17

Here lies in hope of a blessed Resurrection James Rhind, late Mason in Aberdeen, who died Feby., 28th, 1808, aged 80 years.

Here lys in hopes of a glorious Resurrection ye Bodies of these children of James Rhind, Mason in Ab^{dn.} and his spouse, Margaret Reid.

Margaret died of none age, 1751
Margaret, Novr. 1756,
   aged 3 years.
Arthur, Nov., 1758,
   aged 9 months.
Christian, Ma^{r.} 1759,
   aged 4 years.
John, of none age,
   May, 1763.
Susanna, Decr. 1765
   Aged 15 months
James, Sept., 1767,
   aged 10 months.

M.R.   67

Here lies in the hopes of a blessed Resurrection Margaret Reid, spouse to James Rhind, who departed this life October 3rd, 1769, aged 45 years.

My dear and lovely wife lyes here.

Her none can excell, I am sure,
In love to her Relations dear;
Kind to all—much so to the poor.

Mary Rhind, who died July 19th, 1786, aged 3 years.

James Rhind, who died Feby. 6th, 1797.

Alexander Rhind, who died June 6th, 1813, aged 26 years.

As I die in my Youth
Like a forest choked Tree,
Like it, may my relics
No vulgar eyes spy.
The bloom on yon heath
Is an emblem of me,
For its fame and its fragrance
Together will die.
The Angels they do sing the praise
Of their eternal King;
These children, I hope has
Joint their Chorus,
Eternaly there to sing.

For I know y^t my Redeemer liveth, and, though after my skin worms destroy this body, yet in my flesh shall I see God.

<small>There are several ornaments upon this stone, including an angel blowing a trumpet.</small>

(10) Erected by Alexander Aiken, Townhead of Ardoe, in memory of his daughter, Euphemia, who died 9th January, 1860, aged 18 years. Also his wife, Euphemia Lyall, who died 26th November, 1869, aged 63 years. And the said Alexander Aiken died 23rd May, 1881, aged 87 years.

> Reader, look on as you pass by,
> As you are now so once was I—
> In youthful bloom and vigour strong,
> But now I'm laid in silent tomb.

(11) In remembrance of William Smith, Lax Fisher at Bridge of Don, who, when living, behaved himself as an honest man; he died the 18th of November, 1781, aged 53 years; also of Henrietta Duncan, his spouse, aged 40 years, who died in child-bed . . .

(12) In memory of Alexander Beverley, Shoemaker, Aberdeen, who died on the 4th April, 1829, aged 72. Erected by his sister, Jean. Also interred here, Jean Beverley, who died 10th March, 1852, aged 85 years. Blessed are the dead that die in the Lord. For I know that my Redeemer liveth. Them, also, which sleep in Jesus will God bring with him.

On Table Stones.

(1) Erected to the memory of the late William Milne, Farmer in Balquharn, who departed this life December 5th, 1837, aged 71 years. And of his son, James, who died in infancy, August, 1827. Likewise his daughter, Margaret Milne, who died 26th December, 1849, aged 33 years. Also his spouse, Helen Fiddes, who died 18th September, 1862, aged 74. Also their son, William, who died 26th August, 1872. aged 58 years.

(2) In memory of John Ferris, sometime Merchant in the Parish of Alford, who departed this life on the 18th February, 1816, aged 80 years. This stone was erected by George Duncan, Laxfisher in Coults. Also his son, Alexander Duncan, Gardener, who died, 11th September, 1835, aged 21 years. Also Margaret Ferris, wife of the said George Duncan, who died 10th June, 1839, aged 66 years.

(3) Erected by Wm. Spring, in Mains of Ardoe, in memory of his sister, Isabel, who died the 1st May, 1827, aged 12 years. Also of his Father, Wm. Spring, who died the 12th of December, 1845, aged 78 years. Christian Mennie, his Mother, who died 29th October, 1858, aged 69 years. Also his Cousin, Agnes Leslie, who died 26th November, 1878, aged 74 years. The said William Spring, Farmer, Lochend, Ardoe, died the 2nd August, 1879, aged 61 years.

(4) In memory of Margaret Greig, Spouse to John Webster, Merchant, Aberdeen, who died February 20th, 1833, aged 55. Also the said John Webster, who died 18th March, 1849, aged 81.

(5) In memory of Elspet Mennie, who died 24th September, 1834, aged 42 years. This stone was erected by her husband, John Masson, Farmer, Brandsmyres, Banchory . . . The said John Masson died 17th January, 1876, aged 81 years.

(6) This stone is erected by Mary Will in memory of her late husband, Alexander Crocket, once in Easter Ardoe, who departed this life on the 27th October, 1819, aged 68 years. Also interred here the said Mary Will, who died 29th March, 1825, aged 74 years.

(7) In memory of Alexander Philip, Flaxdresser in Aberdeen, who died 18th April, 1820, aged 68 years.

(8) Erected by John Dunn, Tailor, Burgess in Aberdeen, in memory, of his sons, Alexander, who died 23rd January, 1813, aged 7 years. And William, who died 7th January, 1815, in his 7th year. Also of his daughter, Elizabeth, who died 14th February, 1821, aged 7 months. Here also is buried the said John Dunn, Merchant Tailor in Aberdeen, who died on the 15th of November, 1845, aged 64 years. Also John Dunn, Advocate in Aberdeen, son of the said John Dunn, Merchant Tailor, who died on the 19th day of August, 1853, aged 38 years. Also Ann Dunn or Birse, who died on the 27th February, 1841, aged 28 years. Also Ann Farquharson Carr or Dunn, wife of the said John Dunn, Merchant Tailor, who died on the 21st December, 1870, aged 83 years.

(9) Erected by George Morison, D.D., the Minister of this Parish, as a tribute to the many Christian Virtues of his deceased wife, Margaret Jaffray, who died 11th June, 1837, in her 80th year. In the same grave are deposited the remains of her husband, Dr. Morison of Elsick and Disblair, the revered pastor and munificent benefactor of this parish during 60 years, who, on the 13th July, 1845, died Father of the Church of Scotland, in the 88th year of his age, and 63rd of his ministry.

(10) In memory of David Hutcheon, Farmer, Old Bourtrie Bush, who died 25th August, 1843, aged 72; and his daughter, Margaret, who died 14th March, 1844, aged 29. Also Jane Calder, spouse of David Hutcheon, who died 12th January, 1862, aged 90. Also their son, David Hutcheon, Farmer, Old Bourtrie Bush, who died 26th October, 1868, aged 58 years.

(11) Here lies George Hogg of Shannaburn, Merchant in Aberdeen, who died on the 28th day of November, 1826, aged 78.

(12) Erected by Joseph Walker, Baker in Aberdeen, in memory of William Walker, Weaver in Hillside of Findon, who died the 4th of January, 1831, aged 84 years. And Elspet Collie, his spouse, who died in the year 1802, aged 55 years. Also of their children, George and James, Andrew and Margaret, buried here. And Isabel Collie, his second spouse, who died in the year 1829, aged 72 years. Also of the said Joseph Walker, Baker, Burgess in Aberdeen, who departed this life on the 25th day of December, 18 . ., aged 56 years.

(13) Here lies the remains of Jannet Gerrard, Spouse to William Knowles, Farmer in Robslaw, who departed this life the 5th of March, 1765, aged 63 years. Here lyes William Knowles, Farm*r* in Robslaw, he died October 29th, 1777, aged 73 years, and Alex. Knowles, his grandchild. Also George Gordon, some time Blacksmith in the Hardgate, Aberdeen, who died 27th December, 1799, aged 65 years; and four of his sons. Also Christian Knowles, Spouse of George Gordon, who died 18th August, 1809, aged 69 years. Also Agnes Moir, Spouse of Thomas Knowles, Robislaw, who died 29th June, 1816, aged 75 years. Also

Thomas Knowles, some time Farmer in Robslaw, who died 6th October, 1818, aged 79 years.

(14) In memory of Adam Low, eighteen years Baker in Aberdeen, who died 11th July, 1823, aged 47; and his son, Adam, Student of Medicine, a young man of promising abilities, who died 9th July, 1823, aged 17. Also Ann Gordon, his spouse, who died 21st Feby., 1824, aged 45. Likewise Alexander Gordon, Flaxdresser in Aberdeen, who died on the 18th day of June, 1831.

(15) Erected by John Middleton in memory of Isabella Middleton, his daughter, who was born 24th December 1784 and died 4th December, 1806, aged 22 years. And of Alexander Middleton, some time Cooper in Aberdeen, his son, who was born 21st April, 1787, and died at Aberdeen the 17th May, 1822, aged 35 years. Also Isabella Duncan, Spouse of John Middleton, who died the 12th August, 1828, aged 83 years. And John Middleton, her husband, who died 26th June, 1834, aged 84 years.

(16) In memery of Peter Donald, who departed this life the 10th of April, 1814, aged 19 years. John Donald, Dams of Banchory, died 27th July, 1841, aged 93 years. Margaret Reid, wife of William Donald, Glazier, Aberdeen, died 3rd January, 1840, aged 38. John, their son, died 18th September, 1840, aged 3 years and 6 months. And the said William Donald, who died 9th January, 1850, aged 49 years.

(17) Erected by Joseph Walker, East Cookstoun, in memory of his wife, Elizabeth Mollison, who died 12th April, 1833, aged 47, and their children, Margaret died 10th May, 1829, aged 14 years, George died 10th March, 1830, aged 14 months, also their daughter, Jean, who died the 8th November, 1836, aged 13 years. And their son, the Revd. James Walker, Late Assistant Minister at Arbuthnot, who died the 16th December, 1848, aged 21 years. The said Joseph Walker, who died the 21st March, 1868, aged 81 years.

(18) Erected by James Strachan, late Blacksmith at Lowersbanks in memory of his wives, Christian Still, died 5th May, 1791, aged 30. Vio ete Walker, died 26th February, 1822, aged 54 . . .

(19) In memory of Jean Collie, Spouse to Wm. Troup, Lax-fisher in Temple of Pitfodels, who died the 6th of January, 1780, aged 65 years, and the said Wm. Troup, who died the 6th of February, 1808, aged 92 years. . . .

(20) Here are interred the remains of the following persons:— William Martin, some time in Braeside of Pitfodels, who died the 16th September, 1766, aged 88 years. Also Margaret Donald, his spouse, who died the 16th November, 1750, aged 52 years. Likewise their children, William, who died the 8th May, 1738, aged 27 years. Alexander, some time in Fulmuir in the Parish of Old Machar, who died the 2nd November, 1754, aged 51 years. Also Marjory Harrow, his spouse, who died the 1st August, 1780, aged 63 years. And George Martin, Shipmaster in Aberdeen, who died the 21st April, 1782, aged 75 years . . .

(21) To the memory of James Gibb, late at the Fords of Dee, who died 13th May, 1811, in the 75th year of his age. And Margaret Troup, his wife, who departed this life on January 7th, 1821, aged 84; also six of their children.

(22) Erected by Charles Mathison, Burgess in Aberdeen, to the memory of his Father, Charles Mathison, late Shore Porter in Aberdeen, who died the 13th day of August, 1809, aged 65 years; and also his Spouse, Elizabeth Garden, who departed this life on the 21st day of May, 1825, aged 86 years. And also to the memory of Margaret, daughter of the said Charles Mathison, Burgess, who died in infancy. Also of the said Charles Mathison, who died 2nd February, 1844, aged 64 years. And his spouse, Elspet Anderson, who died 30th April, 1844, aged 67 years . . .

(23) Erected by David Keith, late in Tollohill, in memory of his family—James died 4th December, 1824, aged 31. Margaret, spouse of George Sharp, died 23rd January, 1825, aged 29. And of his spouse, Janet Freeman, died 10th November, 1829, aged 74. The said David Keith died 6th July, 1832, aged 66. David Sharp died 28th January, 1835, aged 12 years. . . .

(24) In memory of John Fraser, late in Hilldountree, who died in January, 1772, and Elizabeth Mair, his spouse, who died in March, 1776. Also their children—two sons, John and Charles, and four daughters, two Elizabeths, Barbara, and Mary. Likewise Janet Fraser, his sister. Below lies Alexander Walker and his wife. Also of Ann King, aged 64, wife of William King, Wright, Huntly Street, Aberdeen.

(25) Here lies, in hopes of a blessed resurrection, the remains of Rebeca Leiper, spouse to Alexander Knowles in Findon, who departed this life the 9th April, 1781, in the 46th year of her age; and the foresaid Alexander Knowles, Whitefisher, who departed this life 16th October, 1814, aged 81 years.

(26) Here are interred the body of Alexander Leiper, Whitefisher at Findon, who died 1st June, 1804, aged 72 years, and John his son. This stone is erected to his memory by his affectionate spouse, Agnes Knowles, and Alexander, George, James, Ann, and Jean, their children.

(27) Erected by John Watt, Farmer, Ardoe, in memory of his Wife, Isobell Keith, who died 27th January, 1828, aged 64 years. Also his daughter, Helen, who died April, 1812, aged 12 years. And his Daughter, Margaret, wife of James Adamson, Wright, Aberdeen, who died 29th October, 1831, aged 22 years. Also of his son, James, who died 3rd August, 1832, aged 25 years.

(28) To the memory of David Robertson, late Lax-fisher in Braehead, Bridge of Dee, who departed this life the 7th January, 1816, aged 45 years. This stone is erected by Jane Ross, his spouse, as a grateful tribute of her regard and affection for his departed worth.

(29) In memory of William Duthie, Brewer, Aberdeen, who died 10th August, 1849, aged 68 years. Also his children—John, who died 2nd May, 1809, aged 1 year. John, who died 7th May, 1811, aged 3 weeks. William, who died 22nd September, 1815, aged 9 years. James, who died 24th April, 1827, aged 9 years. Ann, who died 11th July, 1827, aged 18 years. Mary, who died 15th April, 1833, aged 19 years. Helen, who died 28th May, 1838, aged 18 years. Charles, who died 31st July, 1845, aged 22 years. And his son, Alexander Still Duthie,

Brewer, Aberdeen, who died 7th January, 1851, aged 36 years, also Ann Millar, his Spouse, who died 19th August, 1852, aged 34 years.

(30) In memory of James Sim, late of Gilcomston in the Parish of St. Machar, Feuar, who departed this life the ninth day of February, MDCCXCIV, in the eighty-sixth year of his age. And of Isabel Milne, his wife, who died the fourth day of October, MDCCLXXX, in the seventy-first of her age. Likewise Ann, their eldest daughter, who died MDCCLVIII, aged XIX years. And Thomas, their youngest son, who died MDCCLVII, aged V years. "Blessed are the dead who die in the Lord, for they rest from their labours and their works do follow them."— *Rev.* XIV, 13.

(31) In memory of George Scott, Farmer in Middletown of Pitfodels, who died 16th January, 1766, aged 76 years. Also of Isabel Patterson, his spouse, who died 29th September, 1737, aged 35 years. Also is interred here, their son, Alexander Scott, Shipmaster in London, who died 9th April, 1778, aged 54 years. Also of Alexander Duncan, Farmer in Middletown of Pitfodels, who died 27th October, 1800, aged 73 years. Also of Isabel Scott, his spouse, who died 15th February, 1805, aged 78 years. Also of George Duncan, their son, Ship Master in Aberdeen, who died at sea, 18th November, 1795, aged 29 years, and he is interred at North Berwick. Also to the memory of Alexander Duncan, Shipmaster in Aberdeen, who died 30th March, 1819, aged 62 years. And of his son, Alexander Duncan, likewise Shipmaster in Aberdeen, who died at sea in December, 1817, aged 29 years, and is interred in the Churchyard of Stronsa. They both lived respected, and died lamented by all who knew them. In memory also of Jean Troup, spouse to Alexander Duncan, Senr., who died 21st November, 1822, aged 65 years.

(32) Erected by Alexander Gildawie, Builder in Aberdeen, in memory of his Mother, Christina Ogilvy, who died 9th December, 1774, aged 60 years. Also his Father, James Gildawie, Builder in Aberdeen, who died October, 1788, aged 78 years. Also his spouse, Ann Logan, who died 3rd November, 1828, aged 77 years. The above Alexander

Gildawie, Esqr. of Gateside, died 4th May, 1832, aged 86 years. Also Isabella Seller, wife of Alexander Gildawie, Junr., died 25th December, 1857, aged 72 years. This said Alexander Gildawie, Junr., died 19th April, 1867, aged 88 years.

(33) Erected by William Pirie, Farmer in South Loirston, in memory of his family. Alexander died 9th July, 1824, aged 23. Catherine died in infancy.

(34) Erected by William Emslie in memory of his Father, Charles Emslie, late Farmer in Cove, who died 26th November, 1819, aged 76 years. Also of his mother, Margaret Bruce, who died 12th April, 1821, aged 70 years. Also Francis their son, died in London the 15th April, 1824, aged 31 years. The said William Emslie, Farmer, South Loirston, Parish of Nigg, died the 5th March, 1834, aged 60 years; and his spouse, Elspet Pyper, who died 18th March, 1817, aged 30 years. John their son, Merchant in Aberdeen, who died 16th Jan., 1845, aged 34 years. Also the children of William Emslie, Farmer, Keir, Belhelvie— John died 19th April, 1848, aged 13 years. Margaret died 29th Jan., 1849, aged 3 years and 6 months. The said William Emslie of Keir died 19th April, 1850, aged 42 years.

(35) This stone is placed here to the memory of Alexander Walker, son of William Walker, Baker, Burgess in Aberdeen, who died 9th September, 1819, aged 12 years. And of his daughter, Margaret, who died 18th May, 1820, aged 6 years. Also of the said Wm. Walker, who died 18th July, 1839, aged 65 years, and of his third son, John Simpson Walker, Medical Practitioner in Kincardine O' Neil and surrounding district, who died 26th July, 1844, in consequence of a fall from his horse at Knowes of Birse the 16th of that month, aged 30 years. And Jean Reid, spouse of William Walker, who died 18th December, 1849, aged 69 years. Also Alexander [R.H.O.] Walker, youngest son of the said William Walker, who died 15th March, 1877, aged 56 years.

(36) In memory of David Spring, late Farmer, in Mid Ardoe, who died the 27th of July, 1814, aged 85 years. Also his wife, Margaret Williamson, who died the 27th February, 1821, aged 83 years. Also

their daughter, Christian Spring, who died on the 1st day of March, 1829, aged 50 years. Also their son, William Spring, died 7th January, 1835, aged 64. Likewise of Ann Nicol, spouse to their son, John Spring, Farmer in Mid Ardoe. She died the 13th October, 1883, aged 38 years. Also Janet, daughter of the said John Spring; she died 16th November, 1837, aged 7 years. The said John Spring died 11th September, 1839, aged 62 years.

(37) Erected by James Spring, Farmer in Mid Ardoe, in memory of his daughter, Agnes, who died 5th September, 1807, aged 2 years. Also of his wife, Mary Ferries, who died 24th September, 1832, aged 57 years. Also the above James Spring, who died 23rd December, 1854, aged 88 years. In the same grave are interred the remains of their son, James Spring, Farmer, Easter Ardoe, who died on the 15th October, 1873, aged 71 years. Also in memory of his son, James, late Farmer, Sunhoney, Midmar, who was accidentally drowned in the Aberdeen Bay, on the 3rd June, 1881, aged 39 years. Likewise Mary Martin, Widow of the above James Spring, Farmer, Easter Ardoe, who died 6th December, 1883, aged 69 years.

(38) Erected by James Martin, Farmer in Mains of Banchory, in memory of his daughter, Jean, who died the 7th September, 1828, aged 5 years and two months. The above named James Martin died the 14th April, 1850, aged 38 years. Jessie Martin, who died the 27th February, 1837, aged 8 years. Mary Martin, who died the 2nd March, 1837, aged 10 years.

(39) Here are deposited the remains of Matthew Martin, who died 27th July, 1835, aged 55 years. Likewise his daughter, Isabel, who died 19th May, 1833, aged 14 years. Also his son, Robert, who died 7th October, 1841, aged 30 years; and his spouse, Isabel Donald, who died 11th July, 1854, aged 71 years. Also their son, Alexander Martin, who died 13th March, 1879, aged 70 years.

(40) Erected by John Martin, Flesher in Aberdeen, in memory of his wife, Mary Spring, who died 2nd July, 1839, aged 31 years. Also the said John Martin, who died 15th May, 1870, aged 63 years.

(41) Here rests in the Lord, the body of Robert Craig, Laxfisher in the Fourds, who departed this life the 17th of July, 1733. And of Age 39 years. And Jean Craig, His Daughter, of Age 3 years . . .
1763 . . . .
Also Jane Wilson, spouse of William Craig, Master of Dredge Maschine, Aberdeen Harbour. She died 24th June, 1869, aged 58 years.

At the foot of this stone, which is dated 1736, and initialed R.C. I.S., are several ornaments, including a man's hand holding a salmon by the tail.

(42) R. R. I. M. Here lies ye Body of Robert Reid, late Tenant in Kinkorth. He died ye 13 of Nov., 1750, aged 67 years. John Caie, who died the 17th December, 1818, aged 74 years. Margaret Hogg, His spouse, who died the 16th May, 1830, aged 77 years. Isobel Martin, his spouse, she died the 19th of Nov., 1750, aged 57 years. George Reid, their son, he died the 19th of Novr., 1750, aged 16 years.

(43) The burying Place of William Michie, sometime in Easter Ardoc, who died August 29th, 1807, aged 58 years. And of Ann Michie, his wife, who died April 5th, 1809, aged 42 years. Also of their son George, who died December 12th, 1812, aged 21 years. Alexander, who died March 8th, 1818, aged 18 years. And William, who died December 14th, 1818, aged 22 years.

(44) In memory of George Fiddes, Late Farmer Fiddestown, who died 25th July, 1832, aged 35. Also his spouse, Jean Knowles, who died 23rd May, 1832, aged 39 years, and their daughter, Elizabeth, who died in infancy. Also their son John, who died April 11th, 1847, aged 19 years.

(45) Here Lyes Magnus Martin, son to William Martin, Greenlauburn, who departed this lyfe dec^r 23rd, 1739, aged 40 years.

This stone has several rude carvings upon it, including a skull and cross bones.

(46) This stone is erected by Isabella Milne, relict of Peter Kelman, late Marinar in Aberdeen, in memory of her parents and family, Alexander Milne and Jean Harrow, Spouse, and their infant children; likewise Alexander Kelman, aged 16 years, Jean Kelman, aged 25 years, who are all interred here. Underneath lies Jean Milne, her sister, who

died 12th August, 1826, aged 50 years. The said Isabella Milne died 26th June, 1828, aged 56 years. Also her son, John, who died in Van Diemans Land, 31st December, 1841, aged 44 years. Also William Flett, Baker in Aberdeen, son-in-law of the foresaid Isabella Kelman, who died 16th May, 1853, aged 46, and 3 of his children:— Robert, who died 22nd August, 1848, aged 7; Martha, who died 28th September, 1848, aged 8; William, who died 5th October, 1848, aged 13.

On Headstones.

(1) Erected by Joseph Wattie, Gardener, in memory of his Father, George Wattie, who died at Aberdeen, 14th November, 1824, aged 79. And of his wife, Isabella Maconochie, who died 18th December, 1836, aged 74. And of their son, John, Shipmaster, Aberdeen, who died 14th December, 1845, aged 56 years. Also James, who died 12th December, 1856, aged 67 years. Also Elizabeth, who died 2nd July, 1868, aged 68 years. Also of James, son of Joseph Wattie, who died 9th February, 1875, aged 33 years, Also Isabella Taylor, wife of Joseph Wattie, who died 6th May, 1878, aged 64 years. Also Joseph Wattie, who died 22nd February, 1886, aged 82 years.

(2) In memory of Isabel Mitchell, wife of George Glegg, Confectioner, Aberdeen, who died 12th July, 1849, aged 46. And of the said George Glegg, who died 3rd May, 1863, aged 86. Erected by their sons, William and James. Also of their son, William Dovertie Glegg, who died at sea, near Singapore, June 23rd, 1876, aged 39 years.

(3) In memory of Robert Collie, late Carter in Aberdeen, who died 6th September, 1832, aged 68. Also his son, Adam Collie, Seaman, who died 5th September, 1854, aged 64 years. And his daughter-in-law, Euphemia Finnie, who died 10th September, 1854, aged 30 years.

(4) In memory of Margaret Nairn, Spouse of William Dunn, in Mains of Banchory, who died August, MDCCCXXIII, aged 76. And of the said William Dunn, who died July, MDCCCXXIV, aged 82. Here also is buried their son, Alexander, Shore Porter in Aberdeen, who died 29th September, MDCCCXXXIV, aged 48.

(5) Erected by William Paterson, Turniemiddle, Portlethen, in memory of his son John, who died 12th September, 1878, aged 28 years.

(6) Erected by John Shepherd in memory of his Father, George Shepherd, Farmer, Cairn Robin, who died 3rd of March, 1857, aged 73 years. Also his mother, Catherine Davidson, who died 7th January, 1859, aged 68 years. Also Ann Shepherd, his sister, who died 31st October, 1863, aged 45 years. Margaret Shepherd died 24th January, 1875, aged 55 years.

(7) Erected by M. F. Anderson, M.A. and M.R.C.S.L, late H.E.I.C.S., formerly of Deebank, in memory of his infant daughter, born March 22nd, died March 24th, A.D. 1871.
"Thy will be done."

(8) In loving memory of The Reverend William Paul, D.D., for 57 years the revered Minister of this Parish. Born 27th September, 1804, Died 27th April, 1884. And of Jessy Stewart, his Wife, who died on the 2nd of February, 1866, aged 58 years. Also in memory of their children—George Morison, who died 3rd August, 1838, aged 13 days. James Stewart, who died 2nd September, 1845, aged 5 days. Alexander, who died 24th November, 1846, aged 9 years. John Thurburn, who died 26th November, 1867, aged 25 years, and is buried at Ventnor. Alexander, who died 2nd April, 1871, aged 23 years, and is buried at Moka, Mauritius.

(9) In memory of Anne Margaret Grant, who died at the School-house of Nether Banchory, on the 12th of October, 1839, in her 37th year.

(10) In affectionate remembrance of Richard, Fourth son of James William Parris, Esqr., born at Glendale, in the Island of Barbadoes, West Indies, the 1st November, 1845, died at Cults, in this Parish, the 18th April, 1871.
"I shall go to him but he shall not return to me."—ii Sam., xii. 23.

(11) In memory of George Jamieson, Jeweller in Aberdeen, and of Drumgarth, in this Parish, born 18th January, 1819, died 25th

November, 1874, and of his youngest son Robert Thomas, born 21st July, 1860, Died 29th October, 1869.

(12) Erected by Elspet Donald, in memory of her husband, John Knowles, Farmer, Blackhill of Findon, who died June 4th, 1853, aged 67 years. And of their daughter, Margaret, who died in infancy—The said Margaret Donald, died 19th July, 1873, aged 73 years.

(13) In memory of James Alexander, late tenant in Mill of Findon, who died 26th October, 1849, aged 79 years. Also Mary Duncan, his wife, who died 23rd March, 1860, aged 90.

(14) Erected by Wm. Findlay, Farmer, Bishopstone, Portlethen, in memory of his children, David and Charles, who died in infancy.

(15) In loving remembrance of Margaret King, who died 2nd December, 1887, aged 57 years. This stone is raised by her sons. Also to the memory of their sisters, Margaret, who died 3rd October, 1879, aged 22 years, and Annie, who died 5th January, 1884, aged 16 years.

(16) In memory of Isabella Webster, wife of John Thomson, in Mill of Cults, who died 10th December, 1878, aged 59 years. And their son Andrew, who died 11th May, 1860, aged 1 year and 2 months. "Blessed are the pure in heart for they shall see God." This stone is erected by their son James, E. I. C. S. Madras, in grateful remembrance of a loving and careful mother.

(17) Here lies the remains of William Morice, once Miller in Mill of Cults, who died 1st March, 1802, aged 60 years. Also his children, George, aged 16 years, Margaret, aged 5 years, John, aged 1 year, Alexander, aged 17 years, and Jane, aged 17 years.

(18) In memory of George Seller, who died on the 2nd March, 1821, aged 57 years, also six of his children who died in infancy, also Elizabeth Seller, who died 16th October, 1829, aged 13 years.

Likewise of Elspet Mitchell, spouse to the above George Seller, she died 21st December, 1833, aged 82 years. Also Elizabeth Urquhart, grand daughter of the above, who died 5th February, 1882, aged 75 years. On small granite heart on same grave.

In loving memory of those we love.

(19) Here lyes Andrew Smith, who departed the 23rd November, 1732. . . .

(20) Erected to the memory of Ogilvie Duthie, Mason, late in Stonegable, who died 15th June, 1874, aged 81years. Helen Henderson, his spouse, who died 4th April, 1875, aged 75 years. Also their sons, Ogilvie, who died 9th November, 1858, aged 23 years, and David, who died 9th Jany., 1866, aged 34 years.

(21) In memory of Robert Duthie, Crofter in Hillhead of Blairs, Parish of Maryculter, who died 2nd Sept., 1823, aged 67 years. Also of Mary Robertson, his first spouse, who died 23rd April, 1798, aged 32 years, and John Duthie their son, who died 28th Jany., 1815, aged 17 years. Allerdyce Duthie, who died 9th March, 1860, aged 67 years, also Jane Gibson his spouse, who died 30th August, 1875, aged 75 years.

(22) To the memory of Robert Mavor, Farmer, in Hillhead of Skaterow, who died the 8th March 1811, aged 55 years. Also his daughter, Jean, who died the 8th December, 1811, aged 10 years. Also Jane Craig, his spouse, who died the 17th January, 1826, aged 59 years. And of their children, Christian Mavor, who died 16th August, 1794, aged 6 months. Betty died 20th December, 1799, aged one year. Robert died 10th March, 1807, aged 10 years. Elizabeth died 20th November, 1845, aged 37 years. Susan died 28th November, 1871, aged 64 years. [On back of same stone]—To the memory of Alexander Mavor, once tenant in Cobleboards, who died 7th March, 1807, aged 92 years. And his spouse, Agnes Duthie, who died 8th February, 1794, aged 82 years.

(23) Here lies John Thomson, and Margaret Donald, his wife, who died 24 October, 1803.

(24) Sacred to the memory of John Knowles, who died in 1776, and his spouse, Margaret Collie, who died in 1799, also their daughter, Elspet, who died 12th July, 1826, aged 68 years.

(25) This stone was erected by Robert Youle, John Youle, and John Bridgefoord, to the memory of their father, Robert Youle, late in Cove, who died 1798, aged 74 years. Also Elspet Milne, his spouse, died in

1769, aged 36 years. Likewise James Youle, son to John Youle, who died in 1796, aged 2 years. Also Mary Youle, spouse to John Bridgefoord, who died in 1790, aged 38 years. Likewise George Bridgefoord, died in 1797, aged 2 years, also Thomas Bridgefoord, who died in 1808, aged 18 years.

(26) W. W. 1798. J. M. In memory of William Williamson, Farmer in Burn of Pheppie, who died 25th March, 1814, aged 73 years. Jean Milne, spouse to William Williamson, in Burn of Pheppy, she died 9th Feby., 1778, aged 37 years. And of their children, James, aged 12, Christian, aged 20, and William Williamson, who died 19th June, 1849, aged 76 years.

(27) Erected by James Webster, Middleton, Pitfodels, in memory of his daughter, Agnes. She died 8th December, 1826, aged 3 years; and two who died in infancy. Also his brother Andrew. He died 16th Decr., 1836, aged 66 years. The said James Webster, died 31st July, 1843, aged 76 years. Agnes Lyon, wife of the above James Webster, who died at Milton, Murtle, 28th September, 1876, aged 87 years.

(28)—This stone is erected by Andrew Paterson, Farmer in Coukstown, in memory of his family. Ann, who died in infancy, in the year 1824. Also Margaret, who died the 2nd July, 1832, aged 22 years. And James, who died the 15th of the same month, aged 18 years. The said Andrew Paterson died 13th April, 1856, aged 73 years; and his wife, Annie Angus, died 27th November, 1875, aged 87 years.

(29)—Erected by his widow. Sacred to the memory of John Reith, once Blacksmith at Hilldowntree, he died 7th March, 1838, aged 41 years. Also his children—William died 8th February, 1836, aged 4 years. Andrew died the same day aged 8 months. Ann died 28th Aug., 1836, aged 6 years. Peter Hutchison, Blacksmith, Aberdeen, who died 13th November, 1869, aged 70 years. In memory of Jane, daughter of the above John Reith and deeply lamented wife of Captain John Twaits, who died 27th June, 1875, aged 37 years.

(30) Sacred to the memory of Robert Mennie, who died at Cults, 19th July, 1848, aged 45. Isobella, his daughter, died 1839, aged 3

months: and Margaret died 1861, aged 15 years. Also Ann Kiloh, wife of the above, died Jan. 25, 1887, aged 82.

(31) Erected by William Anderson, Quarrier, in memory of his father, James Anderson, Farmer, Quarry Lodge, who died October 18, 1873, aged 71 years. Also his mother, Isabella Pirrie, who died August, 1837, aged 32 years. And of his sister, Isabella, who died March 6, 1857, aged 27 years. Also the said William Anderson, who died at Cairnvilla, Buxburn, 6th of December, 1878, aged 44 years, is interred here.

(32) The burial place of Alexander Cromar, Esq., who died 2nd March, 1840, aged 43 years. He was House-Surgeon in the Royal Infirmary, Aberdeen, for 20 years. This stone is erected by a few of his friends as a tribute of respect to his memory.

(33) Alexander Duthie, Jr., erected this stone to the memory of his mother, Christian Jameson, and his brother, William Duthie, who are both interred here. Also his father, Alexander Duthie, who died 8th October, 1828, aged 60 years.

(34) This stone is erected by Jean Carnie in memory of her sister, Elizabeth Carnie, who died 26th May, 1818, aged 20 years.

(35) Here lyes William Harrow, son of James Harrow, Salmon Fisher. Agnes Craig, his spouse, who departed the 1st of March, 17 . . [On small enamelled plate inside glass shade placed on the grave]—In affectionate remembrance of Elizabeth Harrow, who died 28th July, 1888, aged 48 years. A token of respect from her fellow workers at the Aberdeen Jute Co. (Ltd.).

(36) Erected in memory of William Reid, Flesher, Aberdeen, who died in October, 1819, aged 22; and of his wife, Margaret Addison, who died 28th July, 1856, aged 56. They are both interred in the second grave left of this.

(37) 1792, M.S. To the memory of Margaret Shepherd, the wife of George Weir, in berryhill. She died the 29th September, 1790, aged 26 years. Also their daughter Jean, who died in infancy. [On back of same stone]—In memory of Ann Fife, spouse to George Weir, who died

10th October, 1808, aged 40 years. Also their son, John, who died in infancy.

(38) Erected to the memory of Helen Milne, Wife of Thomas Smith, who died at Alma Cottage, Cults, 15th March, 1878, aged 56 years. Also of the said Thomas Smith, who died 26th December, 1886, aged 78. And of their son Robert, who died 20th April, 1888, aged 33.

(39) Erected by Charles Souter in memory of his beloved Brother, James H. Souter, School-master, who died at Bankhead of Portlethen, 27th October, 1877, aged 25 years. Deeply regretted.

(40) Erected by George Freeman, Drumduan, in memory of his son, James, who died 21st June, 1849, aged $3\frac{1}{2}$ years. Mary Ann, who died 10th March, 1877, aged 27 years. And Andrew, who died 3rd January, 1883, aged 20 years.

(41) In memory of	Born.	Died.
Alexander Donald,	1800	1877
Christina Barclay, his wife,	1804	1878
Alexander, \} their sons	1826	1843
John,	1833	1833
Duncan,	1838	1871
Alexander,	1845	1874

(42) Erected by Andrew and Francis Milne in memory of their Father, Alexr. Milne, who died 1857, aged 70 years. Also their Mother Rosan Allan, died 1844, aged 53 years. Also of Helen Milne, grand-child of Andrew Milne, who died 16th July, 1875, aged 18 months. Also Jane Paton, grand-child of Andrew Milne, who died 27th August, 1876, aged 2 years.

(43) This stone is erected by George, James, and William Keith, to the memory of their Father, George Keith, late in Cookston, who died on the 3rd February, 1825, aged 92 years. Also of his grand-children—Elizabeth Keith, who died on the 22nd March, 1815, aged 11 years, and Christina Keith, who died on the 18th July, 1818, aged 16 years. James, son of William Keith, Farmer in Banchory, who died on the 6th

Jan., 1831, aged 21 years. Also the said William Keith, who died on the 7th December, 1840, aged 69 years. And also George Keith, Crofter, Blairs, who died on the 5th of June, 1871, aged 70 years. And also his Wife, Isabella Elrick, who died on the 14th March, 1873, aged 67 years.

(44) In memory of John Watt, Leather Merchant, Aberdeen, who died 1st July, 1859, aged 57 years. Erected by his sons, John and Thomas.

(45) In memory of George Barclay, Builder, Cults, who died 29th May, 1858, aged 73 years. Margaret Massie, his wife, who died 25th June, 1866, aged 73 years. John Barclay, their son, who died 10th February, 1836, aged 10 years. Jane Barclay, their daughter, who died 3rd July, 1885, aged 61 years.

On the South side of same stone—

In memory of Jane Smith, spouse of James W. Barclay, Aberdeen. She was born at Strathdon, and died at Aberdeen on 3rd November, 1865, aged 35 years. Of James Smith Barclay, their only son, born 23rd October, 1865, died 9th June, 1875.

On the North side of the same stone—

In memory of Isabella Hepburn, who died 13th September, 1847, aged 3 years, and Williamina Hepburn, who died 8th August, 1860, aged 9 years, daughters of Alexander Hepburn, Cults, and of his Wife, Isabella Barclay. Also the said Isabella Barclay, who died 23rd August, 1889, aged 69 years, and Alexander Hepburn, who died 7th October, 1889, aged 72 years.

(46) Here lies George Wilson, late of Bottomfauld, who died 25th December, 1759, aged 55 years. Also his children, William and Helen, who died in 1746. Also George Wilson, Mariner, who died 9th September, 1827, aged 77.

(47) 1791. Here lies Alexander Reid, Alexander Walker, and Elizabeth Walker.

(48) James Rhind, Junr., died the sixth of February, 1797, aged 16 years.

(49) Erected by Charles Lawson, Farmer, Deebank, in loving

remembrance of his daughter, Elspet Lawson, who died on the 15th of Feby., 1883, aged 21 years.

(50) In memory of James Duncan, Farmer, Tillyhowes, who died 16th December, 1878, aged 80 years. He was during 40 years a member of the Kirk-Session of the Parish. In all the duties of public and private life he was most exemplary, and was universally respected and beloved by his many friends. His sorrowing widow erected this stone as a tribute of her loving remembrance.

" Blessed are the dead who die in the Lord."

Also his wife, Ann Webster, who died at Cockley, Maryculter, 27th May, 1884, aged 84 years.

(51) In memory of Maria Sinclair, daughter of the late John Sinclair, Esq. of Barrock, who died at the Manse of this Parish on the 9th March, 1876, aged 87 years. "Blessed are they that die in the Lord, they rest from their labours and their works do follow them."

(52) Erected by Robert Walker, Farmer, Mains of Portlethen, in memory of his father, William Walker, Farmer, England, Portlethen, who died 23rd October, 1826, aged 80 years. Isobella Williamson, his mother, who died 15th February, 1851, aged 88 years. Elspet Bartlet, his wife, who died, 8th April, 1849, aged 31 years. Annabella Walker, his daughter, who died 21st Sept., 1851, aged 8 years. Here also are interred the remains of the above named Robert Walker, who died 28th October, 1873, in the 71st year of his age. Also of Anne Walker, his sister, who died 16th January, 1885, aged 89 years.

(53) In memory of David Maver, late Blacksmith, Hardgate of Aberdeen, who died 13th December, 1820, aged 79 years. Also his Grandson, Joseph Maver, who died in infancy.

(54) Erected by their daughters to the memory of their Father, William Eddie, Seaman in Aberdeen, who died at Hull, 31st August, 1836, aged 36 years. Also of their Mother, Hannah Stephen, who died at Aberdeen, 10th March, 1855, aged 53 years.

(55) Erected by Robert Grant in memory of his family, viz. :— William, died 5th Sept., 1833, aged 4 months. James S., died at Singa-

pore, 27th December, 1846, aged 15 years. Robert, died 23rd March, 1847, aged 8 months. Elspet, died 8th Sept., 1848, aged 6 years. Also his sister-in-law, Mary Reid, who died 23rd November, 1858, aged 32 years. The said Robert Grant, who died 1st May, 1864, aged 72 years. Also Isabella Reid, Relict of the said Robert Grant, who died 27th December, 1877, aged 67 years. Also John Grant, Book-keeper, son of the said Robert Grant, who died 17th April, 1885, aged 38 years and 9 months.

(56) To the memory of Alexander Ogston of Ardoe—died 11 December, 1869, aged 70 years. And of his wife, Elliot Lawrance, died 1 August, 1886, aged 72 years.

(57) Erected by Peter Robertson in memory of his son, Peter, who died 23rd January, 1872, aged 7 years; also of his daughter, Catherine, who died 7th February, 1885, aged 22 years.

(58) In loving memory of Margaret Walker, beloved wife of Andrew Anderson, Farmer, Jockston, Ardoe, who died 28th August, 1886, aged 53 years.

(59) In loving memory of Mary Anderson, daughter of James Anderson, Farmer, Mid Ardoe, who died 9th June, 1882, aged 20 years.

(60) In memory of John Henderson, who died at Heathpark, Heathcot, on 8th May, 1887, aged 70 years; and of his son, James, who died 21st November, 1888, aged 23 years.

INDEX OF NAMES.

Aberdeen and London Steam Navigation Co., 29
— Bishop of, 6, 11, 38, 102, 292
— Committee of, 15
— Presbytery, 44-46, 51, 55, 59-62, 83, 201-203, 214, 216
— Town Council, 9, 18, 102-105, 132, 265
Abergeldy, Laird of, 108
Aboyne (Oboyne) Lord, 112, 113, 116, 118-122, 124
Adam, Bishop, of Aberdeen, 204
Adams, Robert, Teacher, Banchory-Devenick, 82
Airlie, Earl of, 54
Albert, Prince Consort, 27
Alexander, Earl of Sutherland, 174
— of Seton, 205
Allan, David, of West Cults, 195
Ancrum, Lord, 257, 258
Anderson, Rev. Mr., Kippen, 197
— Katherine, w. of Rev. G. Ogilvie, 55
— M. F., of Deebank, 274, 311
— Elder, John, 102
— Rev. Wm., Cults Free Church, 197, 198
Angus, Earl of, 13
Anson, Commodore, 94
Antiquaries' Society, Edinburgh, 10, 219, 222
Arbroath (Aberbrothock) Abbot of, 3, 5, 266-268
Ardoch, Laird of, 213
Argyle, Duke of, 127, 181
Arthur, Rev. D. F., Banchory-Devenick Free Church, 68, 69, 196
Athole, Earl of, 3
Auldjo Family, 150
— Provost of Portlethen, 150

Baddie, Barbara, 214
Baillie, of Jerviswood, 24
Baird, John, Aquhorthies, 278
Balkarne, Adam of, 138
Balmuto, Lord, 158, 159
Balquhain (Balquhane) Laird of, 119
Banchory-Devenick Kirk-Session, 22, 41, 201, 202, 211, 227-229, 275-277, 293
— Parish Ministers, 42-62
— Parochial Board, 226-231
— School Board, 70, 97

Banffe, Laird of, 123
Bannerman, Sir Alex., of Elsick, 21
— of Crimonmogate, 58
Barbour, Geo. F., of Bonskeid, 199
— Rev. R. W., Cults Free Church, 199, 200
Barclay, George, Builder, Cults, 57, 65, 278, 317
Bennin, Thos de, Rector, Aberdeen Schools, 6
Bewglass, Dr. Wakefield, 89
Bissett, Patrick, 9
Black, John, Teacher, Banchory-Devenick, 86-88
Blaikie, John, Plumber, Aberdeen, 273
— Provost Thomas, 130, 133
— Rev. W. G., D.D., Edinburgh, 196
Blakhal, Father Gilbert, 107, 182
Blinshell, Barbara, w. of Thos. Merser, 92
— Elizabeth, w. of Provost Thos. Chalmers, 205
— William, of Kirktown of Banchory, 11
Boece, Hector, 105
Boog, Alex., of Burnhouses, 149
— Jean, d. of Alex. Boog, 149
Bonar, Captain, 114
Bosville, Sieur de, 159
Boswell Claude, Lord Balmuto, 158, 159
— John Irvine, of Kingcausie, 83, 159, 160
— Margaret Irvine, of Kingcausie, 160
Brown, ——, w. of Rev. D. F. Arthur, 69
— Margaret Dyce, w. of David Stewart of Banchory, 30
— Principal, Aberdeen, 30
Bruce, David, 143-145
— Robert, Goldsmith, 144, 145
— Rev. Wm., Portlethen, 156
Bryanis, James, 216
Buchan, Alex., Earl of, 5, 136
— George, Lublin, 147
— Gilbert, of Dorbshill, 147
— Mary, w. of James Gordon of Banchory, 20
— Robert, of Portlethen, 147, 152
— William, Earl of, 5
Buchanan, Dr., Glasgow, 68
Buk, Andrew, of Murtle, 206
— Thomas s. of Andrew Buk, 207
Burke, 11
Burness, John, *Thrummy Cap* Author, 150

INDEX OF NAMES.

Burnett (Burnet), Archbishop, 49
— Capt., yr., of Monboddo, 219
— John, of Countesswells, 194
Burns, Robert, Scottish Poet, 148
Bute, Marquis of, 68

Cabell, Alex., Minister, Banchory-Devenick, 43
Cadogan Family, 53
— Lord, 53, 54
Calder, Alex., s. of James Calder, 239
— James, Wine Merchant, Aberdeen, 238, 274-277
Calderwood, 49, 112
Camera, Wm. de, or Chalmers, of Findon, 137, 138, 145, 158
Campbell, of Glenlyon, 12
— Alex., Prebendary, Banchory-Devenick, 43
— Dr., of West Cults, 195
— Grizel, of Broughdearg, 10
— Principal, 18
Cant, Rev. Andrew, 46
Carse—Fish Cadger, 154
Catto, James, Cliff House, 190
Cay, Charles, Teacher, Banchory-Devenick, 78
Chalmers, Provost Alex., of Murtle, 205
— Alex., of Cults, Tarland, 205, 206
— Alex., s. of Alex. Chalmers of Cults, Tarland, 206
— Alex., s. of Alex. Chalmers of Cults, Tarland, 206
— Charles, of Portlethen, 149
— Rev. Dr., 26
— George, of Cults, 193
— Gilbert, 206
— Rev. Jas. Kirkpatrick-Fleming, 149
— Rev. James, 148
— Marjorie, w. of Gilbert Menzies, 169
— Marjory, d. of Alex. Chalmers, 206
— Thomas, of Murtle, 205
— Thomas, 206
— Rev. Wm., Boyndie, 148
— William, of Findon, 138, 204
Chawmers, John, Rector, Aberdeen, 42
Chen, Sir Reginald le, 136
Cheyne, Patrick, of Danestown, 92, 207
— Thomas, s. of Patrick Cheyne, of Danestown, 92
Chisholm, of Cromlicks, 149
Christie, Rev. Chas. S., Cults, 203
— James, of Durie, 160
Clark, James, Teacher, Banchory-Devenick, 79
Clatt, John, Vicar, Banchory-Devenick, 42
Club, Gilbert, Burgess, Aberdeen, 11

Cochran, Provost, Aberdeen, 19
Collie, George, Balnagarth, 190
— James, Viewbank, 190
— Robert, Woodlands, 190
Collison, Baillie, Aberdeen, 171
— Catherine, w. of Rev. Jas. Gordon, 50
Columba, St., 2, 32
Consort, Prince, 27
Corbet, Rev. Dr. Adam, Drumoak, 195
— Dr. James, of Bieldside, 195
— William, of Bieldside, 195
Cormack, Robert, Teacher, Banchory-Devenick, 81
Couts (Coutts) Alexander, Dog Officer, 235
— Margaret, w. of Robt. Irvine of Cults, 191
Covenanting Lords, 14
Cowan, Rev. Dr., 203
Crab, John, Flemish Engineer, 136-138
— John, Murtle, 204
— Paul, Burgess of Aberdeen, 138
Craigievar, Laird of, 118
Crawford, Earl of, 111
— Margaret, w. of Provost Reid, 167
Crombie, Sir Thomas, 210
Cromwell, Oliver, 53, 148, 208
Cruickshank, Alex., Little Banchory, 214
— Elspet, w. of John Johnston, 18
— George, Advocate, Aberdeen, 18-20
— Helen, w. of Rev. John Whyte, 18
— Dr. James, 18
— John, Burgess, Aberdeen, 17
— Robert, of Banchory, 17, 18-20, 265, 269, 270
— Robert, s. of Robert Cruickshank of Banchory, Merchant, London, 18
— Robert, s. of Geo. Cruickshank, 20
Culan, Margaret of, 96
Cullane, Mariot, w. of Provost Reid, 167
Cumberland, Duke of, 21, 257
Cumyn, Agnes, 5
— Alexander, Earl of Buchan, 5, 136
— William, Earl of Buchan, 5
Cunningham, Bishop David, 176
Cushnie, Wm., 66

Dalrymple, C. S., of Westhall, 219
Darg, Jean, 215
Daveny, Williame, 178
David, Earl of Huntingdon, 102
Davidson, Agnes, Westertown, 188
— Alexander, Woodbank, 190
— Andrew, Brae, Pitfodels, 188
— George, Wellwood, 190
Dempster, 101
Devenick (Devenicus, Dewynik), St., 2, 32-37, 43

INDEX OF NAMES.

Dingwall, John, 192
Dominican Friars, 6
Donaldson, Dr. James, Aberdeen, 192
— George, 57
Dougatt, Williame, 178
Douglass (Douglas), Elizabeth, w. of Alex. Chalmers, 206
— John, of Tilwhilly, 94
— Lady Margaret, of Kemnay, 13
— Sir Wm., of Kemnay, 13
Duffus, Janet, 17
— J., & Co., Contractors, 57
— Lord, 17
Duguid, Williame, 178
Dunbar, Bishop Gavin, 99-101, 105, 108, 130, 131, 279
— Patrick, Minister, Banchory-Devenick, 43
Duncan, James, Tilly-hows, 278, 318
— Lizzie Milne, w. of Rev. Wm. Lawrence, 62
— William, Quarry Owner, 62
Dundee Presbytery, 54
Durward Family, 3
— Lord Alan, 3-5
— Elizabeth, 5
— Thomas, 3
— William, of Cults, 193
Dwn, William, Dean of Guild, 111

Edmond, Alex., Garthdee, 190
— Francis, Advocate, Aberdeen, 277
Elphinstone (Elphinstoun, Elphingstoune), Bishop Wm., 98-100, 103, 105, 130, 279
— Rev. Robert, of Kincardine, 105
Emslie, Mrs., d. of James Calder, 238
Errol (Erroll), Earl of, 111, 206
Erskine, of Dun, 44
Ewen, Charles A., Portlethen, 151, 278

Farquhar, Rev. John, Nigg, 254, 255
— Johnne, 178
— Sir Robert, of Mounie, 148
— Captain Robert, 58
Farquharsons, of Invercauld, 10
— of Finzean, 10
Fedarg, Sir Philip de, 5, 6
Findlater, Rev. —, Cairnie, 211
Findon (Fyndon), Philip de, 136
Forbes Family, 12, 17
— of Druminnor, 118
— Alex., s. of John Forbes of Leslie, 13
— Alex., of Aberswithark, 13
— Alex., of Pitsligo, 174
— Alex., heir-apparent of Brux, 171
— Alex., of Morkeu, 190

Forbes, Sir Alex., of Craigievar, 12
— Sir Alex. of, 138
— Anna, of Craigyvar, 147
— Anna, d. of Sir Wm. of Monymusk, 13
— Bathia, d. of Sir Alex. Forbes, 12
— Christian, w. of John Skene of Dyce, 17
— Elizabeth, w. of Rev. Jas. Gordon, 50, 93
— Elizabeth, w. of Thos. Menzies, 174, 176
— Francis, East Middleton, 215, 216
— George, Farmer, Maryculter, 66
— James, s. of Wm. of Monymusk, 178
— Jean, w. of Rev. Alex. Lunan, Monymusk, 13
— Jean, Lady Hatton Meldrum, 17
— John, of Asloun, 13
— John, of Leslie, 13, 14, 140, 178, 182
— John, grandson of John of Leslie, 17
— John, slain at Bridge of Dee, 114, 115
— Sir John, of Monymusk, 140
— Lord, 170, 174, 288-291
— Margaret, w. of M. F. Anderson of Deebank, 274
— Master of, 171
— Robert, of Barns, 13. 140
— Robert, s. of Wm. of Monymusk, 178
— Violet, w. of George Menzies, 174
— William, of Monymusk and Portlethen, 139, 177, 178
— Sir Wm., of Monymusk and Banchory, 12, 13, 146
— William, s. of Sir Wm. of Monymusk and Banchory, 13
— William, s. of John Forbes of Leslie, 13-15, 140
— Sir William, of Craigievar, 15, 147
— William, Professor of Law, 50
— Rev. Wm., Mannofield, 161
Fordyce, Agness, of Ardoe, 94, 95, 274
— John, of Ardoe, 94, 274, 294, 295
Forsyth, Henry, Minister, Banchory-Devenick, 43
Fortescue, Archer Irvine, of Kingcausie, 160
Fotheringham, Margt., w. of David Menzies, 169
— Thomas, of Powrie, 169
Fowler, Sir Robert N., M.P., 199
Fox, Right Hon. Chas. Jas., 53
Fraser, Sir Alex., of Durris, 184
— Alex., Provost of Aberdeen, 26
— Elizabeth, w. of Gilbert Chalmers 206

INDEX OF NAMES.

Fraser, Hugh, of Lovet and Kynnel, 138
— Lord Hugh, of Lovet, 175
— Jessy, w. of Alex. Thomson II., of Banchory, 26
— John, of Ferryhill, 92
— Katherine, w. of Patrick Cheyne, 92
— Thomas, of Durris, 92
— Thomas, Master of Kirk Works, Aberdeen, 133
French, Thomas, Mason, 101
Friends Society, 56
Fyfe, Rev. John, Professor of Moral Philosophy, Aberdeen, 61

Gairdin, George, 178
Galfridus Dompnus, Abbot of Arbroath, 267, 268
Galloway, Rev. Alex., of Kinkell, 101
Gammack, Dr., Aberdeen, 37
Gammel Family, 150
— Jas., of Countesswells, 238
Garden (Gardyne), Family, 8
— Alexander, 105
— Alex., s. of Arthur of Banchory, 11, 12
— Alex., s. of Alex. of Banchory, Major, 12
— Alex., of Troup, 12
— Arthur, of Banchory, 9, 11
— Beatrix, w. of Findla Mhor, 9, 10
— Elizabeth, or Eliza, w. of Geo. Merser, 92
— George, of Banchory, 8, 92
— John, Teacher, Banchory-Devenick, 88, 89
— Peter, of Delgaty, 12
— Thomas, 53, 54
Gardenstone, Francis, Lord, 12
Garioch Presbytery, 55
Geddie, Elizabeth, w. of George Cruickshank, 18
Geillis, James, 178
Gellatly, Rev. —, Aberdeen, 73
Gibb, Alex., s. of G. G. S. Gibb, of Cults, 194
— Elizabeth, w. of Rev. E. T. Vernon. Arbirlot, 194
— George Gibb Shirra, of Cults, 194-196
— George, s. of G. G. S. Gibb, 194
— Lillias Jessie, w. of J. R. Russell, Dunfermline, 195
— Mary, w. of Rev. Jas. Cameron, 194
— Robert, s. of G. G. S. Gibb, 194
Gillan, Rev. James, D.D., Alford, 95
— Rev. James, Alford, 95
Gordon, Family, 16

Gordon, Alex., Bishop of Aberdeen, 99
— Anne, of Banchory, 20
— Lady Anne, w. of Sir Gilbert Menzies of Pitfodels, 179
— Duke of, 129
— Elizabeth, or Elspet, of Gight, 11
— Francis, of Craig, 188
— Francis, s. of John Gordon, of Craig, 21
— George, M.D., s. of Rev. James Gordon of Banchory, 51
— George, Earl of Huntly, 172, 177, 291
— Isobel, w. of Rev. Wm. Robertson, of Banchory, 45
— James, of Ardoe, and Minister of of Banchory-Devenick, 39, 46-51, 78, 93, 94, 217, 226, 272
— James, of Ardmellie and Banchory, 20, 21
— James, of Craig, 21
— James, Episcopal Clergyman, Montrose, 50, 94
— James, Parson, Rothiemay, 105, 114-116, 165, 172, 181
— James, of Haddo and Methlick, 176, 288-291
— Sir John, of Gilcomston, 177
— John, of Craig, 20
— John, s. of John Gordon of Craig, 20
— John, great-grandson of Rev. Jas. Gordon of Banchory, 93, 94
— John, of Murtle, 211, 238
— Madame dē, 182
— Lady Mary, w. of Alex. Irvine of Drum, 209
— Mary, w. of Sir. Alex. Bannerman of Elsick, 21
— Nathaniel, 128
— Sir Robert, Tutor of Sutherland, 96
— Dr. William, Professor of Medicine, 46
— William, Physician, Montrose, 93
— William, of Arroudale, 120
— William, Surgeon, Aberdeen, 144
Gordoun, Alexander, 183
— William, of Gordoun's Mills, 114
Grant, Rev. A. R., Portlethen, 156, 157, 294
— James, 134
— Patrick M'G., Teacher, Banchory-Devenick, 82, 83
Gray, Rev. Alex., Footie, 243
— Lord, 10
— Marjory, w. of David Menzies, 11
— Robert, Teacher, Banchory-Devenick, 89, 90
Great North of Scotland Railway, 29, 30

INDEX OF NAMES. 325

Gregory, Dr., Aberdeen, 144
— Helen, w. of Alex. Thomson of Portlethen, 149
Grey Friars, 138
Grub, Dr. George, Aberdeen, 47
Guild, Matthew, Armourer, Aberdeen, 207
— Dr. William, Aberdeen, 93, 207, 208
Gun (Gunne), Colonel, 113, 116, 120, 185

Haddington Presbytery, 53
Haliburton, George, Provost, Edinburgh, 54
— Janet, w. of Rev. James Nicolson of Banchory, 54
Hall, —, Inspector of Schools, 88
Hamilton, Helen, w. of Andrew Thomson II., of Banchory, 25
— Dr. Robert, 25
Hardie, Elizabeth, w. of Alex. Livingston, Provost of Aberdeen, 193
— John, Aberdeen, 193
Harvey, Ann, Peterculter, 215, 216
Hatt, Alex., Haughton, 278
Hay, Agnes, w. of Alex. Chalmers of Cults, 206
— Alex., "persoun of Turref," 102
Henderson, Colonel, 117
Henry, Bishop of Aberdeen, 205
— George, Master of Kirk Works, 133
Hepburn, Adam, of Craggis, 43
— Alex., Birchfield, 224, 317
Herodotus, 105
Highland Railway Company, 30
Hill, Mathow, 214
Hogg, George, of Shannaburn, 79, 302
— James, Teacher, Banchory-Devenick 79
Holland, Lord, 53
Hostiarius, Lord Alan, 3-5, 266, 268
Hugo, Bishop of Aberdeen, 136
Humbert, General, 259
Huntly, George, Earl of, 207
Hurry, General, 128
Hutcheon, Rev. John, Fetteresso, 58

Innes, James of, 96
— of Pethnak, 96
Inneses of Drainie, 96
Irvine (Irving, Irwing), Alex., of Drum, killed at Pinkie, 209
— Sir Alex., of Drum, Sheriff, 209
— Alexander, s. of Sir Alex. of Drum, 209
— Alexander, of Murtle, 209, 210
— Alexander, of Kingcausie, 14-16
— Anne, w. of Lord Balmuto, 159
— Bettie, d. of Robert Irvine of Cults, 191

Irvine (Irving, Irwing), Charles, 209
— Gilbert, of Colairlie, 209
— Hellen, d. of Robert Irvine of Cults, 191
— Issobell, w. of Dr. Jas. Donaldson, 192
— James, s. of Robert Irvine of Cults, 191
— James, Drum, 206
— Janet, w. of Alex. Chalmers, 206
— Jean, w. of Alexander Irvine of Murtle, 209
— Jeane, w. of Robert Irvine of Cults, 191
— John, of Murtle, 191
— Margaret, w. of Gilbert Menzies, 177, 178, 209
— Margrat, d. of Robert Irvine of Cults, 191
— Marie, d. of Robert Irvine of Cults, 191
— Mary, w. of John Stewart of Banchory, 30
— Robert, of Cults, 94, 191, 192
— Robert, s. of Robert Irvine of Cults, 191

Jaffray, Margaret, w. of Rev. Dr. Morison, 55
Jaffrays of Kingswells, 55
Jamieson, Mrs. George, Drumgarth, 190
— Robert, Assistant, Banchory-Devenick, 39, 78, 253
Jervise, Andrew, 132, 133, 189, 220
John, Earl of Sutherland, 174
— of Levingston, 98
Johnson, Dr., 141
Johnston, Arthur, Poet, 98
— Colonel, 113-115, 119, 120
— George, Dean of Guild, 176
— John, Baillie, Aberdeen, 18, 20
— John, Latin Poet 44
— Patrick, 176
Joyner, Lieut-Colonel, 230, 231

Keith of Ludquharne, 176
— Dr., Ovariotomist, 80
— Alexander, D.D., St. Cyrus, 80
— Alexander, s. of H. Earl Marischal, 80
— Captain, 128
— George, Banchory-Devenick, 67
— Geo. Skene, Teacher, Banchory-Devenick, 79-81, 193
— James, Causie Port, 278
— Rev. John, Keith-hall, 80
— Margaret, w. of Gilbert Menzies, 177
— William of, 137

INDEX OF NAMES.

Kennedy, Alex, "Minorite," 100
— Thomas, of Auchorthies, 158
— of Kearmuick, 158
— Author of *The Annals of Aberdeen*, 42, 108, 138
Kennedy's *Constables of Aberdeen*, 158
Kerr, Dr., Inspector of Schools, 89
Keyth, Isobell, of Troup, 8
Khan Ayoub, 212
Kinghorne (Kinghorn) Earl of, 122, 180
Kinninmonth, Bishop Matthew, 204
Kirkton, Mr., Edinburgh, 24
— Margaret, w. of Dr. Andrew Skene, 25
Kirton, Hilldowntree Hostelry, 71, 72
Knowis, Dauid, 178
Knox, John, Scottish Reformer, 24, 28
— William, Craigton, 190

Lamberton, Wm., Rector, Turriff, 6
Langlands, 50
Law, Rev. Wm., Portlethen, 155, 156
Lawrance (Lawrence) Elliot, w. of Alex. Ogston of Ardoe, 95, 319
— James, Manufacturer, Abdn., 95
— Rev. William F., Banchory-Devenick, 61, 62, 201, 202
— William Farmer, Kirkbuddo, 61
Leask, Rev. Alex., Maryculter, 217
Leinster, Duke of, 53
Leith, Patrick, of Edingarroch, 14
Leslie (Lesley) Bishop, 7, 101
— Lairds of, 281
— Elizabeth, w. of Alex. Menzies, 169
— George, of Leslie, 13
— George, Shipowner, 197
— Janet, w. of Alex. Chalmers, 206
— Jean, w. of John Forbes, 14
— John, yr., of Pitcaple, 14
— John, of Balquhane, 174, 288-291
— John, of Buchquham, 175
— John, 206
— Sarah, w. of Robert Cruickshank of Banchory, 17
— Dr. William, Principal, King's College, 208
— William, Contractor, 133
Liddell, Marjory, w. of Gilbert Menzies, 165
Lighton, John, Middleton of Pitfodels, 188
Lindores, Lord, 14
Livingston, Alex., of Fornet, 192
— Alex., of Cults, 192, 193
Logy, Margaret de, 7
Lorimer, Ann, w. of John Fraser, 92
Lower Deeside Road Trustees, 97
Lummisdane, Robert, of Clova, 175
Lumsden, Alexander, of Auchenlett, 52

Lumsden, Henry, of Pitcaple, 52
— Henry, grandson of Henry Lumsden of Pitcaple, 52
— Janet, w. of Alex. Chalmers, 206
— John, Minister of Banchory-Devenick, 52, 53
— Matthew, 17
Lunan, Rev. Alex., Monymusk, 13
Lundie or Lundin Family, 3
Luther, Martin, 170
Lyell, David, Minister of Banchory-Devenick, 46
— Walter, Town Clerk, Montrose, 46
Lyon King, 96

Macdonald, Alexander, Contractor, 133
Machar, St., 32-36
Maclaine, Lieut. Hector, 212
— Thurburn, of Murtle, 212
— Wm. Osborne, 212
Makintosche, Lauchlin, of Dunnauchtane, 175
Makkanzie, Colin, of Kintaill, 175
M'Donald, General, 128
M'Kenzie, William, Aberdeen, 192
M'Leod, Captain, Rum, 68
M'Lure, Dr., Aberdeen, 86
M'Pherson, Rev. Mr., Liverpool, 196
Main, Dr., Kilmarnock, 68
Maitland, Rev. James, of Sorbie, 52
— John, Minister of Banchory-Devenick, 51, 52, 256
— Rev. Richard, of Nigg, 243
Mar (Marr), David, Baillie, Aberdeen, 92
— Earl of, 149, 243
— Thomas, s. of David Mar, 92
— William, Teacher, Banchory-Devenick, 78
Marischal (Mershall), Earl, 125, 127, 128, 135, 179, 181
— Second Earl, 80
Martin, David, Teacher, Banchory-Devenick, 78
— George, Shipmaster, Aberdeen, 237
— James, 143, 144
Marykirk, Joanna Carolina, 250
Master of Kirk Works, Aberdeen, 19
— Mortifications, 22
Maxwell, Marion, w. of John Menzies, 188
— William, of Kirkconnell, 188
Mearns, Rev. Dr., Kinneff, 58
— Professor Duncan, 58, 277
— Rev. D. G., Oyne, 58
Meldrum Family, 4, 7, 91
— Sir George, of Banchory and Fyvie, 7, 8
— George, of Fyvie, 92
— Lady Hatton, 17

INDEX OF NAMES. 327

Meldrum, William, of Banchory, 6
— William, of Hatton, 8
— William, of Fyvie and Ardoe, 91
Melgdrum Family, 5
— John of, 267, 268
— Sir Philip de, 5, 6
— Sir William de, 6
— William of, 4, 5, 267, 268
Mellit, Janet, 217
Melvill or Melvin, Andw., Minister of Banchory-Devenick, 45
Melvin, Dr., Grammar School, Aberdeen, 85
Menzies (Mengzeis, Menzeis, Menzes), of Pitfodels, 53, 139, 164, 165
— Alexander, of Middleton, 167, 169
— Alexander, s. of Provost Gilbert, 139, 177
— Andrew, of Pitfodels, 167
— David, Burgess, Aberdeen, 146, 165
— David, 169
— David, s. of Robert Menzies, 11
— David, Minister of Nigg and Banchory-Devenick, 43, 44
— Elizabeth, w. of Francis Gordon, of Craig, 188
— George, grandson of Provost Thomas, 174, 177
— Gilbert, Provost, Aberdeen, 165, 166,
— Gilbert, "Banison, Gib," 169-172
— Gilbert, s. of Provost Thomas, 174-177, 291
— Gilbert, s. of George, 177-179
— Sir Gilbert, 93, 140, 179-188
— Gilbert, s. of Sir Gilbert, 182, 183
— Gilbert, of Pitfodels, 188
— James, Minister of Dunnet, 176
— John, of Pitfodels, 188
— John, the last of his race, 188, 189, 294
— Katherine, w. of Geo. Johnston, 176
— Marjory, w. of Rev. Andrew Milne, 11
— Marjory, w. of James Gordon of Haddo, 176
— Mary, w. of Thos. Chalmers, 206
— Matilda, w. of Andrew Buk of Murtle, 206
— Patrick, Burgess, Aberdeen, 175
— Paul, Lieut.-General, 188
— Sir Robert, of Weems, 165
— Robert, of Kirktown, Banchory-Devenick, 11
— Thomas, Provost of Aberdeen, 172-176, 288-291
— Thomas, of Durn, 177, 291

Menzies (Mengzeis, Menzeis, Menzes), William, s. of Sir Gilbert, 93
— William, of Pitfodels, 188
Merser, George, Old Aberdeen, 92
— Malcolm, Rector, Crieff, 44
— Robert, Minister, Banchory-Devenick, 43, 44
— Robert, Minister, Banchory Devenick, s. of Rev. Robert Merser, 44, 45
— Thomas, s. of Rev. Robert Merser, 44
— Thomas, Old Aberdeen, 92
Mersers of Meiklour, 44
Meston, Charles, Teacher, Portlethen, 151
Mhor Findla, 10
Michael, Saint, 7
Michelet, Musician, 9
Middleton, Colonel John, 119
— Major, 117
Miller, Rev. Pat. Leslie, 212
— Rachel Hay, w. of Thurburn Maclaine, 212
— — of Dalswinton, 212
Milne, Alex., jr., Aberdeen, 192
— Alex., Eastertown, 188
— Rev. Andrew, Maryculter, 11
— Cruden, & Co., Aberdeen, 192
— George, Eastertown, 188
Mitchell, Alexander, 143
Moneypenny, Alex., Mason, 128
Monro, Major, 125, 126
Montrose, Marquis of, 112-116, 119, 121, 122, 127, 128, 162, 163, 180, 182, 183, 186, 187
Monymusk, Lairds of, 281
Morison, Geo., D.D., Minister, Banchory-Devenick, 39, 55-59, 69, 72, 78, 79, 99, 135, 151, 154, 155, 196, 273, 277-279, 292-294, 302
— Provost James, of Elsick, 55
— Dr. Thomas, 56
Morrison, Rev. Hugh, of Cults Free Church, 200
Mowat, James, of Ardoe, 92, 93, 280
— James, s. of James Mowat, 93
— John, Mill of Finnan, 234
— Thomas, s. of James Mowat, 93
Muir, Margaret, w. of Andrew Thomson, 24
Munro, Robert, of Fowlis, 175
Murray Family. 164
— Alex of, 164, 166
— Andrew, of Ardoe, 91
— David, s. of Andrew Murray, 91
— James, of Murtle, 207
— Thomas, of Murtle, 207
— William, s. of David Murray, 91

INDEX OF NAMES.

Napier, Mark, 116
Nelson, Lord, 259
Nicol, Dyce, of Ballogie, 219
— Dr. Wm., Stonehaven, 141
Nicolson, Rev. Charles, Amsterdam, 54
— George Haliburton, 54
— James, Minister, Banchory-Devenick 53, 54
— Mr., of Glenbervie, 219
Niven, Professor Charles, 31
Northern Steam Coy., 29

O'Connor, Feargus, 259
Ogilvie, George, Minister, Banchory-Devenick, 54, 55
— Robert, Teacher, Banchory-Devenick, 87, 88
— Rev. Skene, 55
— W., Farmer, Rothiemay, 87
Ogston, Alex., of Ardoe, 95, 319
— Alex. Milne, of Ardoe, 90, 95-97, 223
— Alexander Gordon, s. of Alex. Milne Ogston of Ardoe, 96
— Amelia, d. of Alex. Ogston of Ardoe, 95
— Charles, s. of Alex. Milne Ogston, 96
— Elliot, d. of Alex. Ogston of Ardoe, 95
— Elliot Mabel, d. of Alex. Milne Ogston, 96
— Helen, d. of Alexander Ogston, 95
— James, s. of Alexander Ogston, 95, 190
— James Norman, s. of Alex. Milne Ogston, 96
— Katherine Emily, d. of Alex. Milne Ogston, 96
— Sarah, d. of Alex. Ogston of Ardoe, 95
— of that Ilk, 96, 97
Ogstoun, Alex., of that Ilk, 96
— John, s. of Alex. Ogstoun of that Ilk, 96
Oliver, Rev. Wm., Greyfriars, Aberdeen, 62
Orem, Wm., Old Aberdeen, 38

Paterson, Rev. Dr., Montrose, 85
— Rev. Wm., Nigg, 151, 238, 239
Paton, John, of Grandholm, 17
Patrie, Elizabeth, w. of Robert Farquhar of Mounie, 148
— Elizabeth, w. of Rev. Jas. Chalmers, 148
— Hendrie, Burgess, Aberdeen, 147
— Marjorie, d. of Hendrie Patrie, 147

Patrie, Sir Robert, of Portlethen, 147-149
Paul, David, Minister of Roxburgh, 61
— Edward B., s. of Dr. Paul. 61
— George Morison, W.S., Edinburgh, 61
— Mrs. Dr., Banchory-Devenick, 273
— William, Professor of Natural Philosophy, Aberdeen, 58
— William, D.D., Minister of Banchory-Devenick, 58-62, 69, 78, 85, 86, 94, 196, 201, 229, 278, 293, 311
— William, Advocate, Aberdeen, 61
Philip de Fyndon, 136
Philp (Philpe), Alexander, Westertown, 188
— David, Westertown, 188
— Johnne, 178
— Thomas, in Pitfoddell, 214
Pirie, Rev. Mr., Portlethen, 155
Pitcairn, 178
Pitfoddles (Petfoddils, Pitfodels), Lairds of, 281, 288
Porteous, Captain, 257
Porthill Company, Aberdeen, 192
Pyot, Lawrence, Archdeacon, 138, 146

Raeburn, Rev. Gordon, Keig, 85
Rait (Raitt), Helen, w. of Alex. Chalmers, 206
— George, 178
Ramsay, Capt. Andrew, 119
— Rev. Gilbert, Dyce, 243
— Johnne, 178
Rankilour, David, 143
Ray, Sir William, 106, 107
Reid (Rede), of Pitfodels, 172
— Alex., of Pitfodels, 167, 168, 172
— Andrew, grandson of Wm. Reid, 166, 167
— Marion, w. of Provost Thomas Menzies, 168, 172, 173
— William, of Pitfodels, 164, 166
— William, Teacher, Banchory-Devenick, 90
Rennie, Charles M. II., Aberdeen, 96
— Katherine A. M., w. of A. M. Ogston, 96
Richmond, Duke of, 53
Rizzio, David. 9
Roberts, General Sir Frederick, 212
Robertson, Alexander, 213
— Johnne, 213
— William, Minister, Banchory-Devenick, 45
Rolland, John, of Disblair, 208
— Katherine, w. of Dr. Wm. Guild, 207-209
Rowell, Joseph, 28, 29

INDEX OF NAMES.

Rutherford, George D., Lynwood, 224
— Sir John, of Tarland, 170
Rutherfurde, Patrick, Burgess, Aberdeen, 175

Salmond, Rev. C. A., Cults Free Church, 198, 199
— Mr. Manufacturer, Arbroath, 198
Sandilands, Sir James, 166, 167
Scharcheburg, Roger, 6
Scorgie, Rev. Mr., Portlethen, 155
Scot (Scott), Helen, of Ardross 17
— Sir Walter, 124, 141
Selbie, James, Blacksmith, 71, 72
Seton, Alex., of Meldrum 171
— Sir John, of Pitmedden, 116-118, 162, 163
Shank, Rev. Alex., Drumoak, 256
Shepherd, George, Cairnrobin, 278, 311
— James, Barclay-hill, 278
— John, Findon, 144, 145
— John, Cairnrobin, 145, 311
Shirra, Rev. Robert, Yetholm, 194
Silver, David, Teacher, Portlethen, 151
Skene Family, 21
— Dr. Andrew, 24
— George, of Rubislaw, 21, 150
— John, of Dyce, 17
— Katherine, w. of Alex. Thomson I. of Banchory, 21
— Mary, w. of Andrew Thomson I. of Banchory, 24
— Robert, of Ramore, 192
Skinner, William, Teacher, Banchory-Devenick, 85
Smeaton, Rev. George, Edinburgh, 25
Smith, —, Teacher, Keith, 88
— George, Aberdeen, 73
— Isabell, 216
— John, Architect, Aberdeen, 57, 133
— Margaret, w. of Rev. Dr. Paul, 61
Spalding, John, 14, 47, 113-116, 119-121, 125, 127, 140, 179-181
Spark, Mrs., Aberdeen, 64
Spence, William, 213
Spens, Bishop Thomas, 103
Stainforth, Roger, Vicar, Banchory-Terny, 6
Stephen, Dr. William, of West Cults, 195
— of Balrony, 166
Stewart (Stuart), Rev. —, of Oathlaw, 219
— Alexander, Earl of Mar, 42, 205
— Alexandra C. D., d. of Lord Provost Stewart, 31
— Baillie, Aberdeen, 61
— Charles, s. of Lord Provost Stewart, 30
— David, of Banchory, Lord Provost of Aberdeen, 30, 265

Stewart (Stuart), David Brown Douglas, s. of Lord Provost Stewart, 30
— George Irvine, s. of Lord Provost Stewart, 30
— Jessie, d. of Lord Provost Stewart, 31
— John, of Banchory, 28-30
— Dr. John, 223
— Julia Charlotte, d. of Lord Provost Stewart, 31
— Margaret Isabel, d. of Lord Provost Stewart, 31
— Mary, d. of Lord Provost Stewart, 31
— S. R., & Co., Aberdeen, 30
— William Dyce, s. of Lord Provost Stewart, 30
Still, Rev. Jas. I., Banchory-Devenick Free Church, 70
Strachan, Alex., of Glenkindy, 12
— Betty, of Glenkindy, 12
— Colonel, 183
— Elizabeth, w. of Thomas Buk of Murtle, 207
— William, of Tibbertie, 207
Strahan, Rev. Mr., Aberdeen, 87
Straquhan, Janet, w. of Alex. Garden of Banchory, 12
Strathachin, Agnes, w. of David Murray of Ardoe, 91
Strickland, Miss, 9
Sutherland, Earl of, 179
— James, Precentor, 260
— John, Father, 108
Syme, Mr., Dollar Academy, 160
Symmers, George, of Cults, 194

Tait, Rev. Thos., Old Machar, 80
Tamson, Betty, Aberdeen, 71, 72
Taylor, Capt. G. S., R.N., of Inchgarth, 190
— Rev. Jas., Cookney, 154
Teavnick, St., 37
Tennent, Jas., of Lynhouse, 167
Thom, Helen, w. of Rev. Jas. Nicolson, 54
Thomas, s. of Thane of Cowie, 136
Thomson Family, 21, 28, 135
— Agnes, w. of Rev. John Maitland, 52
— Alexander, of Cults, 191
— Alexander, of Portlethen, 149, 191
— Alexander I., of Banchory, 21-24, 191, 269
— Alexander II., of Banchory, 25-27, 68, 89, 196, 219, 222, 271
— Alexander, s. of Andrew I. of Banchory, 25

INDEX OF NAMES.

Thomson, Andrew, of Cammachmore, 24
— Andrew I., of Banchory, 24, 25
— Andrew II., of Banchory, 25
— Anne, d. of Andrew of Cammachmore, 24
— Helen, of Portlethen, 149
— Helen, d. of Andrew of Cammachmore, 24
— James, s. of Andrew of Cammachmore, 24
— James, of Portlethen, 25, 150
— James, 143
— John, of Cults, 191
— Margaret, d. of Andrew of Cammachmore, 24
— Margaret, d. of Andrew I. of Banchory, 25
Thurburn, Anna, w. of W. O. Maclaine, 212
— Barbara A., d. of John of Murtle, 211
— John of Murtle, 211, 212
— Mrs, w. of John Thurburn, 212
Traill, Loke, Petfoddellis, 213
Troup, Rev. —, Muchalls, 249
— Alex., Westertown, 188
— of that Ilk, 12
— William, Middleton, 188
Turnbull, Rev. Alex., Glasgow, 194
— Margaret, w. of G. G. S. Gibb of Cults, 194

Udny, Laird of, 50
Urquhart, John, of Meldrum, 188
— Mary, w. of Wm. Menzies, 188
— Patrick, of Ardfork and Kilblain, 208
Urrie, Sir John, 206

Vaus, Richard, of Findon, 138
Verney, Earl, 53

Wagrel, Isobel, w. of Robert Williamson. 66
Walker, Alex., Provost, Aberdeen, 18
— Andrew, Aberdeen, 192
— Andrew, Kirk Officer, 261
— George J., Portlethen, 151, 294
— Mrs. George J., Portlethen, 151
— Robert, in Findon, 215
Watson, —, Refreshment-Room Keeper, 72
— Andrew, Advocate, Aberdeen, 95, 274
— Andrew, Minister of Tarland, 95
— James, 143
Watt, John, Teacher, Portlethen, 151
Webster, John, Teacher, Banchory-Devenick, 83, 84
Whitehead, —, Comb Manufacturer, 28
Whyte, Rev. John, of Coylton, 18
Wilkins, —, Minister, Portlethen, 153, 154
Williamson, Robert, Wardhead, 66
— Robert, Writer, Edinburgh, 167
Wilson, John, 143, 144
Wishart, Elizabeth, w. of Sir Wm. Forbes of Banchory, 12, 147
Woodford, Dr., Edinburgh, 86
Wright, Katherine, w. of David Menzies, 169

Yeats, John, of Portlethen, 150
Young, Bishop, Edinburgh, 149
— Helen, w. of Chas. Chalmers of Portlethen, 149
Youngson, T. A. W. A., Southfield, 190, 293

INDEX OF PLACES.

Aberdeen (Aberdeene, Abirdein, Aberdein, Aberdeine, Aberdene, Abirdene, Abirden), 1, 6-9, 11, 14-18, 20-22, 25-30, 37-39, 43-46, 48, 52, 55, 59, 61, 64, 67, 71, 73, 74, 79, 80, 85, 86, 88, 89, 92-97, 100, 102, 104, 107, 108, 112-114, 118, 121, 123-131, 134, 135, 137-139, 144, 146-150, 157, 158, 161, 162, 165, 167, 170-172, 174-181, 183, 188, 191-196, 204-210, 212, 216, 217, 225, 230-233, 238, 265, 273, 274, 277, 289, 291, 292
— Cathedral, 38, 205
— Free Church College, 27, 70
— University, 25, 30, 31, 55, 56, 70, 83, 84, 86-88, 135, 150, 211, 277
— Waterworks, 161
Aberdeenshire, 1, 60, 141, 161, 165, 296
Aberdour, New, 156
Abernethy, 156
Aberswithark, 13
Aboyne, 138, 167
Achreachan, Glenlivat, 10
Agriculture, 294-296
Alford, 4, 95
Amsterdam, 54
Anderston Church, Glasgow, 151
Angus, 44, 121, 127
Anstruther, Easter, 84
Arbirlot Free Church, 195
Arbroath (Aberbrothock), 89, 198
— Abbacy, 3-5, 91, 136, 266-269
Ardefrie, 43
Ardendracht, 43
Ardfork, 208
Ardlair (Ardlar), Kinnethmont, 102-104
Ardmellie, Banffshire, 20
Ardoe (Ardo, Ardoche), 2, 8, 51, 90-97, 155, 221-223, 272-274, 294, 319
— Stone of, 280
Ardross in Fife, 17
Arnlee, 166
Arroudale, 120
Artamford, 210
Ashallo, 43
Asloun, 13
Athol, 165
Auchenlett, 52
Auchineve, 5
Auchlee, 158, 159
Auchorthies (Achorthies), 2, 158-160, 272

Auchterderran, 83
Auchterhouse, 54
Auchterless, 8
Auquhorsk, 81

Badentoy, 140, 281
Balintrodoch, 167
Balkarne, 138
Balmoral, 212
Balmuto, Fifeshire, 83, 159, 160
Balnacraig, Aboyne, 138, 206
Balnagarth, 190
Balquhain (Balquhane), 119, 174, 288
Balquharn, 21, 22, 138, 270
Balrony, 166
Banchory-Devenick Free Church, 26, 68-70, 89, 90, 196
— Free Church Burying Ground, 30, 197
— Hill, 40
— Parish Church, 26, 32-62, 94, 154, 201, 215, 270-279
— Parish Churchyard, 37, 63-67, 95
— Parish Churchyard Tombstone Inscriptions, 297-319
— Parish School, 75-90
— Savings Banks, 292-294
— School Board, 70, 89, 90, 97
Banchory (Banchorie, Banchorrie) Estate, 2-31, 68, 91, 140, 147, 155, 191, 196, 221, 222, 261, 265-272, 281
— House, 9, 14, 26, 27, 70, 113
— Little, 214, 215, 269
— Mains of, 11
— Mills, 269
Banffshire, 20
Barns, 13, 140
Bath, 197
Berryhillock, 269
Berwick, 136, 137
Bethelny, 5
Bieldside, 191, 195, 272
Binghill, 210
Birchfield, Cults, 224
Birse (Brass), 204
Blairs, 170, 189
Bonskeid, Perthshire, 199
Boulogne, France, 7
Bourtreebush, 158
Bowbutts, 269
Bower, Caithness, 61
Boyndie, 148

INDEX OF PLACES.

Brae of Pitfodels, 188
Braeside, 269
Brandsmyres, 269, 281
Brechin, 46, 266
Broadgreens, 269
Broughdearg, 10
Brussels, 100, 107
Brux, 172
Buchan, 176
Buchquham, 175
Burghead, 90
Burnegranes, 178
Burnhouses, Berwickshire, 149

Cairnie, 211
Cairnrobin (Kairnrobin), 8, 145, 272
— Pot, 280
Caithness, 16, 61
Cameron, Fifeshire, 84
Cammachmore, 24
Candahar, 212
Cardens Haugh, 69
Carmyllie, 61
Castleheugh, Pitfodels, 190, 248
Castlehill of Aberdeen, 158
— of Middleton, Pitfodels, 173
Castleton of Braemar, 10
Catnes, 35
Chanry, Old Aberdeen, 38
Charlestown, 189
Chapel of Garioch, 52   [deen, 88
Church of Scotland Training College, Aber-
Clashfarquhar (Glashfarquhar), 8, 25, 135, 220, 222
Clatt, 85
Cliff House, 190
Clova, 175
Colairlie, 209
Colchester, 59
Coldseas, Burn of, 280
Collison's Aisle, Aberdeen, 173
Cookney, 153
Cookston (Cookstown, Cookstoun), 20, 140, 247, 272, 281
— Wester, 140
Constantinople, 54
Corsinday's Cairn, 281
Cortachy, 54
Cortycrome, Slains, 91
Cotbank, Ardoe, 95
Coull, 4, 85
Countesswells, 1, 193, 194, 238
Cove (Coiff), 178, 237
Covenanters' Faulds, 163
Cow Cairn, 280
Coylton, Ayrshire, 18
Crabstane (Crabestane, Crab Stone, Crab-stone), 14, 16, 118, 137, 182

Craggis, 43
Craig Estate, 20, 188
Craigiebuckler, 30
Craigievar (Craigyvar), 12, 15, 118, 147
Craigton, 190
Cramond, 84
Creich, Sutherlandshire, 37
Creskane, 36
Crieff, 44
Crimonmogate, 58
Cromlicks, 149
Crosta, 34
Cruden, 49
Cullen, 148
Culloden, 257
Cults (Quiltis), 56, 65, 99, 201, 215, 252, 293
— Den of, 164
— Estate, 1, 94, 191-195, 209, 210, 272
— Free Church, 69, 196-200
— House, 69, 216, 220, 221
— Mission Church, 201-203
— School, 194
— West, 194, 195, 224
— in Tarland, 205, 206
Cumber, Londonderry, 200
Cumnock, New, 68
Cupar, 266
Cuprastoune, 104
Cushnie, 206

Dalry, 85
Dalswinton, 212
Danestown, 92
Dee, Bridge of, 19, 20, 71, 98-134, 162, 163, 185, 218, 279
— River, 1, 2, 4, 7, 64, 71, 98-100, 155, 162, 164, 167, 188, 191, 211, 222, 270
Deebank, 224, 274
Deeside Railway, 162
Delgaty Estate, 12
Dennie, 167
Deskry, 10
Disblair, 56, 58, 208
Dollar, Academy, 160
Don (Done), 4, 7, 45
Dorbshill, 147
Dorlaithers, 8
Downies, 135
Drainie, 96
Drum, 127, 128, 206, 209, 210
— Mills, 162
Drumforskie, Hill of, 280, 281
Drumgarth, 190
Druminnor, 118
Drumoak, 79, 195, 256

INDEX OF PLACES.

Drum's Aisle, Aberdeen, 15
Dunbar's Aisle, Aberdeen, 101
Dunblane, 149
Dundee, 114, 146
Dunfermline, 195
Dunnauchtane, 175
Dunnet, 176
Dunnottar, 125
Durie Estate, 160
Durn (Durne), 177, 291
Durris, 92, 184, 206
Dyce's Cairn, 280
Dye, Bridge of, 134
Dynie, Burn of, 280

Earn, or Eagles-heugh, Findon, 143-145
East Church, Aberdeen, 6
Eastertown (Easterton), Pitfodels, 164, 167, 172, 174, 188
Echt's Cairn, 281
Edinburgh, 10, 16, 25, 28, 46, 54, 61, 80, 83, 84, 86, 89, 129, 141, 142, 144, 146, 149, 165, 167, 182, 188, 189, 193, 195-197, 203, 215
Edingarroch, 14
Elgin, 129, 149
— Academy, 89
— Parish Church, 96
Elsick Estate, 21, 55-58
Elsick's Cairn, 280
Ettles, 96

Ferryhill, Aberdeen, 74, 92, 207
— Ward, 265
Fetteresso (fetresio), 2, 59, 152, 228
Findon (Finnan, finnon), 2, 8, 20, 136-146, 158, 170, 204, 215, 219, 220, 239, 252, 272, 280, 281
Finzean, 10, 156
Footdee (Fittie, fody), 73, 101, 232
Forbes Estate, 171
Fords of Dee Fishing, 91
Forfar, 86
Forglen, 83
Fornet, Skene, 192
Fort George, 230
Foveran, 50
Fowlis, 175
Fyvie, 6, 8, 91, 92

Galloway, 181
Gallowgate, Aberdeen, 138
Garthdee, 190
Gateside Croft, 201
German Ocean, 2
Gilcomston, 53, 177, 188, 192
Glasgow, 88, 194, 208
— Free St. Matthew's Church, 199

Glasgow University, 50, 68, 197
Glasterberry, 272
Glenavon, Banffshire, 147
Glenbervie, 206
Glenkindy, 12
Glenrinnes, 86
Glentanar, 90
Gordon's Hospital, or College, Aberdeen, 20, 87, 88
Gordonstown, 96
Gordoun's Mills, 114
Grammar School, Aberdeen, 25, 85, 87, 209
— Old Aberdeen, 59, 61, 90
Grandholm, 17
Greenhead, 67
Greyfriars Church, Aberdeen, 62
— Monastery, Aberdeen, 138
Groundlessmyres Moss, 280
Guestrow, Aberdeen, 21
Gymnasium, Old Aberdeen, 89

Haddo Estate, 176
Halgreen, 206
Hardgate, Aberdeen, 72, 137
Harlaw, 74
Hastings, 159
Hatton Estate, 8
Haughhead, 269
Heathcot, 97
Hilldowntree (Hildountree), 71-74, 269, 281
Hillside House, Portlethen. 151, 294
Hilton, Woodside, 104
Huntly, 94
Hutcheon Street, Aberdeen, 29

Inchgarth, 8, 190
Inchmachan, 167
Inchmarlo, 94
Innerpeffry, 44
Innes Estate, 96
Inuerugy, 98
Invercanny, 4
Invercauld, 10, 11
Invercharron, 182
Inverleith, 266
Inverness (Innerness), 30, 78, 174, 175
Iona, 32

Jerviswood, 24
Justice Mills, 127, 163

Kaimhill (Kemhill), 8, 162, 250
Kearmuick, 158
Keig, 85
Keith, 86, 88, 211
Keith-hall & Kinkell, 52, 80, 81, 101, 105
Kemnay, 13

INDEX OF PLACES.

Kennethmont, 102
Kettle Hills, 38
Kilbartha, 167
Kilblain, 208
Kilmarnock, 68
Kinaldie's Pot, 280
Kincardine, 105
Kincardineshire, 1, 2, 42, 86, 91, 137, 141, 165, 167, 296
Kingcausie (Kincousie), 14-16, 83, 158-160
King-Edward, 208, 209
King's College, Aberdeen, 44, 45, 47, 51, 52, 55, 56, 58, 59, 61, 80, 82, 84, 85, 90, 99, 157, 208, 277
Kingswells, 55
Kinnedar, 96
Kinneff, 58
Kintaill, 175
Kintore, 13
Kippen, 197
Kirkbuddo, 61
Kirkconnell 188
Kirkpatrick-Fleming, 149
Kirktown of Banchory-Devenick, 3, 11, 12, 22, 237, 254, 262
Knockquharney's Cairn, 280
Kynnel, 138

Legart (Leggart), 247
— Burn, 270
Leggatsden, 113
Leslie (Lesly), Castle 17
— Churchyard, 17
— Estate, 13, 14, 140, 182
Licklyhead (Likliheid), 14, 16
Liston, 167
Liverpool, 196
Loanhead, 193
Loirston, 139, 177
London, 18. 30, 39, 80, 94, 199
Lonmay, Aberchirder, 230
Lublin, Poland, 147
Ludquharne, Buchan, 176
Lutzen Battle, 12
Lynhouse, 167
Lynwood, Murtle, 224

Machar, New, 26, 148
— Old, 1, 55, 80
Maiwand, 212
Manchester, 68
Mannofield, 161
— Episcopal Church, 161
— Established Church, 161, 202
Mar, 4
Marischal College, Aberdeen, 21, 25, 87, 89, 143, 144, 148, 192, 207, 209, 223
— Street, Aberdeen, 171

Marnoch Parish, 20
Maryculter, 2, 11, 58, 66, 67, 97, 155, 166, 167, 170, 257
Mcalmarket Lane, Aberdeen, 28
Mechlin, 100
Mcgray Hill, 113
Meldrum, 5, 6, 171, 188, 267, 268
Menie, Belhelvie, 138
Methlick (Methlyk), 32, 176, 288, 289
Middleton of Pitfodels, 164, 165, 167, 172, 188
— Castlehill of, 173
— East, 216
Milltown (Milltoun) of Murtle, 206-208, 272
Milne's Institution, Fochabers, 88
Mondynes, 42
Montrose, 15, 46, 50, 85, 94
Monymusk, 12, 13, 139, 140, 146, 177, 178, 281
Mortlach, 38
Morayshire, 96
Morkeu, 190
Mounie, 148
Muchalls, 153, 249
Murcar (Murcur), 73
Muriecroft, 43
Murtle (Murchill, Murthill, Murthil), 1, 8, 170, 191, 204-212, 238, 292
— Mains of, 210
Musselburgh, 10

Netherkirkgate, Aberdeen, 42
Neville's Cross, 6
Newcastle, 112
Newhills, 1
Newton of Murtle, 210, 272
Nigg, 2, 43, 64, 136, 139, 151, 238, 254
Norwood Hall, 190
Nova Scotia, 13

Ogstoun, 96
Old Deeside Road, 162
Oldfold (Auldfold), 210
Orchardfelde, 167
Orkney, 160
Ostend, 107, 108, 185, 187
Oyne, 55, 58

Paisley, 148
Perth, 28, 30, 112, 138, 146
Peterculter, 1, 79, 192, 195, 202, 211, 212, 216
Pethnak, 96
Pinkie, 10, 209
Pitarrow, 12, 147
Pitcaple, 14, 52
— Castle, 14

INDEX OF PLACES. 335

Pitfodels (Badfothel, Badfothellis, Badfothalis, Pitfodellis, Pitfoddels, Pitfoddells, Petfoddelis, Pitfoddellis, Pitfoddell, Pittfodles, Petfoddils, Pittfoddelis), 53, 93, 129, 139, 140, 164-190, 206, 209, 213, 214, 246, 272, 281, 288, 291
— Lodgings, 171, 179
Pitmedden, 116, 117, 162
Pitsligo, 174
Plewlands of Ogstoun, 96
Population Statistics, 296
Portartown, 167
Portgordon, 90
Porthill, Aberdeen, 192
Portlethen, 2, 8, 21, 25, 139, 146-151, 177, 191, 239, 270, 272, 294
— Church, 56, 150, 152 157, 241, 249. 254, 256, 260, 261
— Roman Catholic Chapel, 152
— School, 56, 151
Powrie, 169
Pyketillam, 269

Raich Fishings, 7
Rainieshill, 25, 26
Ramore, 192
Rathven, 88
Redmyre, 140
Rothes, 89
Rothiemay, 87
Rotterdam, 193
Roxburgh, 61
Rubislaw, 21, 137, 150
Rudrestoun, 103, 104
Rum Island, 68
Ruthrieston Bridge, 18, 19, 101

Saint Andrews, 20, 84, 143, 144
— — University, 88, 203
— Cyrus, 80
— Germains, 107
— John's Church, Edinburgh, 84
— Nicholas Church, Aberdeen, 15, 42,
— Nicholas Churchyard, 20, 93, 165,
— Niniane's Chapel, 158
— Thomas's Hospital, Aberdeen, 42
Sandhaven, 90
Sauchentree, 156
Scotland, (Scottlande), 3-6, 9, 10, 13, 32, 37, 38, 105, 115, 137, 172, 173, 186, 208, 229
Scotstoun Cairn, 280
Seaton of Findon, 141
Shannaburn, 79, 302
Sheriffmuir, 149
Shiprow, Aberdeen, 73
Skene, 4, 51, 55, 192

Slains, 91
Sod Kirk, Fetteresso, 153
Sorbie, Wigtonshire, 52
Southfield, 190, 293
Spital Cemetery, 150
Stewart's Hospital, Edinburgh, 89
Stirling, 88, 167
Stonedykes, 269
Stonegavel, 210
Stonehaven, (Stonehyve), 65, 113, 134, 141, 213, 214, 252
Strathearn, 44
Sutherland, 37
Swanbister, Orkney, 160

Talavera, 159
Tarland, 86, 95, 170, 205
Templar Land, "Badfothal," 166
Temple, Pitfodels, 166
— Church, 167
Thankerton, 167
Thurburn Cooking Depôt, 212
Tibbertie, 207
Tilbunes, 92
Tillyhouses, 269
Tilwhilly, 94
Tollohill, (Tullohill, Tollo Hill), 27, 113, 237, 269
Tomintoul, 156
Torphichen, 166, 167
Torry, (Torrie,) 13, 128, 140, 280, 281
Trinity College, Cambridge, 31
— Friars Convent, Abdn., 93
Troup Estate, 8, 12, 177
Tulliallan, Perthshire, 80, 81
— House, 80, 81
Tulloch, 167
Turriff, (Turref), 6, 102, 208
Two Mile Cross, 162, 163

Udny's Cairn, 281
Ursuline Convent of St. Margaret's Edinburgh, 189

Victoria Lodging House, Aberdeen, 21
Viewbank, 190

Wakefield, 89
Wardhead, Countesswells, 66
Weems, 165
Wellwood, 190
West Church, Aberdeen, 166
— Craibstone Street, Aberdeen, 137
Westertown of Pitfodels, 164, 167, 172, 188
Woodbank, 190
Woodlands, 190

Yetholm, 194
Yorkshire, 50

www.ingramcontent.com/pod-product-compliance
Lightning Source LLC
Chambersburg PA
CBHW020316240426
43673CB00039B/829